Archives of Desire

GENDER AND AMERICAN CULTURE
Coeditors
Thadious M. Davis
Mary Kelley

Editorial Advisory Board

Nancy Cott
Jane Sherron De Hart
John D'Emilio
Linda K. Kerber
Annelise Orleck
Nell Irvin Painter

Janice Radway
Robert Reid-Pharr
Noliwe Rooks
Barbara Sicherman
Cheryl Wall

Emerita Board Members
Cathy N. Davidson
Sara Evans
Annette Kolodny
Wendy Martin

Guided by feminist and antiracist perspectives, this series examines the construction and influence of gender and sexuality within the full range of Americas cultures. Investigating in deep context the ways in which gender works with and against such markers as race, class, and region, the series presents outstanding interdisciplinary scholarship, including works in history, literary studies, religion, folklore, and the visual arts. In so doing, Gender and American Culture seeks to reveal how identity and community are shaped by gender and sexuality.

A complete list of books published in Gender and American Culture is available at www.uncpress.unc.edu.

Archives of Desire

THE QUEER HISTORICAL WORK OF
NEW ENGLAND REGIONALISM

J. Samaine Lockwood

The University of North Carolina Press CHAPEL HILL

Published with the assistance of the Authors Fund of the
University of North Carolina Press.

© 2015 The University of North Carolina Press

All rights reserved

Designed by Alyssa D'Avanzo
Set in Miller by codeMantra, Inc.

The paper in this book meets the guidelines for permanence and
durability of the Committee on Production Guidelines for Book Longevity
of the Council on Library Resources.

The University of North Carolina Press has been a member of the
Green Press Initiative since 2003.

Cover illustration: photograph from unpublished edition of Sarah Orne
Jewett's first novel, *Deephaven*. Sarah Orne Jewett Compositions and Other
Papers, 1847–1909 (MS Am 1743.26 [14]), Houghton Library, Harvard University.

Library of Congress Cataloging-in-Publication Data
Lockwood, J. Samaine, author.
Archives of desire : the queer historical work of
New England regionalism / J. Samaine Lockwood.
pages cm. — (Gender and American culture)
ISBN 978-1-4696-2536-2 (pbk : alk. paper)
ISBN 978-1-4696-2537-9 (ebook)
1. American literature—New England—History and criticism.
2. American literature—Women authors—History and criticism.
3. Women and literature—New England—History—19th century.
4. New England—Intellectual life—19th century.
5. New England—In literature. 6. Regionalism in literature.
I. Title. II. Series: Gender & American culture.
PS243.L594 2015
810.9'92870974—dc23
2015010514

In memory of Maude Samaine Lockwood and Cora Clark Wright and for my mother, Susanne

Contents

Acknowledgments xi

INTRODUCTION
Recollecting New England Regionalism 1

1

Renovating the House of History 25

2

Literature's Historical Acts 57

3

Out of the China Closet 89

4

Spectral Fusions, Modernist Times 117

EPILOGUE
The Intimate Historicism of Late Twentieth-Century Feminist Criticism 155

Notes 165

Bibliography 191

Index 211

Figures

1. Elizabeth Bishop Perkins in colonial dress on staircase 5
2. Emma Lewis Coleman, C. Alice Baker's bedroom 28
3. Emma Lewis Coleman, *Gathering Faggots* 38
4. Susan Minot Lane, *The Junkins Garrison* 51
5. Winslow Homer, *Robert Junkins' Garrison House, York, Maine* 52
6. A. W. Elson & Co., *C. Alice Baker* 56
7. Emma Lewis Coleman, Kate and Helen walking into the woods 73
8. Emma Lewis Coleman, Kate and Helen picking flowers 74
9. Emma Lewis Coleman, Kate and Helen talking with an older woman 75
10. Emma Lewis Coleman, Kate and Helen at the water's edge 79
11. George Washington pitcher 100
12. The Perkins-Davidson colonial garden party, York, Maine 124
13. Joseph H. Hatfield, illustration for "The Yellow Wall-Paper. A Story" 132
14. Joseph Rodefer DeCamp, *The Blue Cup* 144
15. Elizabeth Bishop Perkins in colonial dress on porch 152

Acknowledgments

Though writing a book is most often understood as a solitary practice, it requires the labor and love of many people. I am so grateful for the teachers, mentors, colleagues, friends, and family members who have supported my intellectual life and this particular project. Bernie Baker and Steve Smith introduced me to the joys of American Studies and literary analysis early in my career, and, later, Tony Wohl, Miriam Cohen, Donna Heiland, and the late Donald Olsen and Ann E. Imbrie trained me as a cultural historian and feminist critic attentive to the riches of the archive. I could not have asked for a better set of mentors as a graduate student at the University of California, Davis: Margaret Ferguson, Linda Morris, Karen Halttunen, Fran Dolan, and Catherine Robson provided not only spirited conversation, thoughtful feedback, and great advice but models of intellectual lives well lived. It was my great fortune to arrive at Davis at the same time as Elizabeth Freeman, dissertation director and mentor *extraordinaire*. I do not exaggerate when I say that her generosity, intellect, and good humor made every step of the dissertation process, and every step of our relationship beyond that, a joy.

At George Mason I am lucky to be part of a supportive, vibrant department. In particular, Tamara Harvey, Debra Lattanzi Shutika, Eric Gary Anderson, Keith Clark, Robert Matz, and Zofia Burr have helped me navigate the life of a junior faculty member and encouraged my research. Mason's College of Humanities and Social Sciences provided me with the Mathy Junior Faculty Award in the Arts and Humanities, which funded an additional semester of writing and research, and Mason's English Department gave me the funding to hire two talented research assistants—Heather Hilton and Ryan Sheehan—whom I thank for their excellent work. Sharing my passion for nineteenth-century culture and archival work with Mason students has been a great privilege; I have benefited from many animated discussions with graduate students in my American literary regionalism and Gothic literature courses, and I am particularly grateful for having had the chance to mentor many superb undergraduate scholars into feminist-historicist scholarship.

Late in the life of this book project, I was infused with fresh energy thanks to the inaugural First Book Institute (FBI) hosted by the Center for American Literary Studies at Penn State University. I am grateful to the members of FBI's generous and genial first cohort; Adrienne Brown, Danielle Heard, Ted Martin, Christen Mucher, Todd Carmody, Sarah Juliet Lauro, and Sonya Posmentier provided me new ways of thinking about this work. What Sean Goudie and Priscilla Wald make happen at FBI exemplifies what professional development and collegial practice can and should be; I cannot thank Sean and Priscilla enough for believing in this book.

I have appreciated the detailed feedback on my work offered by various readers and editors, Linda Rhoads, Denise Knight, Cynthia Davis, Jennifer Tuttle, Robert Caserio, and anonymous readers for the *New England Quarterly* among them. I want to especially thank the anonymous readers for the University of North Carolina Press whose excellent comments and questions helped me clarify further the stakes of this project and prompted my writing of the epilogue; their intellectual generosity enriched this book. I feel myself very fortunate to have worked with Mark Simpson-Vos, editor at UNC Press. I cannot imagine having had a better first-book experience: Mark has understood what I have been trying to say and do in this project and has guided me masterfully through the process. Lucas Church and Jay Mazzocchi were also instrumental in making my work with UNC Press a pleasure at every stage. I have also been helped by a number of curators and librarians, often from afar. Thanks to David Bosse at the Pocumtuck Valley Memorial Association Library at Historic Deerfield, Jeanne Gamble at Historic New England, and Virginia Spiller and Nancy Moran at the Museums of Old York. I am grateful also for the aid of Kevin D. Murphy and Tom Johnson, the director of the Victoria Mansion in Portland, Maine, who corresponded with me about Elizabeth Bishop Perkins when I needed the information most.

I have had the privilege of being part of two writing groups over the course of this project, and it is through them that some of my most important ideas have been formed and sharpened. Tiffany Aldrich MacBain and Katie Kalpin Smith helped me to tease out early readings and, perhaps more important, commiserated with me regarding the pleasures and pains of conceptualizing a new project. If it had not been for Joan Bristol and Tamara Harvey, who have provided not only feedback but also food and friendship, this book would be a paler version of itself and the process of writing it would not have been half as fun. To the neighborhood crew in Fairfax who welcomed my family and me into their supportive circle, especially Cheryl Coyne: I have appreciated and needed the breaks from the book you have provided. And a special thanks to Patti Higginbotham who kept running with me no matter how busy or stressed out we became.

Throughout this process I have been supported by all my family members, but I have been especially buoyed by my mother-in-law, Lisbeth, who has helped maintain my well-being through her patience and great cooking; my sister, Sarah, who has consistently given me such good advice that I have felt the younger sister rather than the older; my father, Doug, who has always believed I could do anything; and my mother, Susanne, who has acknowledged my work and my choices at every juncture. Leo, my lover of history and connoisseur of all things imaginative, and Ezra, my detail-oriented performer and fellow gourmet, have kept me singing, laughing, and playing ball through it all. My deepest debt is to Demian who, for the last two decades, has encouraged and unconditionally supported every one of my projects. I thank him most of all and look forward to seeing what else our enduring partnership will make possible.

Portions of this book appeared elsewhere in earlier versions: some material from chapter 3, "Out of the China Closet," is from "Shopping for the Nation: Women's China Collecting in Late-Nineteenth-Century New England," *New England Quarterly* 81 (March 2008): 63–90; and part of chapter 4, "Spectral Fusions, Modernist Times," is from "Charlotte Perkins Gilman's Colonial Revival," *Legacy* 29 (2012): 86–114. I thank the publishers for permission to reprint them here.

Archives of Desire

Introduction

Recollecting New England Regionalism

Thoughts of the colonial New England past shaped the lives of many late nineteenth-century women in the United States. In the years before the Civil War, select writers, collectors, and historians had taken up the project of representing the colonial period, but it was not until the Centennial Exhibition of 1876 that reimagining the seventeenth and eighteenth centuries became a popular pastime.[1] By the turn into the twentieth century, one could not look around the northeastern United States without encountering colonial revivalism: Wallace Nutting built a virtual empire by selling antique reproduction furniture and lithographs of women in staged colonial scenes; historical works set in colonial times were published for adult and juvenile audiences; historical preservation was professionalized, with William Appleton's Society for the Preservation of New England Antiquities (SPNEA) leading the movement; and businesses sprang up along the region's thoroughfares that sold colonial antiques to tourists.[2] The colonial revival involved mostly white, leisured northeasterners celebrating and trying to materially reshape the New England landscape and its stories according to an idealized and often ill-understood colonial past. This effort had its roots in what the historian Stephen Nissenbaum has called the sectionalist "culture wars" from earlier in the nineteenth century wherein New Englanders asserted the ongoing moral, racial, and cultural superiority of their white, so-called native region over the South in particular.[3] Colonial revivalism was, in many ways, a nostalgic, racist, and nativist love affair with a regionally specific past, part of an ongoing bid to secure for white New England the spotlight on history's stage.

Colonial revivalism, however, is not quite so easily reducible, so overdetermined in its historical imagination, its features, or its effects. I argue in this book that colonial revivalism formed part of a larger regionalist movement, one that provided a range of women cultural producers a sanctioned framework within which to rethink the relationships among gender, social-sexual forms, history, racial affiliations, and collective identities. Women dominated colonial revivalism in New England as well as the regionalist literary production and domestic tourism to which it was inextricably tied. "Yankee women were largely responsible for cultivating the movement," Joseph Conforti asserts in his examination of the colonial revival.[4] The list of American literary regionalists who focused their work on New England, meanwhile, features women: Rose Terry Cooke, Mary Wilkins Freeman, Sarah Orne Jewett, Alice Brown, and Annie Trumbull Slosson.[5] Women were also in the majority among vacationers to New England: tourists summering on Cape Cod, Henry James's narrator in *The Bostonians* assumes, are all women who rent houses, as Olive Chancellor does, or are "anxious lady-boarders wrapped in shawls."[6] Women's magazines such as *Good Housekeeping* and *Ladies' Home Journal* proffered advice for success in summer boarding, the precursor to the bed-and-breakfast industry, suggesting that women were its central players both as landladies and boarders.[7] By 1900, the figure of the imperious urban woman tourist terrorizing provincial and rural climes was so familiar to audiences that Freeman based her laugh-out-loud novella *The Jamesons* on it. And again and again across colonial revivalist, literary regionalist, and tourist practices northeastern white women wrote and performed intimacies with the past in ways that troubled mainstream versions of history.

The case of Elizabeth Bishop Perkins exemplifies the imbrications of colonial revivalism, regionalist literary production, and tourism that I examine in this book and demonstrates the capaciously queer, feminist cultural work New England regionalism performed.[8] In 1898, at the age of nineteen, Perkins, along with her mother, purchased an eighteenth-century house in York, Maine, now known as the Elizabeth Perkins house, that they would summer in and renovate extensively during the following thirty-five years.[9] The Perkins women were New Yorkers who became central players in the project to make York Village what it remains today: a culture-rich heritage tourism destination. Architectural restoration was at the heart of their endeavor. Within just a year of moving into the Perkins house, the cosmopolitan Mary Perkins joined a local York resident, Elizabeth Burleigh Davidson, to lead the restoration of York's Old Gaol, the famous eighteenth-century prison that inspired Nathaniel Hawthorne's *The Scarlet Letter*.[10] The

Perkins women undertook the renovation of the dilapidated four-room-and-ell Perkins house in the same historical spirit, turning it, piece by piece, into "a spacious colonial revival home incorporating neo-Palladian, Georgian, and federal architectural elements."[11] To this day, tourists visiting Old York can explore the Perkins house as part of their journey through "old" New England.[12]

At first glance, the story of Elizabeth Perkins—privileged white daughter, urbanite, tourist, and colonial revivalist trying to reshape the features of a small New England village—seems a relatively straightforward, even familiar one. It was to an idealized, gentrified construction of the colonial era that Perkins dedicated herself by way of home renovation and community work. She helped establish the Piscataqua Garden Club, an organization committed to maintaining gardens and trees, reducing litter, and banning unsightly marks of modernity like billboards from southern Maine's public spaces.[13] Perkins also shared many goals of the Old York Historical and Improvement Society, an organization of mostly summer residents aiming "to beautify the village and to preserve York's past."[14] Believing, as did many late nineteenth-century Americans, that colonial New England villages had been comprised of white buildings clustered around a central green, Perkins campaigned for shop owners in the Village to paint their buildings white.[15] The nucleated settlement form Perkins and her peers wanted replicated, with its orderly fences and large houses, did not accurately reflect colonial New England, however. As the cultural geographer Joseph Wood has shown, the white village ideal prevalent in the late nineteenth century, the same one that persists in our own cultural imaginary, reflected early nineteenth-century, rather than colonial, settlement patterns. Far from building white villages, settler colonials in New England scattered their small, brightly painted houses across the landscape.[16]

Nonetheless, Perkins's relationship to history was more complex than the familiar narrative of genteel antimodernism allows. Perkins's passion for the past was what we might call a queer historicism: she was deeply invested in recording her embodied relationship to New England history, one that involved a range of desires and erotic expressions. According to the architectural historian Kevin D. Murphy, Perkins's restoration of the Perkins house rendered it a queer, heterotopic space.[17] Rather than purchase a luxurious home in the socially prestigious summer resort of York Harbor, a place where young, well-to-do white Americans often found suitable spouses, the Perkins women chose a historic restoration project off the beaten path.[18] The house itself contained a trace of Perkins's history of erotic intimacies with women despite her private papers having been destroyed soon after her death: Murphy explains, "A postcard was found wedged behind her dresser in which her female correspondent spoke of sneaking up to Elizabeth's room, perhaps by the nearby servant's staircase, where the two fell into one another's arms."[19] The Perkins house, however, was more than an alternative sociosexual space, just as Perkins's erotic imaginings included more than what the seemingly proto-lesbian postcard suggests. As important as those modes of queerness are, the Perkins house also became a stage that Perkins constructed and on which she performed an embodied, sensually charged relationship to the colonial past.[20]

The desire for belonging by way of intimacy with history-rich architectural spaces shaped Perkins's work. In her short story "The Codfish Ghost," Perkins represents an early twentieth-century character achieving sensual climax by way of renovating an old house. This unnamed "modest home-hunter" watches "in excited ecstasy" as the mason she has hired chips away at an interior wall of an aged house she has just purchased.[21] No longer able to contain her enthusiasm, she "grabbed the tool from his hand and commenced herself to hack furiously at the wall" until her penetrations expose hand-beveled boards, a discovery that renders her "breathless with exhaustion and surprise."[22] Another of Perkins's short stories, an unpublished manuscript titled "'Almaqui' The House in the Woods," further explores the passion involved in engaging colonial spaces. This work depicts an unnamed twelve-year-old girl who, "very prone to tale spinning by herself," is orphaned and raised in a boarding school.[23] Once an adult, she lives alone working as a schoolteacher, her only pleasure "the hour when she could . . . take off her dress and shoes, and wrap her self in a blanket in winter and lie on her bed, while her thoughts flew to her house in the woods" (3). In the private space of the bed wearing only undergarments, this young woman is transported not by dreams of lovers and marriage proposals or by the return of her parents but by fantasies of dwelling in a sensually rich old colonial, what the narrator calls the "oldest house in the State" (9). After years of garnering pleasure exclusively from the hours spent undressed in bed imagining an alternative habitation, the girl, who is poor, comes into some money and visits an old house with

FIGURE 1 Elizabeth Bishop Perkins in colonial dress on staircase, ca. 1898–1900. Photograph. Courtesy of the Museums of Old York Collections, York, Maine.

an eye to purchasing it, only to realize that it is literally the house of her dreams, for it is the one she has somehow been haunting all these years. The unmarried young woman of "'Almaqui'" turns out to be both a modern and a ghost, her identity a fusion of being across time and space. Though the girl was unaware of her simultaneous existences for many years, during that time, the disjunction between past and present registered itself in and on her desiring body.

Is this not the same vision of temporal multiplicity offered in the striking photograph of the young Perkins in figure 1? Dressed from head to toe in white colonial garb, even her face a wan pallor, photographed from below as she apparently floats down the stairs surrounded by an assemblage of objects that cite the colonial past (the rail-back chair, the oriental rugs) as well as the early twentieth-century present, Perkins performs the ghost of an abstracted colonial woman embodied in the modern moment. As in "'Almaqui,'" Perkins stages the simultaneity of past and present by way of a white, spectral body. Her bosom lifted up and out, her colonial dress meticulous, Perkins seems to yearn physically for and toward the viewer who occupies the position of whoever has just entered the house. This performance welds the colonial to the modern: it registers a racially loaded temporal dissonance and depends on the presence of aged and contemporary things. Perkins's historicism was not a cultural aberration, nor was it the rule. But it formed part of a larger, section-specific cultural movement dominated by women, a movement that emphasized the embodied engagement of the past and the present and hints at both the queer and the performative components of women's historical practices in the latter part of the long nineteenth century.

In this book, I demonstrate how New England women of the period between 1865 and 1915 made history by way of a regionalism that included but reached far beyond fiction writing.[24] When we reassemble a section-specific frame through which to view the regionalist moment and look again, we see that not just fiction but history writing, antique china collecting, colonial home restoration, colonial fancy dressing, and heritage-based tourism constituted the practice in New England.[25] This women-dominated cultural mode shaped how Americans at the turn into the twentieth century understood New England, which was repeatedly personified in the period as feminine and spinsterly, as well as New England womanhood, which included in its conception alternative erotic forms such as the Boston marriage.[26] New England regionalism wrote the unmarried daughter into a dominant narrative of national history just as it constituted a critique of the nation as the ideal political form of belonging for women, offering in its stead unmarried women's membership in a community of New Englanders committed to cosmopolitan dissent. Such dissent reiterated what were thought to be radical colonial values, ones tied to the body's pleasures and pains. The New England regionalists theorized this cosmopolitan identity as rooted in colonial times and as defiant and distinctly Anglo, usually Anglo-Norman. Far from being closeted, avant-garde, mainly melancholy, or marginalized, New England regionalism—an interdisciplinary movement of women interested in thinking historically—was mainstream, culturally formative, collaborative, and emphasized women's history making in particular as pleasurable labor, labor opposed to marriage and maternity.

Like Elizabeth Perkins, many of the New England regionalists who practiced history making as pleasurable structured their sociosexual lives in ways we would now call queer. Some were members of Boston marriages, others formed long-term same-sex relationships and married late in life, and some refused permanent sodalities altogether, but all explored a host of alternative affiliations and erotic encounters that exceed any simple notion of queer as designating only modern homosexuality. Jewett, most famously, was in a Boston marriage with Annie Fields, the influential widow of the publisher James Fields. The Jewett-Fields relationship allowed for the independent living of each and the proliferation of intimate friendships outside the couple form.[27] The fiction writer Alice Brown had a lifelong partnership with the poet Louise Imogen Guiney, and though they maintained separate households, they collaborated and traveled together throughout their lives.[28] The historian and collector C. Alice Baker's first life partner was a fellow educator and visual artist, Susan Minot Lane. Later in their relationship, Baker and Lane expanded their family to include the photographer Emma Lewis Coleman. Together, Baker, Lane, and Coleman restored Frary house in Deerfield, Massachusetts, conducted extensive historical research into colonial women's lives, and helped construct Deerfield as a heritage tourism site, which it remains to this day.

Of the remaining half of these New England regionalists, only two—the historian-collector Alice Morse Earle and the fiction writer and collector Annie Trumbull Slosson—had what appear to have been successful, fairly traditional marriages to men, though Slosson was widowed within the first five years of marriage and did not wed again.[29] The other fiction writers, Cooke and Freeman, remained unmarried for most of their lives. Cooke had a deep and abiding love for her mother and did not marry until she was in her mid-forties, and this marriage was a troubled one.[30] Freeman lived with Mary Wales for nineteen years and also had an intense relationship with Evelyn Sawyer Severance.[31] In 1902, Freeman married Dr. Charles Manning Freeman, but she ended up estranged from her husband.[32] All told, the lives of the New England regionalists evidence the range of affiliations forged by women in the late nineteenth century.

Texturing the New England regionalists' lives and cultural productions, meanwhile, are intimate forms that exceed human-centered celibate, same-sex dyadic, and same-sex triadic models. Ecstatic relations with ghosts, old houses, and antique objects make for just a few of the impassioned pleasures we can trace across the fabric of New England regionalism. This range of relations further evidences what Peter Coviello calls the "varied passions" of the nineteenth-century imaginary, ones that "placed a countervailing emphasis on the erotic as a mode of being not yet encoded in the official vocabularies of the intimate."[33]

Across this diversely threaded tapestry of intimacies practiced and represented in New England regionalism we find a pattern of self-aware historicism, a commitment to the project of making history.

Archives of Desire plumbs the queer, feminist sensations and sensibilities that lie at the heart of the culturally imperialist, racially charged notion that New England among U.S. sections is uniquely historical. New England regionalism as I have recollected it here did not constitute a bid for the unmarried New England daughter and her desires merely to be included in history. Much more powerfully, it conceptualized the unwed daughter as specially embodying in the present and generating into the future a transtemporal white, liberal democratic dissent expressed by way of social-sexual practices. New England regionalism had within it a radical historicist strain by which the regionalists, through a range of performances, recast the scorned spinster as the unmarried New England daughter who, whether genealogically or adoptively linked to the region, embodied in the present a queerly colonial character, one made manifest in her refusal to affiliate along expected, heteronormative lines and in her insistence on exploring vastly configured pleasures.[34] In placing unmarried, often older women 'rather than the young, fertile protagonists of realism and naturalism center stage to history's revolution, the New England regionalists rescripted the legacy of democratic subjecthood as one of defiant New England womanhood. So while the various projects of the New England regionalists formed part of the ongoing mainstream effort among northeastern elites, from Barrett Wendell at Harvard University to William Dean Howells at *Harper's*, to have Anglo-dominated New England history become U.S. history writ large, they also cast the queer New England daughter as star in their tale of sectional superiority. This New England daughter undertook historical labors of myriad sorts, engaging the past in an effort to shape the present and the future. I call this method of doing history intimate historicism.

Intimate Historicism

In her 1925 preface to Sarah Orne Jewett's regionalist novel *The Country of the Pointed Firs*, Willa Cather recollected how Jewett "once laughingly told me that her head was full of dear old houses and dear old women, and that when an old house and an old woman came together in her brain with a click, she knew that a story was under way."[35] Cather delineates a legacy of literary production in which Jewett, a renowned fiction writer and queer woman interested in history, shares her generative process with another aspiring fiction writer and queer woman interested in the past, Cather herself.[36] Jewett's reported statement also replaces a central feature of literary narrative—the plot of heterosexual coupling—with a story of old women and their relationships with historical spaces. In so speaking, Jewett refashions dominant ideas about spinsters as either unproductive and pathological or realizing their worth through heterosexual pining and/or adoptive motherhood, ideas that pervaded discourse in the nineteenth century and beyond.[37] Considered in the context of New England regionalism—a regionalism constituted by colonial revivalism, tourism, and literary production—Jewett's comment names a specifically gendered practice wherein the house becomes the stage for a different sequence of embodied gestures and accompanying sensations. The domestic sphere, moreover, serves as a sensual site *to which* the unmarried woman relates intimately. This imaginative fitting together of old women and old houses well encapsulates how Jewett labored to generate history, writing her vision into the archive of published work.

Crucially, Jewett was not alone in her interest in history making and her focus on old women, subjects perceived as aged by virtue of being outside the heteronorm's circuit of reproductive labor.[38] Yet, as Stephanie Foote has pointed out, "it is Jewett who provide[s] the touchstone" for scholarship on American literary regionalism and, I would add, for queer literary scholarship focused on the age of romantic friendship.[39] Jewett was a member of a loosely affiliated group of women cultural producers that included, at a minimum, fiction writers Mary Wilkins Freeman, Rose Terry Cooke, Annie Trumbull Slosson, and Alice Brown, visual artists Susan Minot Lane and Emma Lewis Coleman, and colonial revivalists/historians C. Alice Baker, Alice Morse Earle, and Elizabeth Perkins.[40] Most of the five fiction writers were friends or had mutual acquaintances.[41] Jewett and Freeman, for instance, corresponded.[42] Cooke dedicated her 1891 volume of short stories, *Huckleberries Gathered from New England Hills*, to "my dearest friend, Annie Trumbull Slosson as a slight expression of my deep love and gratitude." Jewett was close acquaintances with Brown and her partner, the poet Guiney, whom Jewett mentored.[43] Important, too, were the intimate, often collaborative, relations between the fiction writers and the colonial revivalists. Jewett's friendship with Baker and Lane, for example, began in the 1870s and involved correspondence and frequent visits.[44] Baker, Lane, and Coleman bought a house in Kittery Point, Maine, and, during the summer, saw much of Jewett and Fields, Jewett's house being in nearby Berwick. The two families' friendship led to Coleman, Jewett, Baker, and Lane collaborating on the photographs for a special edition of Jewett's novel *Deephaven* that never reached print.[45] Jewett was a good friend of Elizabeth Perkins and her mother, Mary, as well as of Elise and Emily Tyson, another mother–unmarried daughter house-renovating team that restored a colonial mansion called Hamilton house, the setting for much of Jewett's Revolutionary-era novel *The Tory Lover*.[46]

Like Jewett, Freeman knew Baker, Lane, and Coleman. In an 1891 letter to Coleman, Freeman wonders (for the second time in their correspondence) whether Baker, a historian of colonial-era women's history, has "any old Deerfield-tale, which I could use" as inspiration.[47] One year later, Freeman wrote what was, presumably, the product of such cross-fertilization, "Silence," "a Deerfield massacre story" that she "hope[s] [Baker] will like."[48] Freeman corresponded with the historian of colonial times Alice Morse Earle as well. In one letter, Freeman thanks Earle for her book on colonial dress, noting "I . . . shall garb my heroine according to your fashion book."[49] These women visited one another's houses, read one another's writings, inspired one another intellectually, and collaborated occasionally, all of them sharing a specific interest in writing women, especially unmarried women, and their desires into history.

Intimate historicism is the method by which these New England regionalists rethought women's sociosexual sensations and forms of collective belonging in historical terms. Yet my use of this phrase is meant to encapsulate more than the actual social intimacies forged among members of the New England regionalist group and the closeness of their creations. I intentionally join "intimate" (which seems to be about privacy, personal relation, and the domestic) to "historicism" (which seems to be about public narrative, collectivity, and public labor) in an effort to capture both the friction and the affinity between the two terms. In part, the New England regionalists' historicism was intimate in that it represented and explored women's desires and labors. "Intimacy," Lauren Berlant reflects, "names the enigma of [a] range of attachments . . . and it poses a question of scale that links the instability of individual lives to the trajectories of the collective."[50] This notion of intimacy's scale, its active troubling of private and public somewhat misleadingly laid over the individual versus collective, belongs to the word's very denotation, for "intimate," as a noun, means "one who intimately belongs to something; a typical representative or example."[51] The seemingly closest, most private of exchanges have the potential to power public forms of belonging.

The New England regionalists themselves posited a relationship between the intimate desires and generative labors of the unmarried New England woman and her membership in a historicized, regionally specific community. For the regionalists, this membership was achieved not through the patriotic and supposedly progressive labors of marriage and maternity, but through a differently theorized, specifically New England character, one wedded to the sensual and intellectual labors of historical generation as a form of dissent. The New England regionalists represented this historically minded unwed daughter as central to New England's historically rooted identity being passed into a temporally tangled futurity; they implicitly posited her as essential, or intimate, to articulations of freedom. In many ways, the unmarried New England daughter of regionalism's refusal to thoughtlessly affiliate, echoed the efforts of the mythologized Anglo-American colonial citizen willing to throw off kin ties to the mother country in the name of ideology and with the hope of forging new, freer, only partly imaginable bonds. This assertion of the unmarried regional daughter's racially inflected character implied, in turn, another bolder intimation: that queerness itself was essential to democratic life, that so-called old maids were representative of a not yet realized democratic state, or better put, given New England regionalists' decided critique of the nation, a not yet realized free community of white, cosmopolitan dissenters.

The historicism in "intimate historicism," meanwhile, signals that the New England regionalists' work involved historiographical as well as non-literary cultural projects.[52] One way to frame it is to say that their historical work included not only the archive, the supposedly stable, preserved texts and objects of the past, but also the "performances, gestures, orality, movement, dance, singing—in short, all those acts usually thought of as ephemeral, nonreproducible knowledge" that make up what Diana Taylor calls the repertoire.[53] Taylor delineates the repertoire as part of a needed effort on the part of scholars to rethink performance as involving "participation in the production and reproduction of knowledge," specifically the reiteration and reinterpretation of cultural memory.⁵⁴ There are many repertoires the regionalists generated, from the countless history lessons Baker offered adoring students in Deerfield, Chicago, and Cambridge to the performance of Madame de Remusat undertaken by Charlotte Perkins Gilman when in attendance at a colonial tea party in 1890s Pasadena. The women whose works I examine here performed the past in formal and informal settings, sharing and collaborating on their interpretations of history.⁵⁵ Those, like Perkins, who self-consciously dwelt in old houses and integrated antiques, historical wallpapers, and other objects into their home spaces also remade cultural memory. The New England regionalists consistently wrote repertoires into the archive of materials they generated—the fiction, the photographs, the antique china collections, and the renovated houses—thus insisting on the embodied aspect of their history making. The New England regionalists alert us to the places where the repertoire becomes indistinguishable from or embedded in the archive, for intimate historicism tries to capture the felt experience of historical encounter as occasioned by and articulated in the archive understood as a material space.⁵⁶

New England regionalists, moreover, emphasized the sweat and ecstasy involved in the project of making history. Intimate historicism was a practice attuned to temporal asynchrony and the sensations of the variously impassioned or pleasured body. The New England regionalists seem to have understood Louise Fradenburg and Carla Freccero's notion that "history—and not just family history—is an erogenous zone"; at times, they were practitioners of what Elizabeth Freeman calls erotohistoriography, wherein one "sees the body as a method, and historical consciousness as something intimately involved with corporeal sensations."⁵⁷ But the example of the New England regionalists hones Freeman's notion of erotohistoriography, emphasizing how a specific group of women from the past pursued intimacies with historical matter and how they imagined such intimacies as generative. Across the pages of New England regionalism we see history staged (e.g., the laborious efforts of women characters to organize a town centennial celebration in Freeman's *The Jamesons*), crafted (e.g., the thoughtful renovation of Frary house undertaken by Baker, Coleman, and Lane), and hunted down (e.g., Earle's long, dusty searches for valuable Staffordshire plates). By archiving their often erotic repertoires as work, the New England regionalists foregrounded the unmarried woman's body, divorcing it from the labors of heterosexual reproduction understood as the ideal expression of white female citizenship while linking democratic action to the pleasures of recollection. These pleasures were not the same as but seem akin to the forms of grief that, as Dana Luciano so convincingly argues, "At once underwrote the social arrangements that supported its [the temporal imaginary's] standard chronologies and sponsored other ways of advancing history" in the nineteenth-century United States.[58] By the end of the period I examine in this book, a new generation of women writers—Gilman, Brown, and Pauline Elizabeth Hopkins—drew on New England regionalism in generating modernist counterhistories. Once understood as a larger cultural project rather than solely a short chapter in literary history, New England regionalism can be heard echoing across the past century, problematizing both teleological narratives of literary history that have regionalism dead by 1900 and contemporary scholarly accounts that assume the present exists in progressive superiority to regionalism as an antimodern intellectual movement of the past.

Archives of Desire grows out of and seeks to enrich scholarly traditions with which it is necessarily intimate, particularly criticism on American literary regionalism and queer studies scholarship on temporality and history. Part of what my analysis of the New England regionalists' intimate historicism allows us to do is trouble the presumed relationship between feminism and historicism within literary studies. This book would not have been imaginable as a project without the dedicated recovery work and intellectual insights of an earlier, late twentieth-century generation of feminist literary critics. Yet some accounts of regionalism's critical history, particularly new historicist accounts as exemplified by the influential work of Richard Brodhead, have oversimplified feminist literary scholarship, casting it as solely celebratory, as emphasizing gender difference without attention to "the real historical world."[59] Rather than emphasize the discontinuity between feminist critics before and after new historicist critiques, I am interested in considering the substantive continuities within feminist literary criticism wherein those critics have engaged rather than, as Brodhead has it, obscured the historical record. In the epilogue, I take up this question in greater depth, but its influence on my thinking about regionalism pervades *Archives of Desire* from its scope to the sorts of intimately historical readings and research it offers. In short, this book joins a scholarly conversation about regionalism as well as the long-standing effort taken up by mostly women scholars to work out a feminist-historicist scholarly practice. Susan Gillman, in her reading of Jewett's nationalism in *Pointed Firs* as linked to gender-based contestation; Kate McCullough, in her insistence on Jewett's and Florence Converse's efforts to "naturalize the Boston marriage as at the heart of 'America' by associating it with . . . the cultural capital of New England"; Sandra Zagarell, in her rigorous analyses of race in Jewett's regionalism; Stephanie Foote, in her attention to problems of citizenship and belonging and her "look[ing]. . .to see what the nineteenth century can tell twentieth-century literary critics"; and Jennifer Fleissner, in placing the American woman and her rhythms at the center of a rereading of fin de siècle U.S. literature have already worked to recollect regionalism.[60] I may emphasize the centrality of section and sexuality, and I may introduce readers to a more diverse archive than most of these literary scholars have, but we work alongside one another in a historically minded feminist tradition.

As a work of queer studies, *Archives of Desire* expands already abundant thinking about temporality, history, and erotic forms as explored in cultural texts while encouraging a more thorough engagement of traditional and nontraditional archives. The readings I offer have been nourished during the past decade by Christopher Nealon's notion that one might "feel historical," by Annamarie Jagose's attention to sequence in accounting for and reconfiguring lesbian representation, by Elizabeth Freeman's theory of erotohistoriography, by Dana Luciano's ever-productive concept of "chronobiopolitics," her careful attention to the spatiotemporal contours of attachment, and her close consideration of how intimate acts might reorganize the human as nonhuman.[61] In this book I join conversations about how we read the past in literary studies by practicing a method that itself echoes intimate historicism. *Archives of Desire* moves between two frames: on the one hand, I try to position texts in their cultural milieu. From this perspective, Jewett and her writings recede as exceptional. Not Jewett alone, but an entire group of women that included Jewett was engaged in the project of archiving its historical acts. On the other hand, I zoom in closely and attend to the textured nuances in the source materials, which for me means close reading as well as close researching: tracking down the material fragments such as the photographs for an unpublished edition of Jewett's *Deephaven*, images of the physical intimacy between the queer characters Kate Lancaster and Helen Denis among them. This method has led me to consider new materials, to not only interpret how imaginative texts of the past represent sexual lives but also examine how subjects in the nineteenth century perceived themselves as doing history by way of a range of impassioned, queer cultural productions.

New England's Empire; or, Regional Cosmopolitanism

By invoking Diana Taylor's theory of the repertoire as a mode by which cultural memory gets reiterated and remade, a theory grounded in her study of the violence of colonization in the Americas, I am necessarily calling forth the specter of imperialism understood across time. Scholarship on literary regionalism in the United States, in the turn to new historicism in the 1990s, proved particularly generative on this topic: June Howard's collection *New Essays on The Country of the Pointed Firs* and Kate McCullough's monograph *Regions of Identity*, for example, took up regionalism in relation to imperial and national formations. The same spirit animates Stephanie Foote's *Regional Fictions* wherein she argues that in the late nineteenth-century United States, "regional writing gave strangers with accents literary recognition at exactly the same moment that accented strangers in the form of immigrants were clamoring for recognition and representation in the political arena."[62] In my reading of New England regionalism, however, it is not the nation that is the primary structure for women's affiliations but a notion of transhistorical character thought to suture New Englandness to white imperialist endeavor on an international stage. This global valence of New England identity was itself rooted in the past—in the Pilgrims' cosmopolitan identification with European Protestantism and in New England's eighteenth- and early nineteenth-century role in overseas trade. It also had much to do with the regionalists' late nineteenth-century present: the United States in this era continued carrying out the destruction and displacement of Native Americans while expanding its imperialist agenda abroad, projects tied to the notion of white New Englanders disseminating their culture across the continent and beyond.[63] The period between 1865 and 1915 was also shaped by the Union' having just forced the South to remain part of the United States as well as by African Americans' work for racial uplift in a white supremacist nation in which ongoing attempts were made to colonize black bodies and their labors. The New England regionalists, it appears, did not advocate American exceptionalism, with "its paradoxical claim to uniqueness and universality," so much as a New England exceptionalism.[64]

In the nineteenth century, New England was often understood as somehow supranational, operating imperially within the United States as a cosmopolitan region associated (erroneously) with whiteness and at the forefront of imperialist enterprise abroad, a notion well captured in the moniker "Yankee" coming to refer to any American in foreign lands rather than a New Englander.[65] Fears of an intranational imbalance of power, of an urban center, one state, or one region dominating U.S. political life had a long history. In the words of the historian Peter Onuf, "New Englanders were the most sectionally conscious Revolutionaries.... No other group of states was well enough defined or had had the common historical experiences or consciousness of distinct regional interests to be confused with a 'nation.'"[66] As Conforti has further traced, New Englanders from the colonial period through the twentieth century promoted their region's exceptionalism.[67] Emily Dickinson, another unmarried daughter of New England, perhaps put it best: "Because I see—New Englandly— / The Queen, discerns like me— / Provincially"—which is to say, thinking provincially or regionally, in the case of New England, was also to see with Anglicized, imperial eyes.[68]

When the New England regionalists I examine in this study looked back to the colonial period, it was less often to identify with a nation's mythically humble beginnings and more often to lay claim to a cosmopolitan notion of dissent and mobility understood as an Anglo-American birthright. Rethinking colonial histories may have allowed for a critique of late nineteenth-century women's ongoing subordinate relationship to the national polity as not yet enfranchised citizens with significantly compromised rights, but claims to belonging within New England regionalism exceeded the desire for national membership or enfranchisement. Across New England regionalist fiction, late nineteenth-century women characters' rebellions echo colonial forms of dissent against the imperial and familial authority of the British Empire. These traditions of dissent were tied to Eurocentric, cosmopolitan notions of freedom.[69] Embedded in New England regionalism, then, is a forward-looking lament about the unrealized potential of the consolidated nation-state, a dream about what the colonial moment might have meant in terms of democratic citizenship for white women, particularly their freedom to affiliate as they might choose. Within New England regionalism such freedom of affiliation, of movement across disparate spaces, cultures, and intimate forms, took the shape not of nationalism, but of cosmopolitanism.

The cosmopolitanism of New England regionalism is more far reaching than the urban elitism Brodhead critiques in his analysis of Jewett's *Pointed Firs*.[70] So, too, is the cosmopolitanism I invoke distinct from the literary cosmopolitanism, "an ethos of representational inclusiveness, of the widest possible affiliation, and concurrently one of aesthetic discrimination and therefore exclusivity," that Tom Lutz argues critics today (such as Brodhead and Ammons) share with the American regionalists of the nineteenth century.[71] Instead, the cosmopolitanism of the New England regionalists drew on Enlightenment ideas about liberal subjects' free economic, intellectual, and affective exchanges across national boundaries, and it was specifically inflected by gender, sexuality, and race.[72] In a sense, the New England regionalists implicitly revisited some of the questions asked by cosmopolitan European and American women from the turn into the eighteenth century up through the early nineteenth about whether and how women's national citizenship might be possible.[73] Baker, in her research into the New England women taken captive during the French and Indian Wars, explores the many ways those women reaffiliated across national and cultural boundaries, thus casting New England daughters as mobile, flexible, and transnational figures, their desires and lives made possible within an imperial framework; Jewett in *Pointed Firs* has Mrs. Todd and Mrs. Fosdick use the term "queer" to refer to earlier eras in which New England's shipping industry linked Maine's coastal villages to the global economy, to cultural diversity, and to imperialist endeavor abroad.[74] The New England regionalists understood structures of gender, kinship, and power in the far-reaching context of a transhistorical world, rather than in the context of a solely contemporary region or progressive nation. They also claimed for themselves a cosmopolitan identity, one rooted in liberal notions of freedom.

Claims to a nonreproductive, racialized exceptionalism proved significant in an era in which, responding to the influx of immigrants and the decline in white birthrates, leaders such as President Theodore Roosevelt yoked white women's reproduction to the progress of the nation, thought of as a white body politic. This was also a period in history when the eugenics movement gained ground and was consistently tied both to women's rights and to sociosexual freedom.[75] Judith Fetterley and Marjorie Pryse suggest, "We might understand the refusal of white women regionalists to place their fiction in the service of reproducing ... white Anglo-Saxon masculinity as a form of antiracist work," and they go on to claim, "To the extent that regionalism engages in white and male critique as a critique of nation, it also challenges turn-of-the-century U.S. imperialism."[76] But I have found that the cosmopolitan modes of belonging that the regionalists imagined as part of their legacy performed distinct, albeit complex, racial and imperialist work not only by defying nineteenth-century popular cultural images of unmarried women as posing a threat to the progress of the white nation-state by way of their assumed lack of productivity but also by reiterating the special value of white character as a distinct inheritance belonging to queer women.

New England regionalism, especially in its literary facet, performed racial work within an imperial frame through its emphasis on character, a word used to designate race in the period.[77] The notion of New England character as ideal shaped and was shaped by many cultural conversations, among them late nineteenth-century literary criticism. Howells's musings on New England in fiction were sectionalist in precisely this way: "It may be that New England character is merely more wonted to literature," he writes, "that we accept an effect of beauty in it more readily than in less familiarized forms of human nature."[78] Howells implicitly links character to New England. In this context it gets imagined as a thing of beauty, a fantasy of democratic individuality and white racial belonging associated with aesthetic pleasure. This is, arguably, the same sentiment we find in Howells's preference for Freeman's realist fiction over that of Mary Noailles Murfree, a southerner. Both writers have their faults, Howells insists, but Freeman's work is superior in its delineation of intimate racialized belonging, or what he calls "community of character"; he continues, "The people [in Freeman's stories] are of one New England blood, and speak one racy tongue."[79]

The cultural context in which such racially charged delineations of sectionalized literary modes abounded was one in which the New England regionalists worked and were understood. In fact, they themselves helped generate it through their emphasis on racial inheritances of character for unmarried white women. Baker stood in front of audiences and asserted that she had coursing through her body the same "dissenting blood" as her French Canadian relatives; the unmarried protagonist, Dilly Joyce, of Brown's short story "A Last Assembling" "held herself remote from personal intimacies; but all the fine, invisible bonds of race and family took hold of her like irresistible factors, and welded her to the universe anew"; Jewett wrote how amid the history of the Normans "everywhere you will catch a gleam of the glorious courage and steadfastness that have won ... the great English and American discoveries and inventions and noble advancements of all the centuries since."[80] New England regionalism responded to and helped generate the cultural discourses of what historian Michael Kammen has called "an age of memory and ancestor worship."[81] The radical, queer dissent portrayed across the range of New England regionalist forms was rooted in an international vision of white women's freedom, privilege, and mobility, a vision tied to an imperialist prerogative. These interconnections animated, even made possible, the New England regionalist's' intimate historicism.

It is worth considering the continuities between the regionalists' historical moment and our own in terms of discourses about life and productivity and the role women are assumed to play within them. As Jasbir Puar has pointed out, it is by way of the nuclear family structure that queer people in our own era have been receiving temporary "measures of benevolence" within the structure of the nation-state.[82] "This benevolence toward sexual others," Puar writes, "is contingent upon ever-narrowing parameters of white racial privilege, consumption capabilities, gender and kinship normativity, and bodily integrity."[83] The same was largely true, though in a perhaps more overtly gendered way in its bald emphasis on white women's reproductive lives, at the turn of the twentieth century. Teddy Roosevelt asserted, for instance, that "no nation can exist at all unless the average woman is the home-keeper, the good wife, and unless she is the mother of a sufficient number of healthy children to insure the race going forward and not backward."[84] Henry Adams, meanwhile, articulated his wish that he could "require of an octogenarian Senate the passage of a law obliging every woman, married or not, to bear one baby,—at the expense of the Treasury,—before she was thirty years old, under penalty of solitary confinement for life."[85] The New England regionalists participated in and contributed to a mainstream movement to instantiate New England at the center of history *with the unmarried woman and her myriad desires, none of them biologically reproductive, at the center of that history* and thus defied the logic of the nuclear family as the route to queer women's belonging.[86] The shift to imagining unmarried women's dissent as on a continuum with colonial forms of dissent and the consistent demonstration of the future and past orientation of unmarried women threatened to undo some effects of the racist, imperialist assumptions at the base of that self-same project.

Rather than producing children or mothering them, the New England regionalists took up the significant work of historical generation, imagining their historicist acts as tied to alternative forms of feeling. They contested the nationally sanctioned terms of collective life, theorizing in their place a regional cosmopolitanism, which we might understand as an early precursor to Puar's notion of "homonationalism," the twenty-first-century "imbrication of American exceptionalism [that] is increasingly marked through or aided by certain homosexual bodies."[87] Puar's focus is recent history: "Homosexual bodies have been historically understood as endlessly cathected to death," she asserts and offers as her example "the AIDS epidemic."[88] Though her topic is the historically specific permutation of homonationalism in our own day, her ideas give contemporary form to phenomena with longer roots: there is, I propose in this book, a history, alternative histories in fact, of how queerness has been thought as tied to national and international sexualized subjects and has inflected the white racial work of imperialist enterprise. Regional cosmopolitanism, a sectionally articulated claim of belonging to powerful imperial networks of exchange, including those that underwrite or constitute a capacious set of passions, energized New England regionalism. Limning the contours of women regionalists' complex recollections, thinking through how queerness has historically been a site of critique as well as of normative claims and creations, helps sharpen our contemporary understanding of the cultural narratives we have inherited and continue to try and revise. It alerts us to how, in the nineteenth century as today, we find "within the interstices of life and death . . . the differences between queer subjects who are being folded (back) into life and the racialized queernesses that emerge through the naming of populations."[89]

Assembling Archives

"Only that historian will have the gift of fanning the spark of hope in the past who is firmly convinced that *even the dead* will not be safe from the enemy if he wins," Walter Benjamin asserts.[90] Across the pages of New England regionalism, especially in the works of the later generation of writers that I examine in chapter 4, the dead are not distanced from the living but, instead, precisely those with whom women imagine themselves to fuse, commune, or collaborate. These women writers trouble the very notion of the pastness of the past, of history as progressive. The unnamed narrator of "The Yellow Wall-Paper" dwells in an old colonial mansion in the New England countryside and becomes part of a cross-generational collectivity of women by way of her eroticized, repetitive contact with old wallpaper. Baker stands on the gravesite of one of the colonial women captives taken to Canada whose history she has uncovered and reflects, "It was as if I had laid the ghosts of unburied shades that had wandered, restless, haunting my whole life."[91] Hopkins's black woman detective, Venus Johnson, cross-dresses and saves two women from imprisonment in a colonial mansion by citing performances of women's revolutionary heroism. These intimate historicisms are vital, and while they are, more often than not, optimistic in their effort to renovate history, they are undergirded by, and at times threaten to reinscribe, the pain and terror of the past and the present. Histories, in *Archives of Desire*, unfold and fold back on themselves at sometimes unexpected angles. I have tried to remain attuned throughout to the possibility of an archive fragmented across not only time but also space, both in my choice to conduct research at little known, underfunded institutions scattered throughout New England and in the materials I have ultimately included in this study.

The story about New England regionalism I tell in this book challenges recent scholarship on regionalist literature by emphasizing regionalism's broad scope and the forward-looking aspect of New England women regionalists' history making. At the same time, it extends scholarship in queer literary studies by considering an earlier period of queer historicism and exploring how nineteenth-century subjects thought themselves into history by way of complex temporal turns and intellectual labors. The New England regionalists made history, experiencing and recording their myriad yearnings and affective knowledge through archival acts. Their history making involved the assembling of fragments, the gathering of materials assembled with an understanding that they might later be reconfigured and reinterpreted. Archives are often thought of as elite collections hidden from sight from which history is extracted. Regionalists like Baker did conduct extensive research in that kind of archive, but they also created new, alternative archives. Baker and her family members, for instance, brought old, discarded items from the regional past together in new assemblages. Both types of archival work involve recollection: the gathering, staging, and storing of texts and objects emphasizes the materiality of history making, as well as the role of the contingent and the fleeting in historical practice. The New England regionalists were buying, hunting down, and interacting with individual objects, sometimes even literal shards, as they worked to historicize women's experiences, author women's history, and construct material spaces and collection-based narratives that accounted for their capaciously queer desires.

With an understanding of cultural fragments as both discrete and situated within various contexts, *Archives of Desire* moves from history writing (chapter 1) to regionalist fiction (chapter 2) to antique china collecting (chapter 3) to fiction again (chapter 4). In each chapter, I position the regionalist practice emphasized in constitutive relationship to at least one, often more, other regionalist practices and therein demonstrate of New England regionalism's reach. I begin the chapter sequence with "Renovating the House of History," an examination of the regionalist recollections of Baker who was a historian in addition to being involved in architectural restoration, antique collecting, and heritage-tourism development. The breadth of Baker's practices well introduces readers to a redefined New England regionalism. I focus, however, on her colonial history writing, including her metacritical reflections on her own methods, to demonstrate how intimate historicism differed from existing historical practices of the age and to begin explicating how it involved performance and collaboration. Baker's intimate historicism, I contend, cannot be divorced from her membership in a triadic, queer family that included the painter Susan Minot Lane and the photographer and historian Emma Lewis Coleman. Throughout their collaborative works we see a theory of women's history emerging: they conceptualized history as a specifically sociosexual historical configuration, a renovated colonial garrison house in which collectivities of women could live and produce while demonstrating that they belonged and were crucial to generating a cosmopolitan, regional past.

Chapter 2, "Literature's Historical Acts," argues that literature already thought of as regionalist—namely, fiction by Cooke, Freeman, and Jewett—was self-consciously historiographical. Herein I reorient existing arguments about literary regionalism as merely nostalgic, ahistorical, or reflective of historical realities. These fiction writers represent unmarried women's relation to colonial history in two significant ways: Cooke and Freeman use historical allusions to imagine late nineteenth-century women as physically reenacting key scenes from the colonial past, while Jewett attends to how late nineteenth-century women echo historical experience by way of their bodies through physical interactions with historicized spaces and matter (colonial houses, old-fashioned gardens, wild landscapes, and "old" women). In this chapter, I expand my reading of regionalist fiction's historicism through analyzing the photographs Coleman and Jewett created for a special edition of *Deephaven*. Considering the photos alongside *Deephaven's* text allows us to understand more fully these regionalists' vision of a queer mobility enabled by New England exceptionalism.

The popular pastime of antique china collecting, particularly the gender blending and bending reveled in by women china hunters, is the topic of chapter 3, "Out of the China Closet." In the late nineteenth century, antique collecting became all the rage. Those who imagined themselves to be the most adventurous antiquers were women who traveled New England's roads, knocking on farmhouse doors hoping to pay low prices for valuable ceramic wares from the colonial, Revolutionary, and early national periods. The literature of women's china collecting represented this china hunter as a bold, savvy woman who garnered great pleasure from seeking out and acquiring rare old pitchers and plates. Modifying existing English stereotypes about china collectors as either oversexed women or emasculated fops, collectors such as Annie Trumbull Slosson and Alice Morse Earle cast the practice as decidedly historical as well as sensually, if not sexually, satisfying. Through fantasy, the crazed state, and the dream, china-hunting guides allowed for the full play of an intimately historical and distinctly regionalist imagination.

Having discussed the diverse generations and collaborations of the New England regionalists in these first three chapters, I turn back to literature in chapter 4, "Spectral Fusions, Modernist Times." Here, I take up the writings of three women left out of most accounts of regionalism: Charlotte Perkins Gilman, who has not been thought of as a regionalist but as a feminist focused on the nation; Alice Brown, whose work has been all but overlooked by scholars; and Pauline Elizabeth Hopkins, who, though consistently identified with New England and black Boston, is rarely read alongside white regionalist writers. Each of these women writers engaged New England–dominated colonial revivalism in her fiction by way of intimate historicism. The uses to which they put history in their texts, their shared explorations of modern women becoming one with female ghosts, or what I call spectral fusions, merged regionalism into modernism. These three writers were part of the generation that came "after" the New England regionalists. Yet their fiction troubles literary history, for it reveals that modernist constructions of the temporally fragmented self were characteristic of New England regionalism. Opening the view out from modernism to contemporary times, in the book's epilogue I examine another significant moment in U.S. women's intellectual history, one that shaped criticism on regionalism: the 1970s and 1980s, which saw the development of feminist literary studies. In that era, which I demonstrate was deeply informed by questions of legacy, generation, and history making, we reencounter intimate historicism.

Archives of Desire explores the repetition of affective experiences and practices across time, attending more often to similitude than to alterity as the basis for the relationship between the past and present. It is itself an act of intimate historicism, one that recognizes its collaboration with contemporary scholarship on queer temporalities, historical materialism, feminism, and the generations of the New England regionalists. This ever-unfolding set of relationships forms part of the larger, always partial and ongoing practice of what Eve Kosofsky Sedgwick calls "reparation": the trying to piece together a future-looking something while recognizing the past, experiencing the affective charge of such labor, and registering the anxiety such creative, analytical acts are always mediating.[92] Each of these acts, *Archives of Desire* among them, attempts to engage the past in and through the present.

1
Renovating the House of History

C. Alice Baker was an early feminist historian dedicated to researching white, colonial New England women's experiences of captivity, survival, and reaffiliation beyond New England's borders. Unlike the influential histories of colonial North America provided by her contemporary Francis Parkman, in which individual men represent clearly demarcated warring nationalities (e.g., Pontiac, Wolfe, Montcalm), and unlike the colonial revivalist accounts of writers such as Samuel Adams Drake, in which New England figures as the innocent victim of Indian savagery and French greed, Baker's one published book, *True Stories of New England Captives Carried to Canada during the Old French and Indian Wars*, tells of eleven women and girls taken captive in the intercolonial conflicts.[1] These New England daughters were unredeemed and went on to reaffiliate in New France, most of them electing to remain with their new communities rather than return to the New England, Protestant ones into which they were born. Significantly, Baker's historical enterprise did not consist only of archival research and writing. She helped spearhead the historic home restoration movement in New England and was influential in the establishment of Deerfield, Massachusetts, the site of one famous attack on the New England frontier, as a heritage tourism destination. Articulating her historical sensibilities across cultural practices and well-nigh ignored within literary and historical scholarship, Baker pursued what we would think of today as a feminist research agenda. Her work exemplifies the collaborative form often taken by New England regionalism as well as its intimate historicism.

Baker's intellectual endeavors formed part of a larger collaboration involving herself and the two other members of her triadic, same-sex family: Susan Minot Lane and Emma Lewis Coleman. At the age of twenty, "all on fire with generous impulses, warm sympathies and ardent longings," Baker fell in love with Lane, a fellow teacher at

Deerfield Academy.[2] Lane and Baker, who was a particularly successful teacher of history, went on to open schools together in Chicago and, later, in Boston. Lane herself was an accomplished painter.[3] Coleman joined the Baker-Lane family in the 1880s, soon after Baker undertook the historical research project that would occupy her for the rest of her life and yield the publication of *True Stories*.[4] Coleman's extensive work in photography was influenced by Lane's artistic sensibilities, and Coleman's two-volume history *New England Captives Carried to Canada between 1677 and 1760 during the French and Indian Wars* culminated from the research she conducted on the intercolonial wars throughout four decades, two in collaboration with Baker.[5]

Baker, Lane, and Coleman were committed to constructing a historical space in which women, whether from the colonial era or the contemporary moment of the late nineteenth century, could dwell. Baker represented her historical research in *True Stories* as renovating the metaphorical house of New England history, readmitting to a communal historical home forgotten women and girls. Baker, Lane, and Coleman also sought to restructure their own relationship with the regional past through recollection. In 1890, led by Baker, the three women took on the project of restoring Frary house, a dilapidated colonial home in Deerfield, Massachusetts. Together they traveled the New England countryside acquiring fragments of colonial buildings and furniture to be used in the house: the "double-door came from [a] . . . house in Greenfield Meadows," drawers came from the room in the Oliver Wendell Holmes house in which "American generals . . . made plans for the battle of Bunker Hill," and the china closet door was "from the Junkins Garrison-house of York, Maine," a famous colonial home represented by a host of late nineteenth-century artists.[6] By the end of Frary house's restoration, it was not only a space that reminded its inhabitants and visitors of the colonial New England past but also a space inscribed with the history of the Baker-Lane-Coleman family's adventurous and collaborative recollection.

Baker's was an intimate historicism, for it recognized history making as an embodied, pleasurable labor as well as a performance. An excerpt from one of the few letters written by Baker that survives in the archive demonstrates as much and demarcates how the restored Frary house served as one of her stages.[7] Corresponding with her

Canadian cousin in 1895, just a few years after Lane's death, Baker wrote:

> I send you with this letter a photograph taken by Emma of my chamber, a corner of my parlor, and a picture of our music room—I rise at 6 o'clock—pull back the short curtains from my short windows towards to *east*. . . . I stand here perhaps ten minutes & I can truly say I *always* think of dear Susan Lane now with the angels. And very very often of Canada for the house reminds me always of that day in 1703 when French & Indians carried my ancestry into captivity—and so of you and of much happiness you have brought to me.[8]

Figure 2 is a photograph of Baker's chamber taken by Coleman, likely the same image enclosed in the letter to this Canadian cousin.[9]

Baker's letter, especially when read alongside Coleman's photograph, evidences how Frary house became a stage for Baker's intimate historicism. First, Coleman's photograph of Baker's bedroom chamber reinforces the text of Baker's letter in expanding the intimacy between Baker and her cousin, allowing the latter a glimpse into the private spaces and rhythms of Baker's daily life. Photographing interior rooms was a popular practice in the late nineteenth century: professionals were often brought in to create such keepsakes, some of which were kept by the house owner as part of an archive of personal history while others were bound into so-called "house books" and circulated among family and friends.[10] This was the case regardless of whether the house was restored or considered special. Baker's inclusion of three photographs by Coleman with the letter seems an abbreviated, informal riff on the house book, one meant to express and advance the relationship with her cousin. Yet Coleman's photograph accomplishes much more: it highlights, as does Baker's letter, Baker's lived experience of multiple temporalities, her felt communion with the dead.

In the letter, Baker constructs a transnational, transtemporal collectivity of New England white women and represents Frary house as the stage on which she performs membership in that collectivity. Baker expresses how she is mindful of her love, Susan (now dead), and her living partner, Emma, as well as members of her extended family, both her Canadian cousin and the Deerfield captives on whom her research centers. Baker's mode of imagining affiliations is not limited to the couple form, to a sense of the biological, nuclear family, or to

FIGURE 2 Emma Lewis Coleman, C. Alice Baker's bedroom. Photograph. Courtesy of the Pocumtuck Memorial Association Library, Deerfield, Massachusetts.

a distinct historical era; instead, it proliferates. Baker, in this letter, also asserts her physical presence in the space—"I rise," "I stand"—with a focus on her body's positions as if she is writing stage directions. Coleman's photograph of Baker's chamber, meanwhile, in foregrounding the open space of the bedroom, encourages the viewer's perception that the photograph depicts an actual stage setting, one we might step upon. In this, Baker's text and Coleman's image together anticipate not only Roland Barthes's notion that photography is akin to theater "by way of a singular intermediary . . . by way of Death" but the notion of domestic spaces as performance spaces.[11] Flooded with eastern light, the photograph of the bedroom highlights visually the presence of absence (large, light open space) as well as gauzy-ghostly white things (the bedcovers, the curtains, a tablecloth). When we imagine Baker into the space depicted in the photograph according to her phrasing ("I rise," "I stand"), her actions seem a ritual resurrection; her standing in the window awash in light would transmute her figure into a ghostly one, something not unlike the spectral image of Elizabeth Bishop Perkins in figure 1. In these two interrelated texts—the letter and the photograph—Baker is both seen and unseen, embodied and disembodied, rendered part of the transtemporal collectivity of women that has been and lingers on occupying multiple temporalities in Frary house.

It was Baker's project to reorient the historical enterprise along intimate lines, transforming it from an exclusively individual endeavor by which the single historian tells the history of a nation (e.g., the United States) or of competing nations (e.g., England and France) by way of exceptional, representative men. Baker focused, instead, on the many women and children taken captive in the intercolonial wars of the eighteenth century who were not redeemed.[12] By means of imagining relationships between proximate bodies, Baker told the history of New England as a globally embedded region while also portraying the dead as remaining in vital and complex relation with the living. Baker and Coleman together rewrote the unmarried New England daughter, particularly her sociosexual history imagined as rooted in a specifically white construct of ideal citizenship, into the larger regional narrative at just the moment when New England escalated its bid to be considered the most historical and American of U.S. regions. Baker pursued this project by productively troubling the distinction between writing and performance; she used written and spoken language as well as her feeling body to represent scenes of history and to inscribe her own intimately felt performance of women's history into the archive.

True Stories's Colonial Haunts

Deerfield, Massachusetts, was well-known in the nineteenth century for having been the site of a major 1704 French and Indian attack on the English frontier. Abenakis, Frenchmen, Hurons, Mohawks, Pennacooks, and other Iroquois cooperated in executing this early eighteenth-century assault on Deerfield wherein fifty English men, women, and children were killed and 112 were taken into captivity.[13] According to Baker's friend and informal biographer Jennie Arms Sheldon, the research that yielded *True Stories* and, later, *New England Captives* began with George Sheldon's request that Baker pursue a project on Deerfield history: "Give me a woman for my subject and I will!" was Baker's spirited response.[14] An advocate of women's rights, including suffrage, Baker consistently emphasized women's experiences of colonial New England history and captivity in *True Stories*. Here are some of the histories she tells. Christine Otis (originally Margaret Otis) entered captivity as a baby, was raised by the nuns of Montreal, married, and had three children with a Frenchman named Le Beau. She was then widowed, fell in love with the English Captain Baker, moved to New England, and ended up an independent tavern keeper in Dover, New Hampshire. Mother Marie-Joseph of the Infant Jesus (originally Esther Wheelwright) was taken captive at about the age of six, lived with an Abenaki Indian for six years, was taken in by the Governor of Quebec, entered the convent, and served as the influential mother superior of the Ursulines of Quebec for decades.[15] Elizabeth Twatogwach (originally Abigail Nims) was taken at age three into the Mohawk community at the Sault-au-Recollet, raised as an Indian, baptized a Catholic, and then redeemed only to run from Deerfield back to Canada to be reunited with her native community, eventually marrying a fellow Iroquois-assimilated English captive.[16] Marguerite Kanenstenhawi (originally Eunice Williams), whose story has fascinated Americans for centuries, in Baker's account preferred her Mohawk culture to that of English New England. Baker asserts that Kanenstenhawi remained mindfully attached to her New England family, citing as evidence her native husband, Amrusus (Ambroise), having taken her last name, their naming their eldest child John, after her father, and that she "thrice revisited the place of her nativity" (154).[17] Even given this attachment to New England, however, Baker, invoking familiar stereotypes about native peoples as savages, asserts that Kanenstenhawi "insisted upon returning to her Canadian home, and finally died there at the advanced age of ninety ... [which serves as] a proof of her preference for savage haunts and modes of life" (154). Baker consistently places these stories of individual women's lives in the larger framework of male-dominated imperial history. Each chapter of *True Stories* begins not with a colonial raid, but with earlier histories of European exploration, imperialism, violence toward native peoples, or religious dissent. And, as I will discuss later in this chapter, this same understanding of gender history echoes between the covers of Coleman's *New England Captives*. As Baker herself put it, "We should not shrink from tracing effects to their causes" (13).

The women's lives Baker writes about in *True Stories* were lived in a queer modality, by which I mean they defied the heterosexist, chauvinist notion that the allegiances of women are straightforward and overdetermined, thought to be coextensive with one's *patria*. The captives' lives also resist late nineteenth-century theories that women best express their patriotism by way of their reproductive bodies rather than as active, enfranchised citizens electing their affiliations. That the female captives who were not redeemed went on to pursue a range of alternative bonds, ones different from those assigned by coincidence of birth, demonstrates that women's allegiances and intimacies are largely constructed and fluid rather than essential and fixed. Baker's attention to common New England white women living on the colonial frontier does not reinscribe an overdetermined notion of nation or reinforce assumptions that women's experiences were somehow confined to the insular, domestic realm of motherhood and marriage.

In this way, Baker's work implicitly resonates with Christopher Castiglia's reassessment of white women's captivity narratives. He argues, "Above all, captivity's epistemological 'contradiction' challenged Anglo-America's assertion that racial and gendered identities are innate, unified, and unchanging."[18] Castiglia goes further to explain his own scholarly commitment to the project of researching white women's captivity narratives: "My interest in the experiences of captives is understandable in these terms: stifled, isolated, bound and often gagged, the captive white woman paradoxically gains a voice, a mobility, and above all a revised sense of collective belonging."[19] Baker imagined her whole life to have been haunted by the subjects of her research—the captives—and it seems she strove for a kind of belonging similar to the one of which Castiglia writes, one that revises and therein critiques the normative configuring of collectivities in the late nineteenth century, from the community congregated around the domestic hearth to the one constituting the nation. Baker and Castiglia differ, however, in that Baker was interested not in those women who were redeemed and who, by way of that experience of captivity and return, "'queer' the language of domination," but in those captives who remained in Canada, most of whom appear only as written about rather than as writers.[20] *True Stories* constructs a transhistorical diaspora of white women who lived in a queer modality across cultures, their lives defined in the interstices of imperial history, regional identity, and intimate bonds. It is this refashioned regional history that, while recognizable to her peers in the late nineteenth century and to us today as history writing in that it is based on extensive archival research, differed quite markedly from the romantic histories of its age. Baker appears as a character in *True Stories*; she wrote into her history the figure of the late nineteenth-century woman historian and so implicitly theorized the relation between the past and present as mediated by a female scholar.

The historiographical terrain on which Baker built *True Stories* was an uneven one shaped by overlapping traditions and new trends. The institutionally sanctioned romantic historicism practiced by George Bancroft and Francis Parkman, the by then rich tradition of women's historical writing, the so-called antiquarianism of the early nineteenth century that fed gently into the colonial revival of the late century, and the emergent efforts of male historians to professionalize history as a discipline were all contexts for Baker's work. Of these, romantic historicism had perhaps the most profound influence. Born in 1833, come into adulthood in the early 1850s, Baker grew up in a region, nation, and culture fascinated by the past and heavily influenced by the vision of history put forth by Sir Walter Scott. This was the period in which, as Nina Baym has shown, U.S. women's historical writing across forms and genres proliferated, just as it was an era in which, in fictional works by writers such as Nathaniel Hawthorne, houses, armchairs, and other object matter that had survived the colonial period whispered the nation's dark secrets.[21] In Europe and the United States at this same time, following the example of Germaine de Staël, women were generating vibrantly felt, Gothic-tinged histories and engaging crucial questions about citizenship, history, gender, and belonging. It is hard not to see in Baker's intimate historicism echoes of de Staël's work, which "executes the Romantic project of attaching affect to the narrative of the past."[22]

But what sort of space existed for the history of the forgotten that Baker wrote or, institutionally, for Baker herself as a woman historian? We can best answer these questions by examining Baker's complex relationship to the work of Parkman, which reflects at almost every level differences of gendered class power. An independently wealthy Bostonian and graduate of Harvard, Parkman had access to the metropolitan archives of France and England, and it was on these holdings, as well as on various New York, Massachusetts, and Canadian sources, that he based much of *France and England in North America*. Parkman was part of an elite network of influential men. A correspondent of Theodore Roosevelt's, to whom Roosevelt dedicated his own *The Winning of the West*, Parkman knew enough politicians in 1872 to get congressional approval for the publication of documents about La Salle gathered by the French archivist M. Pierre Margry even though Margry's 1870 and 1871 requests to Congress had been denied.[23] Parkman's version of colonial history, which foregrounded the glories of British and U.S. imperialism, the destruction of Native American peoples as inevitable and necessary, and a narrative of history based on great men, was suffused with grand and biased notions of U.S., New England, and white racial superiority. Given this, it is perhaps no surprise that Parkman vocally opposed women's suffrage and rarely mentioned women in his extensive oeuvre.[24]

Parkman, however, in the Deerfield chapter of the last volume of the seven-volume *France and England in North America*, includes three footnotes acknowledging Baker's then unpublished research. Parkman's most substantive footnote about Baker reads: "The above is drawn mainly from extracts made by Miss Baker from the registers of the Church of Notre Dame at Montreal."[25] Baker is, Parkman implies, doing something interesting and doing it well, yet in the grand scale of history, it fits within a paragraph, and she emerges more as a secretarial conduit linking the historian to the archive than as a historian in her own right.

In the relationship between Parkman and Baker subtly inscripted in *Half-Century*, we hear echoes of a larger gender dynamic at play, one with its own history. Beginning in the mid-1870s, during the years in which Parkman served as the president of the Massachusetts Historical Society (MHS, 1875–78), the historian George Sheldon consistently tried to get Baker accepted as a member, but was repeatedly denied.[26] According to Sheldon, "if they [the MHS members] 'ever so far deviated from their rules *as to admit a woman to membership*' Miss Baker would stand high as a candidate."[27] Baker's assertion of herself as a historian of New England and Massachusetts history in particular would never be acknowledged by the MHS in the form of an offer of membership. Baker's project, moreover, looked very different from Parkman's as well as those pursued by the emergent cohort of science-minded professional historians who defined themselves through and against Parkman's romantic amateurism.

The cohort of post-Parkman historians who began writing in the late nineteenth century often conceptualized history as a building and thus implicitly characterized the historical enterprise as involving "steady, cumulative progress."[28] In 1907, the historian Edward Cheyney asserted:

> The scientific writer of history builds no Gothic cathedral, full of irregularities and suggestiveness, aspiring arches, niches filled with sacred or grotesque figures, and aisles dim with religious light,—that is work for the literary historian. But he builds a classic temple: simple, severe, symmetrical in its lines, surrounded by the clear, bright light of truth, pervaded by the spirit of moderation.[29]

Endeavoring to reproduce "the past [that] has really been," the scientific historian downplays his own role in shaping the structure of history.[30] In Cheyney's rendering, the "truth" of the past dictates present-day history's design; he thinks of history as replication rather than the renovation of a preexisting edifice. Similarly obscuring his agency as a meaning-maker, the historian J. Franklin Jameson wrote to Henry Adams, "I struggle on, making bricks without much idea of how the architects will use them."[31] As Peter Novick contends, men like Cheyney and Jameson were reacting against the romantic historicism of Parkman and Bancroft, as well as, I would add, following Bonnie G. Smith, a century of amateur history writing which was aligned with the Gothic, literary historians, and women.[32] These new professional male historians of the late nineteenth century also saw history, whether the designs of its buildings were of the past or not yet determined, as an exercise in constructing something from the ground up rather than as an act of architectural renovation; the latter of these was how Baker understood her history writing.

Like her science-minded male contemporaries, Baker conceptualized history in terms of a building, but one that already existed and that it was the historian's mission to inhabit, renovate, and re-member. In the preface to *True Stories*, Baker frames her overall historical project using the implied metaphor of a colonial building: "I have taken upon myself a mission to open the door for their [the captives'] return" (1). Forced to travel across the boundaries of the British colony and into New France, estranged from their original families, less forgotten than never thought of in the first place within historical treatments of the period, the female captives had not been allowed into the traditionally conceived space of male-authored history, according to Baker. As a historian, Baker remedies this by opening the door to the captives just as she literally renovated the colonial dwelling Frary house. Baker, moreover, imagined the existence of a permeable boundary between history as a domestic space and the spatially framed, lived existence of the historian who, herself, was subject to and able to stage and thus revise history. Not objectivity, but an explicitly subjective, embodied experience of the world underwrote Baker's historicism.

Instead of trying to maintain a boundary between the past and the present, between the supposedly objective historian and his subject, which was the design of professional male historians writing at the turn of the twentieth century, Baker formulated a historical practice that productively and problematically imagined the past and present as inextricably linked and rendered her own body an architectural space in which history could be felt, housed, and staged. Baker depicts how she felt the moment that she stood on the ground where one of the captives, Abigail de Noyon, was buried: "It was as if I had laid the ghosts of unburied shades that had wandered, restless, haunting my whole life" (222).[33] Baker represents her historical practice as based on the demands of the restless dead, which insert themselves into and affect the historian's psychic life conceived as a constructed space. As Emily Dickinson, another queer New England daughter, wrote, "One need not be a Chamber—to be Haunted—/ One need not be a House—/ The Brain has Corridors—surpassing / Material Place—."[34] For Baker, the supposedly private interior of the individual woman's life-as-house serves as the psychological and material stage for a haunting that blurs distinctions between private and public, individual and collective. The historian's own body and life can be haunted, therefore, and history becomes, metaphorically, a house one might dwell in, enter, haunt, fortify, or reconstruct altogether. History is where we live, Baker implies. History, thus, cannot be separated from the present or the personal, for the personal and the embodied person are themselves in history and constitute it. Haunted is the name that Baker gives to this dissonant, felt conceptualization of history.

Vital to Baker's intimate historicism is the material form it takes in and through the historian's own body. Ghosts bring the past into the space of present-day life through engaging the senses of the living. Whiffed, heard, intuited, felt, and sometimes seen, ghosts appear as material presences that, like it or not, jar the body, forcing it into relations across colliding times. Baker claims to have for her "whole life" felt some sort of disjunction between her lived existence and her time, one expressed here as a perpetual haunting (222).[35] I want to propose that the disjunctive temporalities registered in Baker's body achieve equilibrium (get "laid" in Baker's words) by way of Baker feeling, through her work with the captives, part of a larger, transhistorical collectivity. But it is not only a collectivity Baker gathers into being and to which she feels linked; the collective sensibility is part and parcel of the pain of feeling individually haunted. In housing captive women living in a queer modality in history, Baker ostensibly redeems herself.

Baker's fascination with colonial houses and her integration of multiple images of colonial dwellings into *True Stories* further elaborate the idea that history is a colonial house, a specifically sociosexual historical configuration in which women live and produce. That Baker's whole life may be read both as an architectural structure and a duration reinforces this reading. To say the captives' ghosts haunt Baker's whole life is to make them central to her lived experience. When considered in light of the notion that this historical house has been passed down, that male-dominated history has taken the figurative form of a domestic space, Baker's haunted condition makes more sense. She has inherited this historical position and something inside her body feels awry, feels out of joint. Baker's response is to renovate the colonial house of history from a conventional domestic space housing a nuclear family to what looks like a colonial garrison house, a private home open to any community members left outside history's walls. A garrison house was a colonial structure in which a single family dwelt in times of peace, but during attacks it was a refuge for members of the community, for it was particularly fortified to stave off penetration and facilitate shooting from the interior. What Baker seems to find at the burial place of de Noyon, what she finds in the "true stories" of captive women of myriad fates, are fellow daughters whose life trajectories defy conventional notions about sociosexual, racial, religious, national, and vocational belonging. She finds, in other words, lives lived in a queer modality that are thought to be unproductive based on age, unmarried state, or disaffiliation from the colony but that, once pieced together into history, prove to have been generative. Baker's own productivity as a New England daughter, meanwhile, grows out from her work with the captives and defies the understanding of the female body's central patriotic labor as an act of biological reproduction. Using her own body to perform and thus generate "true stories" of history, Baker engaged in an impressive history-writing act that preoccupied her for thirty-five years. This building of a communal female space also involved Lane and Coleman. Each contributed at least one image of a colonial house to *True Stories*: Lane her painting of the Junkins garrison house and Coleman three photographs of buildings including the "Homestead of Josiah Riseing [*sic*] and Abigail Nims." Baker both lived and theorized the contribution an unmarried daughter might make to posterity and how she might, through her own performative recollections, reconcile the past with the present.

Embodying the Past

Baker's intimate historicism was performative. She repeatedly used her body as a method of experiencing and thus revising history. In the words of Jennie Arms Sheldon, as a teacher "she made history a living, pulsating thing. . . . No boy or girl in Miss Baker's class could be dull or indifferent. The ozone of that northwest breeze vitalized nerves and muscles till they tingled. 'She can make a cobblestone live!' was the involuntary exclamation of an admiring school-girl."[36] In addition to making students feel the thrill of history by way of her own enthusiastic contact with cultural artifacts, Baker delivered scholarly papers based on her research to friends and colleagues of the Pocumtuck Valley Memorial Association (PVMA). In fact, Baker wrote the essays that eventually comprised *True Stories* with an eye to their performance: most of these chapters originated as PVMA lectures.[37] Likely this original form explains Baker's ongoing use of the first person throughout her history as well as her metacommentary on the historical process; *True Stories* requires its readers to imagine Baker as a distinct material presence in the scene of reading, to imagine her embodied experience of history.[38]

Baker's performativity extended beyond charismatic history lessons for various audiences to include colonial fancy dressing, a popular entertainment in the late nineteenth century that involved putting on colonial-era costumes and performing the past. Baker consistently placed her body in the position of figures of the past, ones quite different from herself, as a way to generate community and art. One example of Baker's effort to build community through historical performance was the 1892 ball she hosted at Frary house, for which she invited "the village people and her other friends to come in eighteenth century costume."[39] Baker also collaborated with Coleman on colonial revival photography projects. Take, for example, *Gathering Faggots*, a photograph taken by Coleman sometime between 1883 and 1886 that depicts Baker dressed as a rural woman in what looks like old-fashioned garb (figure 3). In this photograph we see, first, the influence of French art on late nineteenth-century U.S. culture. Coleman studied in and toured Europe in the 1860s and 1870s, and this image recalls many of the Barbizon school, such as Jean-François Millet's *Women Carrying Faggots* (ca. 1858) and is, arguably, in cultural dialogue with Winslow Homer's various paintings on the same theme, including *Old Woman Gathering Faggots* (1865) and *The Faggot Gatherer* (1883).

But Baker's act of embodying a woman of another class and, potentially, another time does more than reflect romantic notions of traditional rural work.[40] Positioned in the visual crotch created by the two

FIGURE 3 Emma Lewis Coleman, *Gathering Faggots*, ca. 1880s. Photograph. Courtesy of Historic New England.

tallest trees, one at the almost far right of the photograph, the other left of center, Baker's costumed body occupies the imagined, constructed position of a woman from the past, or at least one whose labors repeat those of the past. Her figure complies with the visual line of the road, while her faggots, held in a splay rather than a neat bundle, create visual mass and texture. The faggots also constitute a series of horizontal lines in intersection with and held in tension against the diagonal lines of the trees and the backward curve of the road. Baker's figure, its gaze and movement in line with the sticks, goes against the flow of this road, crossing rather than following the well-trodden space, as if she knows an alternative way through this feminized landscape.

In *Gathering Faggots*, Baker also performs white racial identification, a double kinship articulated by Baker's own body substituting for a French peasant or early New Englander and Coleman's citation of French artists like Millet. As I discuss in greater detail in chapter 4, colonial fancy dressing was one way to lay claim to a racial historical legacy based in the body. These are not the literal genetic repetitions Barthes, in *Camera Lucida*, traces in his personal photos, thus locating the queer in the racialized family, but a more generalized claim to white membership, one that, not based exclusively on genetics, might undermine its own terms.[41] Such claims to whiteness were, according to Shawn Michelle Smith, central to the very technology of early photography: "Over the course of the nineteenth century, the literal whiteness of material objects blurred into the cultural whiteness of subjects, as photography played a central role in establishing race as a cultural identity that could be seen in new ways."[42] We see the same visible invisibility of whiteness in Coleman's photograph of Baker's bedroom (figure 2), where all that ghostly light evokes a white collectivity of women intimate across time—Baker, Coleman, Lane, the cousin, the colonial captives—understood as a transhistorical family.

In her writings, Baker also performed past historical events and identities, emphasizing the role of her body in those pleasurable labors. Diana Taylor's notion of the scenario offers a useful frame for understanding how Baker performed the past. In *The Archive and the Repertoire*, Taylor argues that the repertoire (the uncaptured and uncapturable forms of performance) is just as significant a means by which cultural memory gets transmitted over time as the archive (extant written and visual sources).[43] In proposing a method for how scholars might attend to the repertoire, Taylor suggests thinking in terms of scenarios, which are "meaning-making paradigms that structure social environments, behaviors, and potential outcomes."[44] Within these scenarios, people enact scripts of the past and thus pass on conservative ideologies and disciplinary structures. Such acts, however, also have the potential to revise or resist the conservatism implicit in the scenario, which is itself always inherited.[45] Today, what remains of Baker's historical work is mainly archival: texts, photos, Frary house. But those archival materials contain the trace of and continually point us back toward the repertoire of her history making. The materials Baker generated that have made it into the archive demand that we attend to those traces of her repertoire in her work. *True Stories* is a text in which we find important evidence of her gendered performance of history.

In *True Stories*, Baker places her body in the same environments and improvised relations as were occupied by men associated with the history of the captives from both the colonial past and the late nineteenth-century present. She therein revises male-dominated scenarios that persist across time. Baker goes beyond generating a romantic, nostalgic history of colonial times and, instead, places herself as an unmarried New England daughter at the center of both modern historical practice-as-performance and a discourse of cosmopolitan, democratic citizenship imagined to have historical roots. As I will soon elaborate, part of Baker's use of and attention to her body, its accessing of historically loaded sensations, knowledge, and ecstasies, is bound to an implicit claim about the physical and social mobility of the white New England daughter across national and cultural differences. This cosmopolitan theory of historical identification, one that highlights the constructedness of identity and affiliation and thinks of belonging in terms that exceed the borders of the nation, depends on the performative fluency of the white New England daughter as an ideal, dissenting citizen. That performative fluency is embodied insofar as it involves the New England daughter taking on the postures, gestures, and sensations of other bodies, therein often laying claim to membership in or affinity with other cultures and communities. It is also imagined to depend on a regionally inflected racial inheritance posing under the sign of character. What we have in Baker's intimate historicism is a method of constructing for modern New England white women living in a queer modality a historical membership written by way of the body, part of an implicit theorization of whiteness as inherently and exceptionally democratic and inherently and exceptionally queer.

The history of forgotten captive women, as Baker does it, depends on the female historian performing three scenarios, what I am calling the scenario of heroism, the scenario of the historian, and the scenario of heritage. In the chapter "My Hunt for the Captives," in which she interweaves the recovered story of Abigail de Noyon with that of her own journey to Canada to begin looking for traces of the captives in the archive, Baker depicts her research as a self-conscious reworking of the scenario of heroism, more specifically, the colonial Deerfield resident John Sheldon's early eighteenth-century efforts to redeem the captives. Sheldon was a Deerfield leader not in town during the 1704 raid. His wife and youngest child were killed during the attack, and three of his children and his young daughter-in-law were captured (168). Sheldon undertook three journeys to Canada to find the captives and redeem them. Implicitly fashioning herself a modern-day Sheldon by placing her chapter on Sheldon's winter trek to New France immediately before the chapter on her own winter journey to Canada to find traces of the captives in the archives, Baker expresses her commitment to learn of the "lost" captives as deeply personal: "I have longed to know their fate [and] . . . the longing has become a purpose" (193). She even explicitly links the two journeys, noting the difference gender and history make: "I doubt if Deacon Sheldon himself was thought so demented, when he announced his intention of going to Canada in mid-winter to demand the release of his kinsfolk and neighbors, as I was, when I made known my purpose, to go to Montreal in December" (193–94).

Adventuring forth, exposing her body to the cold of winter, traveling across some of the same land as Sheldon had, Baker performs a significant act of historical gender insubordination through this scenario, one whose fantastic, resistant potential Baker hints at when using the phrase "so demented." In physically imitating Sheldon's trek, Baker lays claim to the power of the scenario of heroism while exposing and remedying its insufficiencies. When Sheldon went to New France, he had meetings and maintained correspondence with key political figures, trying to use a combination of money and political leverage to redeem the captives. In Baker's version of this scenario, she imaginatively engages influential men of the old regime, riffing on Sheldon's many meetings. Once in Montreal, Baker visits an exhibition of portraits of colonial leaders of New France at the Natural History Society. Finding herself "face to face" with the object representations of "the illustrious founders of New France," Baker limns how mediated exposure to the bodies of colonial French leaders define her project and modifies its heroism (194). Her adventure to Canada is, like the portraits, an attempt to imitate through art what once existed—to copy an original—not with the goal of exact replication but with the goal of reenacting and therefore possibly rewriting history. Hers is an affective experience with the portraits: she gazes at the "poor, mutilated hands, and . . . deeply-lined face" of Père Jogues and closely examines the "handsome and noble faces" of the Hertel brothers (194, 195). Rather than having to negotiate the intimate details of colonial political life as Sheldon did during his trips to Canada, Baker can approach these men as inert, contained renderings of individual-character-based male power, as artistic constructions rather than living realities.

Baker revises the scenario of heroism and that revision thrusts her center stage in another scenario traditionally forbidden to women: the scenario of the historian. Baker locates, or figuratively redeems, the forgotten captives in the archival record by thinking about how proximate bodies assumed to be different (men and women, English and French) might defy such assumptions by discerning their likeness. In particular, as she looks at a portrait of the Hertel brothers at the Natural History Society, Baker slows down, allowing her imagination to drift from the details of these male bodies to the scene during the Deerfield raid when one of the Hertel brothers was injured and the Deerfield woman Mary Baldwin Catlin "tenderly raised [the Hertel boy's] head and moistened [his] fevered lips" in response to his begging for water (195). In this precise historical moment of supposedly violent differentiation between English and French bodies to which Baker's historical imagination transports her, Catlin redefines the terms of relationship by replacing national conflict with shared membership in a transnational Christian community. That Catlin forgot her [New] English allegiance in tending to an enemy's physical needs was the "inspiration" that led Baker to realize that the Catholic Church may well have archived the presence of the captives in New France. Baker goes immediately to the church records of the Curé of Notre Dame, where she finds what would become the central archive for her historical research (195). It is in that rich repository, one created by other colonials living in a queer modality—the priests and nuns of New France—that Baker finds evidence of the lost captives' reaffiliations. Records of baptisms, first communions, marriages, participation in church culture, and deaths—all these fragments form the basis for what would become *True Stories* and Coleman's *New England Captives* after it. It is only through performing the scenario of heroism in a different time and as a differently gendered, feeling body contemplating past bodies that Baker uncovers the archive, which, in turn, makes possible her work in women's history.

In the nineteenth century, archives were understood as exclusively male, erotic enclaves. Leopold von Ranke, the European historian who most influenced the development of history as a professional discipline in the United States, described documents sequestered in archives as "so many princesses, possibly beautiful, all under a curse and needing to be saved," and one collection as "absolutely a virgin. I long for the moment I have access to her."[46] Other scholars replicated these sentiments, portraying the archive as the dwelling place of a "harem" and a place of "ecstasy."[47] Of course, there was a fine line between heterosexual archive fever and an archival erotic considered to offer "alternatives to heterosexual pleasures," a concern that dates back to at least the late eighteenth century in English culture.[48] Baker participates in the heteroerotic dominant script of the scenario of the historian, at one point representing herself moving beyond the "impenetrable veil shrouding" the "precious secrets" of the mission records (254). But her meditation on penetration quickly shifts to a different form of contact—digital dexterity—that challenges the heteroerotic scenario of the historian. Baker reflects, "These records are like the photographer's negative. They require patient and skilful [*sic*] manipulation and developing" (255). Baker here moves the erotic labor of and in the archive into the darkroom, transforming it from the penetrative model of discovery to an exercise in modern, manual manipulation, one that emphasizes representation and reveals "the photographic distinctness of every detail of these lives . . . [and thus] almost takes one's breath away" (255). The comparison between archival records and photographic negatives may also be an allusion to Baker's partner, Coleman, who was with her on this research trip taking photographs.

Baker imagines the woman historian as capable of myriad acts and sensations, including those associated with maternity. At another point in her depiction of the scenario of the historian, she represents herself as experiencing maternal sensations; she depicts the moment when she read in the archives of an attack on a colonial New England village. "Instinctively I hold out my arms and whisper, 'Don't be afraid,' to the little Elisha Searle as I see him there . . . just as he was snatched from his mother's side," Baker confides (199). Note how Baker conflates the present and recent past with the colonial past in her use of "hold" rather than "held." Similarly, she "sees" Searle in the present "just as he was snatched"—he both looks just as he did when snatched and she sees him at the moment of being taken captive. The past comes alive, becomes present, felt experience on the body in the archive for Baker. By means of the historian's sensorium, history lives and the historian is a participant, moving between roles, manipulations, and embodied feelings.

The shift from role of husband-hero to dexterous researcher and archival mother takes Baker across erotic, productive territory, a journey that climaxes in the scenario of heritage represented in "A Day at Oka." This chapter depicts Baker visiting the colonial homestead built by Mohawk-assimilated captives Twatogwach and Shonatakakwani (referred to by the priests in the mission community as Elizabeth and Ignace Raizenne). What I am calling the scenario of heritage is one in which the biological descendant, in this case Jean Baptiste Raizenne, celebrates his colonial inheritance. This inheritance includes the descendant's own body understood as the continuation of the ancestor's body. At heart, this scenario celebrates the continuity of bodies through biological reproduction as well as the survival of material inheritances such as houses, land, and domestic effects that once belonged and still belonged to those bodies in the time *True Stories* was written. Baker's performance of history, however, threatens to disrupt this biologically based, largely male-centered progress narrative. She represents herself, a woman and historian, as able to be titillated and transformed just as the male descendant Jean Baptiste is.

The scenario of heritage that Baker depicts in "A Day at Oka" is, at first glance, advanced by an energetic heteroerotics of history. The scenario crystallizes when Baker meets Jean Baptiste Raizenne, the descendant of Twatogwach and Shonatakakwani. After Baker meets Jean Baptiste, she transports her readers to their loud, rhythmic approach to the historic house where the captives had once lived:

> "*Voici la propriété du pauvre Ignace!*" "This is the estate of poor Ignace," he [Jean Baptiste] cried. "This road the captive made with his own hands." When we came in sight of the house, his excitement was intense. "*Marche, donc vite!*" "Go on quick!" he shouted to his horse, and to me, "*Voilà la vieille maison, la maison d'Ignace! oh, que je l'aime!*" "There is the old house, Ignace's house! oh, how I love it!" And it was "*voilà*" this, and "*voilà*" that, and finally, "*Voilà le bébé!*" as the little toddling thing met us at the kitchen door, and here we were under the very rooftree of the two captives.
>
> I shall not attempt to describe my feelings. I was dazed and overwhelmed with memories of the far-off past. (256)

The "volubility" of Jean Baptiste's exclamations, the movement of the horse pulling them along, and the galloping between the exclamations and Baker's translations of them propel the reader as well as the story's participants toward the future and the past as condensed in the colonial homestead (256). For Jean Baptiste, the enthusiasm culminates in the appearance of the baby, who is his offspring. Providing a nearly sentence-by-sentence translation of this male "excitement that was intense," Baker demonstrates her ability to feel and represent, literally and figuratively, masculine ecstasies. Baker does not just share in a sexualized celebration of reproduction that has as its crowning moment the appearance of offspring; she also achieves her own ecstasy—she is "dazed and overwhelmed with memories of the far-off past"—based on intimacy with history (256). It is out of these multiple scenarios that collapse temporal distinctions and engage sexualized energies that Baker generates *True Stories*.

We might fairly read Baker's performances as acts of gendered historical insubordination, the form of drag theorized by Elizabeth Freeman as "a kind of *temporal* transitivity" that might involve "registering on their [some bodies'] very surface the co-presence of several historically contingent events, social movements, and/or collective pleasures."[49] This temporal drag, moreover, is "exteriorized as a mode of bodily adornment or even habitus."[50] It is the "even habitus" that lies on the outskirts in Freeman's account that proves central in Baker's history. The house as habitus with the performing body in it is how the body might also do, even live, history.

In *True Stories*, Baker does not represent herself as wearing the garb of the colonial or contemporary men who traditionally star in the scenarios she performs. But we should not overlook the way in which, for Baker, history is made not just on but in and externalized by the body of the historian. Baker focused not on the habitus as manifested on the body's surfaces, but on the material sensations and transformations experienced within the body as habitus—the body as a house haunted, the body as rendering bare the archive, the body achieving an intimately historical climax—and the body in habitus—in the historically loaded house. In the scenario of heritage, for example, Baker lays claim to being a sort of adoptive daughter to the captives by imitating the sounds emerging from within Jean Baptiste's male body and then materially altering her own body by placing it "under the very roof-tree of the two captives" (256). Baker also integrates into her body the historical foods of the Raizenne homestead. Just after her expressions of ecstasy, she writes of herself, Coleman, and Jean Baptiste: "We drank to the memory of the captives . . . in wine made from vines originally planted by Ignace [Shonatakakwani]. We tasted water from his well; we ate apples from the sole survivor of his orchard" (256). Baker represents how intimacy with the colonial shapes, in fact becomes, incorporated into the historian's body. These ingestions, moreover, expand the range of senses Baker uses to do history: she sees the homestead, she feels the erotic rhythms of Jean Baptiste's words and the pleasurable propulsions forward on his horse, she touches and tastes the juices of heirloom fruits. Amid this scenario, ancestry figures as fluid, not based on direct descent alone, but accessible through a more generalized performance of whiteness.

Dissenting Blood

The scenarios of history and belonging Baker rehearsed in *True Stories* were, as we have seen, embodied, staged through, on, and in the historian's material self. In the late nineteenth century, when scientific racism, eugenics, and obsessions with genealogy were widespread, doing history involved engaging the concepts of inheritance, ancestry, and race. Baker's notion of a racialized, regionalized character proved complicated, however, for it depended on an idea of dissent that though linked to race might be severed from it. Baker was, in part, interested in her own blood-based genealogy: Frary house had supposedly belonged to Baker's great-great-grandfather, Samson Frary, and Abigail de Noyon was her ancestor. But Baker also had an interest in women's possible mobility across identities, across differently gendered bodily situations, and she was drawn to the idea of transtemporal collectivities of women dwelling together. Baker yoked literal and adoptive modes of belonging by way of a few central concepts: character, ancestry, and dissent. Baker's theory of history done in a queer modality relied on a specific construction of white racial exceptionalism defined in terms of dissent, which she applied to New England in particular. Although Baker was interested in the "institutions of the old Aryan stock," and her work "answered nativist anxieties while buttressing both the economic and cultural foundations of Deerfield's white Anglo-Saxon community," that makes for only part of the story.[51] I want to explore how profoundly racial Baker's construct of New England womanhood was, how her emphasis on collectivities, reaffiliation, and performance problematized straightforward claims to legacy like those made by the Daughters of the American Revolution, an organization that, in the same era, "posited American identity as an ancestral heirloom founded in a legacy of blood" and ultimately "reinforced the value of a historically masculinized realm of documented public action as the fount from which their racially inflected ... bloodlines would flow."[52] For though Baker used the rhetoric of blood, she laid claim to a notion of ancestry that exceeded direct descent, emphasized the lives of women and children rather than women's production of children, and depended on a theory of racial character that seems to have contained the seeds of its own undoing.

Throughout *True Stories*, Baker relies on a rhetoric of belonging that blends ancestry, character, and dissent rather than one that focuses on blood alone. The most explicit statement of the interrelationships among these concepts and their centrality to Baker's own historical enterprise occurs at the end of a chapter entitled "A Scion of the Church in Deerfield: Joseph-Octave Plessis, First Archbishop of Quebec." First delivered as a speech in Deerfield on the occasion of its church's anniversary, this chapter implies that history-loving late nineteenth-century Protestant residents of Deerfield should celebrate Plessis, who was a Catholic leader in Canada in the early nineteenth century. Baker first tells of Plessis's New England ancestry, claiming that a girl taken captive in 1704 and not redeemed, Martha, the eight-year-old daughter of Thomas French, a colonial Deerfield town clerk, was Plessis's ancestress. Baker then tells of Plessis's exceptional character, how, raised by a French immigrant blacksmith outside of Montreal, he became a superbly effective, well-loved priest who ascended to the position of archbishop in 1818. Plessis figures in Baker's account as the liberal champion of Catholics in a historical era of strained relations between Catholic Canadians and their Protestant English rulers. According to Baker, Plessis was particularly well-known for rallying Catholic Canadians to defend English Canada against the United States in the War of 1812, for, in other words, helping cultivate national loyalty while honoring religious diversity and thus proving that valuable, trustworthy subjects of England came in various guises (295–96). Though not a colonial, Plessis embodied the principle of mindful dissent Baker imagines to have characterized many of the colonial captives in *True Stories*.

All told, Baker asserts a kinship between Plessis's exceptionalism and her own cosmopolitan radicalism as she argues for Plessis's place in a history of New England:

> Would it have shocked the old man [colonial New Englander Thomas French] more I wonder, to have known that one of his blood should become the most illustrious defender of the Roman Catholic faith in Canada,—or that a woman of the same stock should stand in this place on this anniversary, to ask you to honor this veritable scion of the church in Deerfield?
>
> Who shall dare affirm or deny that to the drop of New England blood in his veins, Joseph-Octave Plessis, owes the grandest traits of his character?
>
> After all,—what matters it? Neither New England nor New France,—Puritan nor Catholic, holds a monopoly of virtue.
>
> Sects perish. Nationalities blend. Character endures. (303)

Saturated with the language of descent—"one of his blood," "a woman of the same stock," "this veritable scion," "the drop of New England blood"—this passage represents racial inheritance as a given. Baker's self-conscious radicalism (i.e., the shocking aspect of her performance of history, her insistence that Plessis forms part of the story of Deerfield), however, appears to defy the rhetoric of belonging that infuses the passage. She is, after all, announcing on this local anniversary dedicated to celebrating New England and Protestant exceptionalism that sectional and national identities are not essential but subject to history, to the human process of manipulating the family tree by means of grafting. (A scion is "a descendant," but its older definition is "a slip for grafting.")[53] Yet one component of Baker's "true story" remains fixed over time: that transhistorical essence is "character" (303).

Character in this context articulates racial belonging. As Cathy Boeckmann puts it, "The most important synonym for *race* in this period, and the term with the most complex conceptual framework, was *character*."[54] Building on Boeckmann's work, James Salazar has posited that what the rhetoric of character allowed in terms of race science was an articulation of "the essential *historicity* of race," namely, that it could be changed over time.[55] Baker, however, does not seem to construe character as changeable but as a transhistorical legacy rooted in white dissent that enables the realignment of one's identity and allegiances. Character thus understood constitutes a racial inheritance, a fixed thing that enables its possessor the open-ended mobility necessary to live in a queer modality, to be grafted. The New England daughters taken captive about whom Baker writes may elect to change their affiliations over time, as Kanenstenhawi and Twatogwach did in remaining among the Iroquois. And, indeed, Baker depicts these women as choosing membership in native communities much as she represents Mother Marie-Joseph as "unshaken" by letters her New England family wrote to her "urging her return" to New England and Protestantism (56). Baker also empathizes with Twatogwach for wanting to escape from New England once she was redeemed. The agency to choose one's family and community results from the sociosexual, cultural mobility of the liberal democratic subject who has inherited the freedom to reaffiliate. Far from being the exclusive property of men, and this perhaps marks Baker's most characteristic regionalist innovation, the ideal character is pervasive among the women of New England, passed down by way of something like blood, and it secures for them membership in history as modern, mobile, distinctly white subjects.

It is in her concept of "dissenting blood," also found in the Plessis chapter, that I find Baker's mode of theorizing ancestry and resistance brought together.[56] This dissenting blood was thought to course through the unique body of New England history from the earliest days of Protestantism through the settling of Massachusetts and from the Revolutionary era through the period of abolitionism and civil war. Even though they had captivity thrust upon them—an example of how imperialist projects affected and were affected by women's lives—the captives' lives in New France demonstrate a capacity for dissent in that their reaffiliations were ongoing. The border-crossings and myriad changes in cultural allegiance Baker celebrates in *True Stories* and in her own intimate historicist practice, for all of her historical attentiveness, depend on dehistoricizing the specifically regionalized white character of New England.

The racial dimension of Baker's theory of women's history forms a significant part of its cultural work. As I read it, *True Stories* participates in debates about women, nation, and citizenship that, according to the historian Teresa Anne Murphy, have been central to women's history writing in the United States since the birth of the nation.[57] From these debates in the late eighteenth century and the early nineteenth emerged the dominant mode of understanding women's citizenship through domesticity.[58] The domestic sphere was understood to encompass the house, a space tied fundamentally to family and religion as well as to specific ideas about women's role in generating and safeguarding the race through reproduction and mothering. When Baker renovates the house of history configured as a domestic space and asserts that it holds within it the stories of various women who reaffiliated beyond what became the United States, when she suggests that the house of history might be modified to shelter collectivities of queer nineteenth-century women, when she reconstructs the house of history through various acts of historical insubordination, she retools an ideal of women's citizenship based not on nation or national belonging but on the expression of a dissenting character imagined as ideally democratic, racially white, and transnational. Rather than explicitly arguing for women's equality as did Abigail Adams and Margaret Fuller before her, Baker finds in the colonial period early precursors for the adaptive, open-minded liberal subject, the ideal citizen who regularly takes the form of the unmarried New England daughter.[59] It is this daughter who contributes to the perpetuation of section-specific values by way of her body—not through heterosexual reproduction but through the embodied, often erotic performance of what were once (and are not necessarily any longer) male-dominated scenarios.

In theorizing women's citizenship and the figure of the New England daughter in particular, Baker implicity synthesizes a national-imperial mode wherein the white daughter has never belonged to the nation or historical time with a backward-looking, regionalized white privilege by way of which she demands reparation. In a sense, the New England daughter's her forced exclusion becomes a spatial and temporal site of radical potential from which she might reconfigure the very terms of contemporary political, sexual, and social belonging and refashion history by rethinking what constitutes ancestry.

Reparative Collaborations

Heather Love, in *Feeling Backward*, turns her attention to the forms queer affiliations between scholars of the present and the subjects of their scholarship from the past have taken. According to Love, there has been a disproportionate tendency among those working in queer studies to think of their subjects in intimate terms: as friends, as lovers, as closeted queers in need of an "emotional rescue."[60] Part of the power of Love's argument lies in its insistence that we remember the roles violence and disaffiliation have played in queer experience across time. It is useful to consider Baker's intimate historicism, which often took the form of eroticized celebration and depended on a rhetoric of kinship and cohabitation, through this lens. We might say that Baker's *True Stories* stages a personally loaded queer redemption from the violent fragments of settler-colonialism in the northeastern United States and Canada. Yet Baker's was not the only model for historicizing the captives' lives. All the members of Baker's triadic queer family—Baker, Lane, and Coleman—represented colonial history across various media. By looking at their individual and collaborative efforts, we glimpse a more varied vision of history, one that registers not only the ecstasies of history making but also its depressing, alienating aspects.

One place in which Baker's, Lane's, and Coleman's work overlapped was in each's concern for colonial history imagined in architectural terms as a garrison house. Lane, for example, painted the

FIGURE 4 Susan Minot Lane, *The Junkins Garrison*, 1875. Oil on canvas; 7 1/2 inches x 14 inches. Courtesy of the Museums of Old York Collections, York, Maine.

Junkins garrison house, which Baker included as an illustration in *True Stories*. Coleman joined Baker in her historical research, and when Baker died, her research continued for twenty more years. Coleman's eventual publication—*New England Captives Carried to Canada*—extends and speaks back to Baker's formulation of history as a house in *True Stories*. The garrison house had special status as a private architectural space that harbored members of the extended community during attack. As a space, it signifies a paranoid architecture, one designed to thwart and survive the violent negotiations and consequences of imperialism.

To elucidate this family's collaborative vision of the garrison house as a figure for history, I want, first, to compare Lane's painting *The Junkins Garrison* (figure 4) to another painted in the same year, *Robert Junkins' Garrison House, York, Maine* (figure 5), by the well-known New England artist Winslow Homer. This garrison house was once located in South Berwick, Maine, and was fairly decrepit when these two artists painted it separately in 1875.[61]

In Homer's rendering, the house, though somewhat dilapidated and thus marking the passage of time, exists amid signs of the present as well as the future. The stone wall seems well kept and the wood fence looks like a recent addition, one that suggests active husbandry. Foregrounded in the Homer painting are what appear to be a mother and son holding hands. In this, Homer's garrison house

FIGURE 5 Winslow Homer, *Robert Junkins' Garrison House, York, Maine*, July 1875. Brush and oil paint on canvas, 22 9/16 x 15 11/16 inches. Courtesy of Cooper-Hewitt, National Design Museum, Smithsonian Institution/Art Resource, New York.

acknowledges history in the landscape coexisting with contemporary generations. The role of the woman here appears to be that of the mother, the creator of new life by way of heteroreproduction. And although the young boy functions as a sign of the future, his presence also asserts the principle of continuing male power and property ownership; structurally speaking, if not literally, this boy may be the next Robert Junkins. Colonial heroism—the defense of New England against the Indians and French—figures in Homer's painting as distinctly male and possessive by way of Robert Junkins's name. Junkins, it is implied, has made possible, fathered even, this contemporary American scene. In the background of the present-day mother and child walking down the country road stands the garrison house, signifying the history and future of the white male defending his right to colonize the world as well as the discourses of fear and victimization central to that project.

Lane's painting, by contrast, depicts the garrison as decrepit. It places the garrison house at a further distance from the viewer and represents it as more in tune temporally with the landscape around it.

The remnant of a stone wall, for example, cordons off the house and the solitary tree, separating them from the viewer by a fairly significant visual field at the front of the picture. Rather than human figures, we have little here except the tree, which shows its age and, partly dead, unpruned, and unevenly shaggy, evidences the distinct absence of husbandry. The apparently uninhabited image Lane offers (excepting the viewer's presence) more firmly places the garrison house in the past and refuses to link the house to a clear future. Unlike Homer's *Robert Junkins' Garrison House, York, Maine*, which depicts the building almost head on, Lane's *The Junkins Garrison* depicts the building at a slant, and it is seemingly more painterly, its aspects more hazy. While we might read Lane's painting, like Baker's *True Stories*, as a more romantic rendering of the colonial past, its Gothicism tends to stress absence and death. Rather than reminding us of the continuity of generations, the garrison house, especially when taken in the context of the captivity histories of *True Stories*, seems to record the failure of its own architectural intent: those who once dwelt here could not, did not, adequately anticipate the surprise of French and Indian attack. Lane's garrison looks haunted; a darkness dominates this take on colonial history. The house itself is not a relic of the past set in a future-oriented scene. Instead, dilapidation pervades the painting, which seems to resist and distance the contemporary viewer who may not easily see herself in this historical landscape.

When read in the context of *True Stories*'s reparative project, *The Junkins Garrison* represents more than an abandoned house in the landscape of an aging rural New England.[62] Lane's painting was reproduced in the chapter dedicated to the stories of Mary and Esther Sayward of York who were not literally taken from the Junkins garrison but for whose York home this image stands in as a substitute. Captivated and never redeemed, the Saywards became French: one took holy orders, and the other married. Lane's painting, when read alongside Baker's history, gives visual form to what is left behind when women are taken captive. The scene is dismal, the house uninhabited. By contrast, Baker's history implies that the renovated garrison house constitutes the figurative architectural space back into which she invites the captives to enter. While we see New England colonial experience reasserted across generations into futurity in Homer's painting, Lane's work focuses on the desolation and alienating aspect of the colonial past.

In Coleman's *New England Captives*, chronologically the last of the Baker-Lane-Coleman family's regionalist recollections, we see not only the theory of the garrison house of history realized fully but also how this historicism got changed over and passed across differently configured generations of queer women. Sixteen years after Baker's death and thirty-two after Lane's, Coleman published *New England Captives*. Quite different from Baker's *True Stories*, *New England Captives* offers a broad historical view and a central thesis. Rather than tell a range of stories of women and children taken captive in detail, Coleman presents a compendium of all the captives to whom she and Baker found references in various sources. Published after World War I, demonstrating the close historical ties among the French, English, and Indians in northeastern North America, *New England Captives* reads like an antiwar project. Here is Coleman's thesis, presented in the first sentences of the first page of the text proper: "'The real cause of contentions among men is the ambition to take what does not belong to them.' In the seventeenth, as alas in the twentieth century, men killed each other for that ambition.... The last intercolonial war ended with the Cession of Canada. In all the wars captives, mostly women and children, were carried from New England to Canada."[63] Coleman's history does not foreground the exceptional democratic character of New England daughters or the power of reaffiliation so much as the gendered costs of war, of imperial endeavor. Yet it is possible, perhaps even inevitable, that Baker's and Coleman's project on the captives, structured in part by a feminist critique of imperial violence, anticipated and could, in turn, be situated a half century after it was begun in relation to World War I.

New England Captives provides a view onto how intimate historicist productions shape-shift over time, particularly in the movement across generations.[64] Coleman's history closely resembles the professional, modern male-authored histories emergent in Baker's time. Gone are the references to "romance," the integration of literary features into the history, the presence of the performing historian as a gendered self. In Coleman, the "I" appears nowhere other than in the preface, and methodology is nowhere discussed. Yet as much as Coleman's work is influenced by the archival, scientific mode—it is a weighty compendium of facts about the captives—it is still productively haunted by the captive women as well as by Lane and Baker, by the prior generation's mode of doing history. Coleman frames her study as a modern work of feminist history driven by an ethic of recovery. Compared to Baker's book,

Coleman's *New England Captives* stands as a more capacious garrison house in that it attempts to include every name and every post-captivity narrative referenced in the archives, even those mentioned only in the Catholic archives. Among the captives presented by Coleman are nearly countless white colonials as well as eighteenth-century colonials such as Jeanne Wannannemim, an Indian taken captive from Northfield in 1695; a "melatto" [*sic*] taken from Exeter in 1706; slaves taken from Canterbury in 1752; Peter Labaree, "a French Huguenot"; "Dorset, a negro"; and Nero Caesar, a black soldier.[65] Progress is not inevitable here, but like Walter Benjamin's angel of history, Coleman keeps her face turned toward the past, paying increasing attention to the wreckage in the form of individuals who were forgotten or considered of less importance among white New Englanders within colonial and, presumably, late nineteenth-century society.[66]

New England Captives self-consciously places itself in the interwoven context of systemic violence (war), systemic violence against women (imperialism and captivity), and the sustaining love and queer genealogy of the Baker-Lane-Coleman family. The book opens with reference to its own intimate history: the first image, opposite the title page, is Lane's *Junkins Garrison House*. Together, Lane's image and Coleman's title emphasize a darker, more deathly and evacuated representation of the New England past than the one *True Stories* presents. Implicitly citing Homer, Parkman, and other cultural producers who insisted on the generative, defining aspects of colonial war, Lane and Coleman seem to refuse a notion of history as progressive, as improving over time. In *New England Captives*, the facing pages just after Lane's painting and the copyright include a photograph of C. Alice Baker on the left (figure 6) and the dedication on the right: "In Memory of C. Alice Baker." Here again we have Baker's body foregrounded in the performance of women's history, this time as herself a ghost of sorts, with her fingers assertively penetrating a book. Coleman recollects and claims to be acting in the spirit of Baker as an intellectual progenitor and lover when she explains, "In memory of her [Baker's] work I have tried to do with it what she would have wished; joining as far as possible the Canadian and New England threads and extending it through the long period of French and Indian warfare."[67]

Taken together, the versions of colonial history produced by Baker, Lane, and Coleman move between the ecstasies of embodied historical performance represented by Baker and the catalogue of death

FIGURE 6 A. W. Elson & Co., *C. Alice Baker*. Photograph. Published in Emma Lewis Coleman, *New England Captives Carried to Canada, 1677–1760*, volume 1.

and disaffiliation painted by Lane and published by Coleman thought as part of the same historical vision. For Coleman and Baker, who researched the captives for forty years each, the intimate historian recollects the fragments of history because the clamoring of the dead, both the unknown and the loved, resounds in the chambers of her very being.

Literature's Historical Acts

New England regionalist fiction performed historiographical work. Sarah Orne Jewett, now the most famous of the New England regionalist writers, had these lines from Gustave Flaubert posted over her writing desk: "Écrire la vie ordinaire comme on écrit l'histoire" ("Write about daily life as you would write history"), and she asserted in her 1893 preface to *Deephaven* that the novel was an "attempt to explain the past and the present to each other."[1] In response to a letter from Hamlin Garland asking whether or not her characters were of a past time, Mary Wilkins Freeman, the most popular of the New England regionalists in her own day, explained, "Yes I do consider that I am writing about the New England of the present day, and the dialect is that which is daily in my ears. I have however a fancy that my characters belong to a present that is rapidly becoming *past*, and that a few generations will cause them to disappear."[2] Both Jewett and Freeman theorize a relationship between the past and modernity. For Jewett, the past, in the form of the aged men and women of coastal Maine, is alive and well, though in miscommunication with the present as represented by urban tourists. Jewett portrays two temporalities as coexisting in the present time while, for Freeman, the present comprises a single temporality, one in process: her characters are "of the present day" and "belong to a present" at a historical moment she perceives as characterized by the speeding up of time. Like the historian and colonial revivalist C. Alice Baker, Jewett and Freeman understood their regionalist productions as historical acts, ones in which temporality and sociality meet. Jewett's past and present need an interlocutor—Jewett—who understands, even inhabits, both temporalities, much like the two main characters of *Deephaven*, Kate Lancaster and Helen Denis. Freeman's characters, meanwhile, "belong" to their time, participating in a temporally based affiliation. These two writers of New England literary regionalism imagined the past in complex relation to the present, and it is in the spatiotemporal context of New England in particular that the unmarried women of their stories act.

Twentieth- and twenty-first-century accounts of literary regionalism, however, have tended to oversimplify regionalism's historical project as nostalgic or ahistoricist. Josephine Donovan, for example, argues that regionalist fiction by Freeman records the mournful process by which "the preindustrial values of that ['woman-centered, matriarchal'] world . . . are going down to defeat."[3] Richard Brodhead asserts that Jewett's Dunnet Landing is meant to function as "a counterworld to 1890s modernity."[4] And though she notes that the Bowden reunion in *Pointed Firs* "flickers between times," Stephanie Foote ultimately concludes that regionalism like Jewett's "constructs regional folk as figures of a receding past . . . as 'ahistorical,'" rendering Dunnet Landing "a kind of timeless frieze."[5] It may well be that, as Valerie Rohy has it, "anachronism, specifically in the form of nostalgia, is a central temporal issue not only for Jewett and Cather, but also . . . for the regionalist writing of their era."[6] Yet declension, counterworld, and ahistoricism were not what Jewett and Freeman emphasized in their writings; rural New England, instead, is contemporary and constitutive.[7] In Freeman's words, she depicts "a present that is rapidly becoming past," and Jewett undertakes an ongoing social negotiation across generations in the late nineteenth-century now. The difference between receding and becoming, between an already achieved past and a history in the process of being generated, while seemingly slight, is, in fact, profoundly significant: the New England regionalists consistently represent New England as the vital and most radically historical of American sections where unmarried female characters of all ages live in unfolding relationship to one another and to history. Rather than "always ask its readers to read outside history," New England regionalism consistently asks its readers to read the contemporary unmarried New England daughter as deeply rooted in regional history, as herself an expression in the present of an ongoing historical and regionalized dissent.[8]

New England regionalist fiction is also historical insofar as it consistently represents the late nineteenth century in relation to colonial times. Scholars, however, have largely overlooked the New England regionalists' direct portrayal of colonial times. Mary Wilkins Freeman's first work of published fiction, for example, was *The Adventures of Ann: Stories of Colonial Times*, and she went on to write two plays, a short story collection, and a novella all set in colonial New England.[9]

Freeman also published a novel of colonial Virginia history, *The Heart's Highway*, that centered on a rebellion spearheaded by an unmarried woman. Jewett preferred *The Tory Lover*, her historical romance set in Revolutionary-era Maine, England, and France, to all her other works, representing it as her life's culminating creative act: "I cannot believe that so much of my heart was put into it . . . I could not have died until I got it done!"[10] Rose Terry Cooke looked back to colonial women's experiences in "An Old-Fashioned Thanksgiving," "Clary's Trial," and her novel *Steadfast*, and Alice Brown wrote works on colonial women such as *Mercy Warren*, a piece of nonfiction.

In this chapter, I argue that emergent in the fiction of Rose Terry Cooke and fully realized in the writings of Freeman and Jewett is a representation of unmarried women as negotiating in the present an intimate relationship to colonial New England history. This negotiation relies on historical allusions and the figuring of the past as recurring across and thus shaping the late nineteenth-century present. It also depends on representations of fictional women who do not get whisked from courtship to marriage to maternity in the traditional plotting of progressive, modern time based in and on women's heterosexual reproduction. Hamlin Garland may well have been talking about all the New England literary regionalists when he wrote to Van Wyck Brooks in 1938 about what he called the "miraculous[ness]" of Freeman's writing: "It is easy to write stories of copulation, any one [*sic*] can do that and most young writers do—but Mary Wilkins [Freeman] presented elderly people or young people in new and puzzling relationships."[11] The New England regionalist fiction writers shared a surprisingly coherent interest in "new and puzzling" intimacies and erotic forms that might emerge for unmarried women. These new intimacies were modern, as Garland's word choice indicates, and profoundly linked to history. The New England regionalist fiction writers imagined these novel bonds as contiguous with a regionally specific and elaborate brand of individuality, and as a means by which history itself might be generated and passed down, over, and back among women.

Cooke, Freeman, and Jewett wrote into existence a differently timed womanhood, one founded not on a progressive, productive model of time—what Dana Luciano has called "chronobiopolitics, or the sexual arrangement of the time of life"—nor on the supposedly cyclical time of the maternal body, or what Julia Kristeva has called "women's time."[12] Instead, they think of the trajectory of older women's experiences as integrating various temporalities and thus reshape the terms those women's material experiences, pleasures, and forms of belonging take. This rehearsal of history, wherein the contemporary woman recalls by way of her present postures the colonial past, I call the queerly colonial; such performances tie the modern and emergent to history in the present-day unmarried daughter's very body through forms that emphasize duration and depend on historical allusion and cross-generational intimacies. Crucially, the unmarried daughters that appear throughout the pages of New England regionalist fiction and inhabit this alternative temporality are not the biologically young female protagonists with reproductive potential that Jennifer Fleissner has argued dominated American literature across modes, including regionalism, at the turn of the twentieth century.[13] Instead, New England regionalism stars the old maid, who, regardless of her actual age or fertility, was considered aged, virtually postmenopausal. I contend that far from stalling out, the unmarried women of regionalism, if they do not marry, often enter an extended, sloweddown time of erotic freedom, of concentrated sensation and affective mobilities engendered by the unmarried state.

The queerly colonial unmarried woman of the late nineteenth-century present that Cooke, Freeman, and Jewett so often imagined also defied existing literary stereotypes of the old maid. The spinsters of New England regionalism rarely adopt children or are foiled in love like their precursors Harriet Beecher Stowe's maternal Miss Mehitable or Catherine Maria Sedgwick's restrained and self-abnegating Esther Downing.[14] Even less do they resemble Nathaniel Hawthorne's fearful Hepzibah Pyncheon of *The House of the Seven Gables* who, obsessed with her status as a gentlewoman, dare not leave the domestic sphere and its proscribed labors and cares. Hepzibah, like other harpooned, pathologized nineteenth-century spinsters, is barren, nearly a ghost herself in her obsession with the past. J. T. Trowbridge's well-circulated 1870 poem "Dorothy in the Garret" offers a popular cultural version of this stereotype wherein the spinster is dried up and ghostly:

> In the low-raftered garret, stooping
> Carefully over the creaking boards,
> Old Maid Dorothy goes a-groping
> Among its dusty and cobwebbed hoards;
> Seeking some bundles of patches, hid

Far under the eaves, or bunch of sage,
Or satchel hung on its nail, amid
The heirlooms of a bygone age.[15]

In "Dorothy in the Garret," the old maid seems to dwell not in the present, but in the past, which is why we find her in an attic filled with objects and spaces—the "bunch of sage," the creviced "eaves," and the womb-like "satchel"—that mirror her body's supposedly wizened, untouched places. Her action—"a-groping"—denotes not only an inability to see and a slowed-down, timid mobility but also a perverse sexual touch, one that usually takes as its object the body of a woman.[16] Trowbridge's spinster is of the past, unproductive, and pathological. By contrast, the old maids of New England regionalism are self-possessed and rebellious.[17] They are depicted as astutely feeling and influencing history in their efforts to reform conditions of gender injustice or to pursue a life path that does not coincide with what one Freeman character calls "the reg'lar road of lovin'."[18] Their range of affiliations evidences an affective mobility, and their unwed bodies often figure as fecund rather than diminished. Contrast Mrs. Todd in Jewett's *Pointed Firs* "press[ing] her aromatic nosegay [of just-picked pennyroyal] between her hands and offer[ing] it to me [the narrator] again and again" with Trowbridge's Dorothy groping for the dried-up "bunch of sage."[19] How different Hepzibah's virtual entombment in Hawthorne's house of the seven gables from the rich writerly legacy Jewett passed down to Willa Cather: "When an old house and an old woman came together in her brain with a click," Cather recounted, "she knew that a story was under way."[20]

The New England regionalists and New England regionalism have largely been understood across literary history in terms of the very stereotypes about spinsterhood as impoverished that they wrote against. Henry James's 1895 epistolary outburst "I hate 'old New England stories'!—which are lean and pale and poor and ugly," offers an early example of a critic constellating agedness, New England, and women's artistic inadequacy.[21] The same sentiment, this time explicitly tied to the regionalists' unmarried status, was reiterated by Van Wyck Brooks who, writing in 1940, portrayed the New England regionalist women writers as mere secretaries of the historically real, bereft of artistic, social, and sexual potential: "Miss Jewett and Miss Wilkins," he claims, "described the Yankee ebb-tide, a world of empty houses and abandoned farms, of shuttered windows, relics, ghosts and silence."[22] Brooks's notion of the regionalist mode as a sort of "ebb-tide" echoes across literary scholarship: in Ann Douglas Wood's account of women's regionalism as a "literature of impoverishment"; in Richard Brodhead's sense that regionalism simply reinforced an "elite formation defined in part through its high-cultural affiliations and vacation practices"; and, more subtly, in Jennifer Fleissner's concurring with Brooks that the female characters of New England regionalism lack in the scope of their experiences, hence their compulsions and manias.[23]

In the readings that follow, I argue that in New England regionalist fiction refusing to marry figures as a form of dissent meant to keep one's mobility and independence intact and that this dissent is imagined to reiterate a regionally distinct counternational radicalism. Built into these literary representations of young New England women considering and often refusing marriage were unsatisfied yearnings for the potential of colonial times, for a sort of liberal citizenship in which white women might have been included at the moment of nation formation but were not and from which they remained excluded in the late nineteenth century. Importantly, the nation, like marriage, was not the affiliative form the New England regionalists hoped their belonging would take. They focused, instead, on the region and the unmarried state as the freest forms of political-historical organization for women. The regionalist fiction writers, however, did not represent all unmarried women's connections to colonial New England in the same way. Cooke and Freeman used historical allusions to place their unmarried, aged protagonists in physical positions that echoed those of their colonial forebears and thus imagined them staging revisions of history that emphasized women's independence. Jewett, meanwhile, found in touristic explorations of new landscapes and friendships a way to represent unmarried women's relationships to larger geological, political, and regional histories. In New England regionalist fiction, we have a section-specific historiographical project that posits the New England white daughter's propensity for dissent as a far-reaching legacy of desirous, queerly colonial citizenship.

Historical Allusions, Bodily Acts

According to Susan Stewart, literary allusions always foreground the relationship between the past and the present and are, implicitly, social figures of speech in that they necessarily allow or exclude readers from membership in an imagined knowledge community: either you know the allusion and so belong to that community, or you do not.[24] Historical allusions also disrupt the very idea of history as progressive, for they invite readers to see how structures and ideologies persist or suddenly resurface across time. And when integrated into a fictional setting or used as part of a figure of speech, historical allusions go even further, encouraging the reader to imagine characters performing the relationship between the past and the present by way of their bodies. Take, for instance, the action and allusion used in Freeman's "The Revolt of 'Mother'" just after Sarah Penn explains to the nosy minister why she will not move out of her husband's new barn: Sarah "arose," the narrator tells us; "the barn threshold might have been Plymouth Rock from her bearing."[25] Sarah takes on, bodily, the parallel posture, affect, and ideological position of the Pilgrim Fathers. The significance of Sarah's rebellion regarding the barn may be in question—left to the reader's interpretation as captured in the word "might"—but there is no question as to her "bearing." She reenacts the embodied presence of colonial male ancestors.

Such historical allusions, rife in Freeman's work, constitute a hopeful historicism, for they acknowledge how colonial New England identities and power structures continue to inflect life in the late nineteenth-century United States and experiment with how such structures might be modified by way of historical reenactments. Through such allusions, the domestic sphere becomes one with imperial spheres as a stage for history-shaping action. Far from a retreat from questions of empire or impoverished by parochialism as some literary critics have it, New England regionalism thinks nineteenth-century white women's experiences in terms of global history.[26] It is the ostracized, impoverished old maid who, more often than not, ends up taking center stage in these allusive acts, her embodied experience of the past in the present fusing personal, gendered histories with regional and imperial ones.

It is no coincidence that in a fair number of works of New England regionalist fiction the unmarried state itself, represented as having a duration of variable length between being controlled by the father and by the husband, is linked to the radical potential of the Revolutionary era through allusion to the Fourth of July. Herein late nineteenth-century women's independence is joined to the liminal form of incipient nationhood. It is on this symbolic date that Jake Hazzard of Cooke's story "Mary Ann's Mind" strands the love of his life, Mary Ann Tucker, on an island, refusing to let her back on his boat until she decides whether or not to accept his proposal of marriage.[27] Emeline Ruggles, the psychologically complex star of Harriet Prescott Spofford's tale "Knitting Sale-Socks" stands up her suitor-cousin Stephen when he comes to visit her in Salem on Independence Day, opting to spend the day picnicking with her fellow factory girls rather than risk having to entertain the question "Will you marry me?"[28] In the time between serving her ungrateful family and marrying Tom Reed, Annie Hempstead of Freeman's "Dear Annie" asserts her independence by moving into the colonial mansion she has inherited from her grandmother, an act that involves feeling "within herself the sensations of a revolutionist."[29]

In the above examples, celebrations of personal proto-national independence end up yielding to the dependencies of marriage. But what of the New England daughters of regionalism who choose not to marry at all but choose, instead, to distend the period of independence and its revolutionary sensations, to defy the temporal trajectory of the traditional bildungsroman as conceptualized for women? So it is with New England regionalist women characters such as Louisa Ellis, Louisa Britton, Martha (of "Martha's Lady"), Kate Lancaster, Helen Denis, Nan Prince, Isabel North, and Dilly Joyce.[30] In being and becoming "old maids," their supposed sexual immobility and lack of reproductive potential ages them, figuratively, before their time. Occupying the resulting queer time, a time outside of heteronormative reproduction supposed to be progressive, these young old maids are almost indistinguishable from the host of older unmarried protagonists of New England regionalist fiction, be it Freeman's Hetty Fifield ("A Church Mouse") or Jewett's Mrs. Todd (*Pointed Firs*).[31] Together, these unmarried characters dominate regionalist fiction. They create, defy, survive, and reiterate the dissenting spirit available to them as white New England daughters.

Rose Terry Cooke's "How Celia Changed Her Mind" exemplifies how the aged New England daughter comes to claim membership in a transhistorical regional collective based on a colonial connection, one articulated through historical allusion. In this story, the kinless middle-aged old maid Celia Barnes goes from yearning to be married to being the wife of a tyrannical "master," Deacon Everts, to longing to return to her prior state of old maidenhood, a return she insists she has achieved when she becomes a widow.[32] Celia, at the story's opening, does not celebrate her unmarried state, for she understands it as the basis of her lack of structural power. Orphaned at a young age and bound out, she has been excluded from her community's systems of property and family even though her body bespeaks her racial kinship with both the New England community and with historicity: "Forty other girls in Bassett might have been described in the same way" as Celia, whose "face was one to improve with age . . . [its features having been] always more the style of fifty than fifteen" (140).

A "typical Yankee," Celia revises personal and regional history in the story's final scene by holding a Thanksgiving Day celebration for all seven of the old maids in town, thus emphasizing how alternative attachments as well as the pleasures of food and celebration after deprivation refer back to a powerful narrative of Anglo-imperialism and historicized, regional belonging (138). Judith Fetterley and Marjorie Pryse have convincingly read Celia's Thanksgiving as "dedicated to welcoming and reproducing queers."[33] Celia's Thanksgiving dinner also implies that unmarried women have a historical claim to membership in New England at a moment when the region, by way of Thanksgiving, had just been set forth as a model for every section of the nation. Established as a federal holiday in 1863, during the Civil War and only a decade before colonial revivalism as a movement took off, Thanksgiving was tied to the effort to center national history on New England.[34] Cooke writes Celia into this idealized version of New England history by placing her in a position historically reserved for the Yankee patriarch and figuring it as having generative potential: "Celia bloomed at the head of the board" (152). The image of Celia as flowering, with its invocation of sexual productivity, aestheticizes and eroticizes Celia's reclamation of old maidenhood while linking her to Rose Barker whose orphans Celia plans to adopt in order to "fetch 'em up to be dyed-in-the-wool old maid" (153). Celia imagines a queer future and asserts her freedom in the pursuit of bodily pleasures—feasting and blooming—through historical recollection. When she declares at Thanksgiving, "I'm so thankful to be an old maid ag'in!," the straight-talking Sally Gillett is technically right when she snaps back, "I thought you was a widder" (153). But Celia is effectively refashioning the formerly derogatory label "old maid," using it to designate those unmarried women who live independently, who, like figurative colonists, refuse to surrender their individual freedom just to be called kin by tyrants. Celia's nominal return to old maidenhood symbolically embraces the prior in an act of defiant remembering.[35]

Mary Wilkins Freeman, like Cooke, gestures to colonial times by way of historical allusions across her oeuvre, from Louisa Britton "struggling to wrest a little sustenance from [her family's] stony acre of land" to rebel against her mother, Mrs. Britton (homophone of Britain), to the late nineteenth-century persecution of Christmas Jenny, which "was a remnant of the old New England witchcraft superstition."[36] Freeman's short story "A Church Mouse" captures particularly well how historical allusions function in her texts, how they power her implicit argument that characters, especially women characters, cannot be understood without reference to history, that the very terms of social relation are dictated by ideological structures that persist over and in time. In "A Church Mouse," as in other Freeman works, the use of historical allusions also invites the reader to remember the transhistorical exclusion of and violence against queer women and serves, ultimately, as the mode by which the ostracized old maid goes from seeming a disruptive, dangerous, dissenting community member to being resituated as an ideal colonial-style white citizen imagined as having an inherent right to live independently and colonize spaces not originally her own.

"A Church Mouse" tells the story of Hetty Fifield, an unpopular older, unmarried woman who insists that her town, which does not have a poorhouse, provide her with a place to live. Unwilling to be bound out to a cruel mistress, Hetty takes the initiative and moves her few worldly goods into the community church, asserting herself and alienating her community further by taking on the role of sexton. (Most agree with Deacon Hale that they "never heard of a woman's bein' saxton.")[37] When the villagers, led by Hale, eventually seek to physically remove Hetty from the church, she garrisons herself in the building. The story climaxes with Hetty delivering a dramatic speech from one of the church windows, after which the villagers, led by the women, decide to allow Hetty to reside permanently in the church and stay on as its sexton. In "A Church Mouse," Freeman not only employs historical allusions in depicting an aged spinster but gives narrative form to the process by which an ostracized old maid who is perceived as witchlike ends up embodying the white colonists who fought in the intercolonial wars against the French and Indians. It is through references to the New England colonial past, both explicit and implicit, that Freeman re-presents the old maid as an ideal, specifically white New Englander and in the same gesture critiques and refashions colonial history, especially the causes that motivated violence against those unmarried women persecuted as witches.

In the way the villagers and even the narrator early on represent Hetty we see echoes of the stereotype of spinster as witch. Hetty is imagined as unproductive, penetrating, and thus threatening the health of the domestic configuration. "Held in the light of a long-thorned brier among the beanpoles, or a fierce little animal with claws and teeth bared," Hetty recalls the folkloric belief that witches were dangerous, different, and transformed themselves into or had special relations to certain animals, including rodents (349).[38] Like the prickly weed in the garden or the rat in the cellar, those women thought in colonial New England to be witches "coveted, demanding assistance, food, lodging, and comfort. They intruded, pushing themselves in where they were not wanted."[39] Freeman seems well aware of how prejudices about gender, age, and poverty shaped New England women's experiences. Like the vast majority of early New Englanders accused of being witches—"79 percent of accused witches between 1620 and 1725 were female, and women represented 80 percent of all executed witches"—Hetty is female, poor, on in years, pushes her way into control over a small corner of the community church, and collects food donations.[40]

Freeman, however, does not present Hetty as intrinsically witchlike. Instead, those qualities, the narrator makes clear, are what the villagers perceive; Hetty's difference has everything to do with her poverty and her sexualized, racialized body. The villagers see Hetty as not belonging based on her apparently non-normative body: she seems physically other, both of another species (i.e., a rodent) and another race (i.e., she is "sallow as a squaw") (345). She also does not belong to an established domestic configuration. The narrator of "A Church Mouse," however, upends the notion of this woman not belonging when, late in the story, she represents the church with Hetty bolted inside as a "feeble garrison" (355).[41] Here, Freeman's narrator places Hetty, and by retroactive extension those persecuted as witches in the colonial period, not in the role of criminal or pervert, but in that of the mythologized white settler of colonial America in his quest for a new home, a space aligned with freedom. It is this settler figure with his willingness to question the authority of the metropole while toiling in poverty on the periphery of empire that, Freeman's text posits, made possible the emergence of New England.

Throughout time, Freeman's story implies, New England women have been committed to the colonial enterprise: they have demanded, individually, the freedom to colonize spaces not originally their own in the name of self-determination conceived as natural right. Hetty does just this in moving herself into the church against Deacon Hale's prohibition, and her decision is naturalized, the result of her being "like some little animal with the purpose to which it was born strong within it" (347). When the men try to break down the church door that Hetty has bolted, she appears in the window and speaks publicly about how she has "had to fight to keep a footin' on the earth, an' now I'm gittin' too old for't" (354). Hetty, in other words, has always been at war in order to establish a place of her own. Not words alone but the historical event to which Hetty's form and gestures allude aligns her with colonial New England grit. As Hetty begins to speak, "her dark old face, peering out of the window, looked ghastly; the wind blew her poor gray locks over it. . . . The magnitude of her last act of defiance had caused it to react upon herself like an overloaded gun" (354). In this textual moment, the church as garrison house expands into an entire scene of intercolonial violence. The image of Hetty fortressed in the garrison house with her hair over her face wielding a figurative gun recalls the colonial women who famously wielded guns and let down their hair to seem like men in a 1706 Indian raid on a blockhouse near Oyster River (now Durham, New Hampshire).[42] Hetty's gun, in this passage, is not an actual rifle, of course, but a figure for her seemingly masculine defiance of gender roles, what Janice Daniel describes as Hetty's "position[ing] herself in extraordinary nineteenth-century places—those that have previously been occupied by men."[43] Hetty speaks in public and, like the Oyster River women before her, performs the role of gritty male colonial. "A Church Mouse" traces how Hetty, though her neighbors first associate her with otherness and a lack of productivity, gets acknowledged as the legatee of a hardscrabble imperialist mentality, one that affords her membership, even a preferred membership, in Anglo-American New England once her story is placed within a larger historical narrative of imperialism. Hetty might be "sallow as a squaw," but when the male leaders of the village lay a crowbar to the garrison's door, the vulnerable settler-colonial fuses with the possible rape victim; the late nineteenth-century male characters become the modern equivalents of French and Indian aggressors determined to kill or capture an Anglo-English colonial.[44]

Singular and lacking kin ties, Hetty comes to live in the transtemporal communal garrison house of white New England history by way of her defiance and public assertions, especially the creative act of speaking in costumeless and partial drag, a historicized performance that has a significant effect on the present and possibly even the future of belonging for women.[45] If not for Hetty's defense of her claim to space in the church through the verbal appeal, the community women of "A Church Mouse" would not have had a chance to reassert their voices, which had been "drowned out . . . by a masculine clamor" as the men debated whether to break down the door and remove Hetty by force (354). In response to Hetty's speech about how desperately she wants to have her own space in this world, "Mrs. Gale's voice rang out clear and strong and irrepressible. 'Of course you can stay in the meetin'-house'" (354–55). Perhaps most important in terms of the future, witnessing Hetty's historicized performance of belonging are "two young girls," one of them Mrs. Gale's daughter (354). As they watch Hetty's conflict with the villagers unfold, these girls "had their arms around each other under their shawls" (354). Freeman here offers an embodied image of who and what the next generation might hold as a result of these stagings of historicized gender injustice and queer white belonging.

Traveling through Deephaven

In the regionalist writings of Cooke and Freeman, the unmarried New England daughter recalibrates history by way of her structural position as a social and political outsider whose independent labor alludes to New England's colonial past and renders her an idealized insider in a community of dissenting settler-colonials. In the regionalist writings of Jewett, historical allusions play a role but more important are the complex processes by which characters live unfolding histories through the sensual engagement of material spaces. In *Pointed Firs*, for example, individuality is historical, tied to cosmopolitanism, and goes by the name "queer." As Mrs. Fosdick says to Mrs. Todd before they collaboratively narrate the story of the unmarried Joanna Todd, "What a lot o' queer folks there used to be about here, anyway, when we was young, Almiry. Everybody's just like everybody else, now; nobody to laugh about, and nobody to cry about."[46] To which Mrs. Todd replies,

"There was more energy then. . . . [A]s for the old folks, they pray for the advantage o' bein' a little different" (64). Aligned with history as well as an individuality energized by eighteenth- and early nineteenth-century New England's relation to global markets, people of the older generation in this passage are more interesting, original, relational, cosmopolitan, and feeling than those of the younger. It is only through cultivating relationships with this older generation of New Englanders that the travelers of Jewett's novels come to recognize themselves as historical, as belonging to a tradition of queer, cosmopolitan affective freedom.

Jewett's first novel, *Deephaven*, launched what became a career-long exploration of alternative intimacies with New England places and people perceived not as ahistorical but temporally dynamic. In broadest brushstrokes, *Deephaven* tells of the summer the twenty-four-year-old protagonist Kate Lancaster and the narrator Helen Denis spend living together in a colonial mansion on the coast of Maine that Kate's mother inherited from her aunt, Miss Brandon. Histories of mobility as well as the main characters' social and physical movements are central to this summer experiment with queer domesticity. When Kate and Helen take up residence in the colonial mansion, which Judith Fetterley reads as "an alternative, lesbian space," they encounter various histories of young women's forced immobility archived in the house.[47] This forced immobility reveals the transtemporality of young unmarried women's desire to assert their mobility. The best chamber, which Helen calls "dismal," or of evil days, is stagnant, filled with cobwebs, and features a picture "of the Maid of Orleans tied with an unnecessarily strong rope to a very stout stake."[48] In the letters the girls find in Miss Brandon's desk from her best friend Dolly we have another example of a young, unmarried woman from the past resisting immobilization. "My dear, delightful Kitten," one letter begins, if father forbids a visit due to rain, "I shall go galloping after him and overtake him when it is too late to send me back" (35). Dolly, it turns out, was immobilized by death at age eighteen, perhaps before her love for Kitten could be fully realized or her father overtaken. Fetterley sees in these letters "a vision of history as progressive. . . . [F]emale friendship has more space in 1877 than it did in 1809."[49] I would argue that the material effects of the Brandon house—its décor, its old letters—not only signify the past but haunt the present and the future, reminding Kate and Helen of the long history of both female friendship and women's sociosexual immobilization.

Kate, meanwhile, contains within herself the possibility of history repeating. Kate seems to be the modern manifestation of the past generation's spinsters—her Aunt Brandon was also named Katherine and between the young Kate and the ghostly old maid "Miss Chauncey" Helen detects "a kinship . . . not of blood, only that they both were of the same stamp and rank: Miss Chauncey of the old generation and Kate Lancaster of the new" (279). But unlike these affluent unmarried women of the past, Kate enjoys a pronounced mobility that is tied to the love she shares with another woman. Kate and Helen renovate the historical house and the history of proto-lesbian domesticity; they change the Brandon house to match their needs, modifying the décor and choosing in which parts of the house to dwell. They designate the west parlor as their favorite parlor, and it becomes, for them, the most frequently used room of the mansion. In that room's decoration we have wedded together the material evidence of New England's prior historic mobility across global markets—"odd china figures and cups and vases, unaccountable Chinese carvings and exquisite corals and seashells, minerals and Swiss wood-work, and articles of *vertu* from the South Seas" and windows with "old stained glass . . . taken from some older English house"—and treasures the girls garner on their own contemporary ramblings in the New England countryside, "immense bouquets of field flowers" and "green ferns in a tall champagne-glass" among them (29–30, 30). Unmarried women have a place in New England history's house; in fact, the house constitutes a mutable space in which historical periods and contemporary practices converge.

It is, in truth, the social and physical mobility of Kate and Helen beyond the domestic space of the colonial mansion that reinforces, naturalizes, and historicizes their love for one another. Note how Helen yokes movement across geographical spaces to the forging of intimacies with New Englanders in this summary of how she and Kate spent the season:

> I am sure that Kate Lancaster and I must have spent by far the greater part of the summer out of doors. We often made long expeditions . . . sometimes being gone all day, and sometimes taking a long afternoon stroll and coming home early in the evening hungry as hunters and laden with treasure, whether we had been through the pine woods inland or alongshore, whether we had met old friends or made some desirable new

acquaintances. We had a fashion of calling at the farm-houses, and by the end of the season we knew as many people as if we had lived in Deephaven all our days. We used to ask for a drink of water; this was our unfailing introduction. (226–27)

Anticipating the passage from *Pointed Firs* wherein Jewett's unnamed narrator asserts that "when one really knows a village like this and its surroundings, it is like becoming acquainted with a single person" (1), Helen links the adventurous exploration of the natural world with the expansion of Kate and Helen's social ties. Their "long expeditions" yield the flowers that revivify the west parlor, making it an ideal environment for their domestic experiment, and their ever-expanding relationships make their historical roots in New England seem deep, as though they have lived in Deephaven "all our days" (226). And here, in the Emma Lewis Coleman photographs meant for a special edition of *Deephaven* that was never published, we have a visual representation of how Kate and Helen's intimacy relies on their mobility, their exploration of the natural world, and their forging of cross-generational relationships.[50]

The first of these photographic illustrations to depict Kate and Helen features their physical intimacy as it is framed by the natural world of New England (figure 7). Walking together toward the sun, Kate's arm around Helen's waist, the girls cast shadows behind them just as they have left the history of unmarried women's violent immobilization in the dismal shadows of Miss Brandon's best chamber. Far afield from domestic confinement, the two move more deeply into the New England woods, their bodies penetrating forward from the bushes of the foreground toward the thicker growth of firs that lay ahead.[51] Giving loose visual form to female genitalia, this photograph depicts the young women's love for one another as both articulated in the natural world and naturalized by way of the landscape's fecundity.

The photograph meant for the facing page, meanwhile, represents Kate and Helen on the way back from their sojourn in the woods (figure 8). Here the girls face the viewer, and Helen leans down to gather the treasures that place her and Kate's own queer and present mobility into the decorative discourses of the west parlor: the flowers and ferns that Kate holds in her basket. Kate's hands, meanwhile, come together in a distinct "V," directing our gaze to her own genital area, which is linked to the blooming flowers and fern tendrils. The circuit from women's eroticized body parts, including Kate's hands, to

FIGURE 7 Emma Lewis Coleman, Kate and Helen walking into the woods. Photograph from unpublished edition of *Deephaven*. Sarah Orne Jewett Compositions and Other Papers, 1847–1909. MS Am 1743.26 (14), Houghton Library, Harvard University.

flowers to fir trees is complete. Helen's act of picking flowers and the presence of collected flora throughout the novel, both the bouquets of the west parlor and the cattails that Kate keeps in her bedroom back in Boston as a symbol of their summer, reinforce these meanings.

Time's passage is marked in figure 8 in the form of the footprints the girls made in the muddy road on their way into the woods, footprints

FIGURE 8 Emma Lewis Coleman, Kate and Helen picking flowers. Photograph from unpublished edition of *Deephaven*. Sarah Orne Jewett Compositions and Other Papers, 1847–1909. MS Am 1743.26 (14), Houghton Library, Harvard University.

FIGURE 9 Emma Lewis Coleman, Kate and Helen talking with an older woman. Photograph from unpublished edition of *Deephaven*. Sarah Orne Jewett Compositions and Other Papers, 1847–1909. MS Am 1743.26 (14), Houghton Library, Harvard University.

that render historical their journey together. Alongside these women whose bodies are turned toward us are physical reminders of the prior image of them walking away from us, Kate's arm around Helen's waist. Their past intimacy, the history of their bodies in this place, is written on the land (in the mud as footprints) and into the archive (by way of the photo). Placed on facing pages, these two photographs encourage us to wonder about what intimate acts may have occured in the span of time and space that remains unrepresented in the images but that is suggested by the language of distention Helen uses in the text to describe their journeys: "We often made long expeditions ... sometimes being gone all day, and sometimes taking a long afternoon stroll" (226).

The third of these photographs (figure 9) makes specific reference to the same passage quoted above even though it appears later in the unpublished book: it depicts Kate about to drink water that the girls have routinely requested as part of their "unfailing introduction" to new people. In this photograph, more clearly than in the passage from the novel itself, we have a proposed connection between the collection of symbolic flowers long rooted in the soils of New England and the expansion of social relations with older people who are the perennial blossoming of New England families that go back to colonial times. Both form part of a dynamic queer practice in the present. When we look back to early in *Deephaven*, to the moment when Helen explains to readers why she loves Kate and how she hopes we, too, will love her, we see how empathy engenders her social mobility: Kate knows "with surest instinct how to meet them [people] on their own ground. It is the girl's being so genuinely sympathetic and interested which makes every one ready to talk to her and be friends with her; just as the sunshine makes it easy for flowers to grow which the chilly winds hinder" (48). Much like Helen in figure 8 leans toward the flowers she collects from the New England roadside to form part of the unfolding history of same-sex domesticity and mobility, Kate, in figure 9, leans in to make contact with an old New England woman figured as one of many flowers she is said to warm. Barriers to this contact with an elderly New Englander, however, are double: there is a fence between the girls and the older woman and a long pole set at a vertical slant divides them visually. Difference is coded, too, in the old woman's light shirt contrasting the girls' dark dresses. Yet the figures come together visually in the repeating images of vessels: the water bucket and water cup, both of which seem to recall the female body as a vessel filled not by the phallus—which is right there in the form of the pole—but by the "feminine" water that the woman offers and that Kate imbibes. The water, moreover, is merely sexually symbolic while being socially significant: the request for water fulfilled, we know from reading the passage, initiates intimacy with the old woman and other Deephaven residents like her. In the end, Kate's meeting people on their own ground writes her, and by extension Helen, into the Deephaven community and thus not only helps explain the past and present to one another, as Jewett has it in her 1893 preface. It also helps ground unmarried women's affective and erotic freedom in a historicized culture of empathy.

Kate and Helen's mobility takes as its precursor the cosmopolitan mobility of eighteenth-century New England where members of coastal communities like the real-life equivalents of Deephaven participated directly in international trade. The imperial past celebrated in Jewett's novels not only concerns "traces of empire" read as signs of "white colonial settlement and dominance," as Elizabeth Ammons has it in her analysis of *Pointed Firs*; it also deals with queerness in particular as imbricated in a cosmopolitan form of empathetic identification, an identification that depends on a much more subtle and complex imagining of whiteness and its presumed mobilities than the charge of racism or imperialism allows.[52] At the same time, when Fetterley and Pryse, in part trying to restore attention to the radical possibilities of regionalist texts in the wake of readings such as that by Ammons, read empathy as "potentially disruptive and transgressive," as constructed but ultimately "a solution for survival in a world of difference," what remains unacknowledged is how empathy as a radical strategy has been historically keyed to white survival and dominance.[53] *Deephaven* imagines the ideal, cosmopolitan unmarried young woman, Kate Lancaster, as "meeting people on their own ground" and as like the sun (or Christ-as-son) in distributing her affective energy. This image implicitly brings to bear a historic notion of white Christian New England women's empathy as the basis for a transformed democracy, one based on an assumption of white racial superiority.

We can best understand part of the literary-historical legacy of empathy found within Jewett's and other regionalists' work by taking a brief detour back to the abolitionist best-seller *Uncle Tom's Cabin*, written by the New Englander and proto-regionalist Harriet Beecher Stowe. In this novel, as Jane Tompkins has famously argued, it is the empathetic, unmarried white daughter, little Eva, who emerges as the Christ figure.[54]

As a child, Eva is, her father St. Clare insists, "The only true democrat," one who "put[s] herself on an equality with every creature that comes near her."[55] Fueled by a radical New Testament understanding of Christ as the champion of the downtrodden, Eva generates an affective energy that is spent loving and thus educating by example the African American slaves and the nascent white republicans of the St. Clare household. Without the structural inequities of slavery and the moral backwardness among whites that it has bred, Stowe's narrator implies, Eva's democratic Christianity would have no basis for its articulation. Not only might the domestic space need to be "divested of men," as Gillian Brown argues, but white and black unmarried women must be present for the seeds of liberal democratic subjecthood to be sown.[56] It is, after all, the unmarried New England women Miss Ophelia and Topsy, who becomes an adopted black daughter of the region, rather than male citizens (the white Augustine) and potential male citizens (the black Tom), who are transformed by Eva and live on into futurity. The flourishing of these seeds, in turn, depends on an empathetic (and arguably imperial) adoptive asexual or sexually transgressive form of reproduction: neither Ophelia nor Topsy, following Eva, give over their independence to a husband. Instead, Topsy "at the age of womanhood . . . by her own request . . . became a member of the Christian church," eventually serving as a mission teacher in Africa (612).

Analyses of queer sexualities in *Uncle Tom's Cabin* have focused on male homosexual desire, but what if we were to read Topsy as queer in her adoption into the community of New England unmarried daughters?[57] That at the age when marriage is expected of young women Topsy asserts her own agency (she is the only St. Clare slave to be manumitted by Augustine before he dies) and "by her own request" becomes part of the New England Christian community demonstrates how, for Stowe, a specially coded New England democratic subjecthood depends on women's freedom of affiliation as opposed to marriage and slavery, which are both predicated on female subjugation (612). As Karen Sánchez-Eppler has argued, in nineteenth-century white feminist writing, "The metaphoric linking of women and slaves proves ubiquitous."[58] Yet, in this instance, Stowe gestures toward how New England daughters, black and white, might maintain their independence by remaining single. This independence, however, is qualified, for it depends on two things: "lowly" black others (Ophelia on Topsy, Topsy on Africans) and a clear identification with the regional-imperial New England family.

FIGURE 10 Emma Lewis Coleman, Kate and Helen at the water's edge. Photograph from unpublished edition of *Deephaven*. Sarah Orne Jewett Compositions and Other Papers, 1847–1909. MS Am 1743.26 (14), Houghton Library, Harvard University.

In offering this brief segue into Stowe's representation of unmarried New England women, I am not suggesting that the older members of the Deephaven community are figured as racially other but, rather, that Kate's exercise of empathetic identification, which for Fetterley and Pryse is a distinct feature of regionalism, depends, in part, on the privilege of white mobility that specifically alludes to the eighteenth-century global markets that made coastal New England queer and cosmopolitan. Participation in such markets included the traffic in slaves and in the products of the slave-based economy like the sugar that Captain Tolland in a later Jewett work, "The Foreigner," brings back to Dunnet Landing from the Caribbean, along with a new wife.[59] It also forms part of the tradition of white liberalism that emerges from the history of abolitionism. In this particular example, white racial privilege founds alternative sociosexual mobilities for white women. The queer cosmopolitanism of Kate, following the Civil War at the moment of the failure of Reconstruction is that of the unmarried, white New England daughter as the ideal imperialist-democrat, as an empathetic regional and world citizen.[60] So profoundly is their affective freedom based on travel that Helen and Kate ultimately decide they cannot settle permanently in Deephaven, even though Kate "laughingly proposed one evening . . . that we should copy the Ladies of Llangollen" and stay living together on the Maine coast (290).[61] As the final Coleman photograph of the hoped-for and never-realized edition of *Deephaven* suggests, the intimacy cultivated during that summer between Kate and Helen depends not on settling into a dyadic same-sex household but on ongoing social and physical movement that engages history just as it looks forward to the future, recognizing both as intertwined (figure 10). Helen gazes out to sea across the Atlantic, and Kate looks down to the apparently limitless world of imaginative literature: traveling and writing are the two ways Jewett imagines a mobile intimate practice that is itself historical and in history, ever-expanding in its embrace.

Tourism's Intimate Historicity

Jewett, throughout her career, moved readers from cross-generational relations historicizing and reinforcing the mobility of young queer women (in *Deephaven*) to cross-generational relations that were themselves the center of an intimate life understood not as ending within a season's time but unfolding unpredictably out into the future (in *Pointed Firs*). In both of these novelistic explorations of women's eroticism, the natural environment figures as a living space, a sort of extension of the unmarried woman's body with its swaths of dense firs, its deep harbors, its fragrant pennyroyal plots, and its gardens of thyme. Alice Brown, an early reviewer of *Pointed Firs* and a queer colleague of Jewett's, gestured toward the novel's use of figures of floral penetration and cosmic fingering: "*Pointed Firs* is the flower of a sweet, sane knowledge of life, and an art so elusive that it smiles up at you while you pull aside the petals, vainly probing its heart.... The pointed firs have their roots in the ground of national being; they are index fingers to the stars."[62] More significant than the sensuality of Jewett's text is its role in the refiguring of intimacy's history. One way that *Pointed Firs* constructs the "salutary historiographic model" of which Peter Coviello writes is by way of summer tourism, a cultural practice for use of which the novel has been consistently critiqued and which is worth revisiting.[63]

Tourism in New England after the Civil War took myriad forms: some leisured Americans frequented resorts such as Bar Harbor and Newport, which were meeting grounds for the rich and marriageable; some purchased summer homes; and others, often those less well off, boarded for part or all of the summer season. In this last practice, a tourist from the city would pay a rural resident for food and a room, and it is this sort of tourism—summer boarding—that *Pointed Firs* depicts. By 1891, a contributor to *Ladies' Home Journal* reported that summer boarding "is said to be the third largest industry in the State of Maine, vying in its results with those of the lumber, ice and hay crops there."[64] Nine years later, New Hampshire reported more than 150,000 summer guests at farmhouses, boarding houses, and hotels; the cash received from those guests totaled nearly 5 million dollars.[65] Jewett, a native of southern Maine, noticed the changes that accompanied the rise of the domestic tourism industry in New England and, later in life, linked it to her writerly mission: "When I was, perhaps, fifteen [c. 1864], the first 'city boarders' began to make their appearance near Berwick; and the way they misconstrued the country people and made game of their peculiarities fired me with indignation. I determined to teach the world that country people were not the awkward, ignorant set those persons seemed to think."[66]

The growth of summer boarding brought urban and rural men and women into intimate and more frequent contact, and these encounters, in turn, gave way to Jewett's pubescent pique as well as to various representations of tourism in the era's popular culture. Across a substantial archive of popular fiction on summer boarding we find two types of plots, one romantic, the other humorous: either the stories begin with tourism and end with an engagement or they depict urban and rural women who simply cannot get along. Two city people might fall in love once boarding in the same house.[67] Perhaps the lovely rural daughter entrances the urban boarder's heart, allowing him a doubly powerful respite from city life: a home and a rural wife.[68] And in some, as in Jewett's understudied novel *A Marsh Island*, the presence of the summer boarder triangulates an existing rural relationship.[69]

According to nonfiction sources, however, summer boarding was not about men and women getting together but about women becoming estranged.[70] Landladies took responsibility for their family's boarders while their husbands, if they had them, worked in shops or in the field. Boarders, meanwhile, were most often women who had the leisure to leave the city for an extended period of time. One contributor to *Good Housekeeping* captured the general sense of frustration to be found in many advice articles on the subject when she called the summer boarder-landlady relationship "a difficult problem."[71] *Pointed Firs* rejects both of these dominant cultural scripts in depicting the narrator and Mrs. Todd doing more than getting along, as forging lasting, sensually infused social ties over time.

In *Pointed Firs*, Jewett sets the temporal dynamism of unmarried women's desires against the stagnation and limitations of marriage. To cite just two examples, poor Joanna's self-exile after having been jilted by a man figures as being on a historical continuum with captivity, and Elijah Tilley's pathetic refrain "poor dear" in reference to his dead wife constellates sentimentalism and compulsion. Limited to the domestic sphere, Elijah's wife died just after she had completed what, in retrospect, seems to have been her life's work—putting together her house (121). As Elijah tells the narrator: "She told me that last summer before she was taken away that she couldn't think o' anything more she wanted, there was everything in the house, an' all her rooms was furnished pretty. I was goin' over to the Port, an' inquired for errands. I used to ask her to say what she wanted, cost or no cost. . . . It kind o' chilled me up when she spoke so satisfied" (125). Travel and myriad forms of sociality *as opposed to* domesticity and marriage offered unmarried women a literal way to meet people and provide a metaphor for the mobility of affect Jewett understood as central to queer intimacy. Rather than presenting historic New England as yielding a quaint or prescribed version of history to the hungry tourist, Jewett imagined tourism itself as giving way to potentially erotic, alternative practices, ones that actively defied the heterosexual love plot that drove most narratives, including the summer-boarding fiction of popular magazines, and gave form to a distended, multiclimactic intimacy expanded across time. This is the sort of history she depicts in her most famous novel.

Pointed Firs offers cross-generational queer love as the basis for an alternative, dissenting epistemology, one that takes friendship distended across an undesignated time as its model. In *Pointed Firs*'s first chapter, the narrator maps the terrain the novel will plot: "When one really knows a village like this and its surroundings, it is like becoming acquainted with a single person. The process of falling in love at first sight is as final as it is swift in such a case, but the growth of true friendship may be a lifelong affair" (1–2). A historicized queerness under the aegis of friendship here becomes a way of knowing for this single person. Coviello emphasizes that the experience of getting to know this part of New England is like "becoming acquainted with a *single* person."[72] "Single" denotes individual just as it suggests unmarried, therein forwarding the notion of a specially individuated New England daughter who is singular (or "queer," to use Mrs. Todd and Mrs. Fosdick's parlance) and an unwed woman available for different kinds of historically embedded intimacies. Engaging a place, this passage proposes, can take two forms. The first is the "process of falling in love at first sight." Taking little time (it is "swift") and rendering fixed one's knowledge (it is "final"), falling in love may well result in the end of history figured as the end of knowledge making. Falling in love, however, may give way to a second social possibility, "the growth of true friendship," which is neither fast nor final but, naturalized as "growth," takes place over a duration, its end time uncertain. Knowledge, we may infer, does not become fixed in this latter form of exchange but remains unmoored, and thus its becoming is future-oriented and free; it has no clear end or destination in sight. It looks forward just as Helen and Kate look to the ocean and the book in Coleman's photograph, just as the narrator from *Pointed Firs* leaves by boat and, in the later Dunnet Landing stories, returns and leaves again and again.

The alternative epistemology *Pointed Firs* theorizes in its opening pages anticipates how it thinks into existence a distended history of cross-generational intimacy between Mrs. Todd and the narrator as well as how the novel revises narrative form. In an 1873 letter to Horace E. Scudder, Jewett famously laments her inability to write a story of length.

> I don't believe I could write a long story as he [William Dean Howells] suggested, and you advise me in this last letter. In the

first place, I have no dramatic talent. The story would have no plot. I should have to fill it out with descriptions of character and meditations. It seems to me I can furnish the theatre, and show you the actors, and the scenery, and the audience, but there never is any play! I could write you entertaining letters perhaps, from some desirable house where I was in most charming company, but I couldn't make a story about it.[73]

Pointed Firs is the project in which Jewett does write a "long story" about "most charming company" in a "desirable house," and she achieves this by focusing not on heterosexual romance but on the movement back and forth between the proximity of intimacy and the distance of solitude involved in a dynamic, at times erotic, relationship between two women: the narrator and Mrs. Todd.[74] Mrs. Todd and the narrator sometimes come together as a dyad, but, more important, they expand their relationship to become triadic (as when Mrs. Fosdick visits) or to incorporate immediate and extended family (as on Green Island and at the Bowden reunion). Amid those various fluctuations, each never ceases to be single and singular. Kate McCullough has convincingly argued that *Pointed Firs* takes as its central metaphor the Boston marriage and thus "locates the homosocial at the heart of the nation."[75] I contend, in turn, that Jewett posits in *Pointed Firs* an alternative narrative of affective mobility expressed through the metaphor not of queer marriage but of travel. Tourism thought as a historical act allows the queer white daughter to be productive and future-oriented, and it forwards a mode of affiliation that both involves and expands beyond the flexible Boston marriage model to include variously configured intimacies as themselves imbedded in and expressed over time.

Pointed Firs stages an erotic "play," to borrow from the language of Jewett's letter to Scudder. Its notion of narrative embodiment, including the important representation of material experience and the use of historical allusions, link it to C. Alice Baker's historical performances as well as to Cooke's and Freeman's fiction writing. The action in *Pointed Firs* is the getting to know a person. This involves not only the older New Englander, Mrs. Todd, becoming the loved one, but also the narrator experiencing Mrs. Todd's body in relationship to New England's natural world, which allows the narrator access to both. Jewett herein offers a different model for narrative. The slowly pulsed plot of *Pointed Firs* tracks fundamental change over time:

the narrator transitioning from the third-person "she," who is a visitor projecting her "affectionate dreams" of Dunnet Landing as a tourist destination onto the town, to the "I" who comes to love Mrs. Todd (2).

The narrator relinquishes the third-person perspective only once some time has passed and she gets to know Mrs. Todd. Having settled for a moment in the second-person perspective in chapter 2, the narrator experiences what I take to be the first of the novel's multiple erotic climaxes: you "learned to know" that Mrs. Todd was trodding "heavily upon thyme," the narrator tells us, by way of the fragrance that makes its way into your bedroom and which you inhale while in the intimate temporal space of lying "half awake in the morning," a quietly private historical pleasure that modifies the visual economy of the narrator's prior "dreams" of Dunnet Landing as quaint, its shores unchanged (3, 2). The viscerally immediate scent of thyme released on the air by the brush of a near stranger's skirt brings a pleasure all its own (and crosses over a century into the thyme-smelling time of the reader's moment). As the friendship between the narrator and Mrs. Todd expands, the narrator transitions to the fully realized I, the point of view used for the remainder of the novel. Inhabiting the body of this I, the narrator inhales the scents of Mrs. Todd's body blended into and through the smells of the Maine landscape over and over again, from the time when Mrs. Todd tells the narrator of the first man she loved "while the strange fragrance of the mysterious herb blew in from the little garden" to the erotic repetition of Mrs. Todd pressing "her aromatic nosegay between her hands and offer[ing] it to [the narrator] again and again" in the pennyroyal plot on Green Island (8, 48). It is over time and, in these last two examples, after Mrs. Todd has narrated her own intimate past that the narrator experiences the land of the country of the pointed firs sensually, by means of its fragrant plants. As Bill Brown insists, smell, which "depends on proximity, on chemical contact, on physical infiltration," is "how Jewett establishes an overwhelming intimacy between natural and human matter."[76] The getting to know another woman in a cross-generational intimacy expanding freely and unevenly over time involves the landscape thought of as an erotic site and the loved one's body in encounter with the landscape as generating scents that enter the lover's body materially. By the novel's climax of belonging—the Bowden reunion—it is not just Mrs. Todd's body in relation to myriad plants from which the narrator garners pleasure; her sense of the New England landscape's erotic potential has graduated, yielding a meditation on the molten heat embedded in the regional character and its sensual life thought in terms of world-historical time.

The Bowden reunion has been at the center of much critical debate in Jewett scholarship. Early feminists often read it as a celebration of matrifocal community, while historicist critics, some feminists among them, have read it as a racist, nativist staging of national exclusivity.[77] I am interested in enlarging the view, recognizing how the reunion places queer New England women's intimacies on a temporal and geographical scales that exceed a national one. "It is very rare in country life," the Bowden reunion chapter of *Pointed Firs* begins,

> where high days and holidays are few, that any occasion of general interest proves to be less than great. Such is the hidden fire of enthusiasm in the New England nature that, once given an outlet, it shines forth with almost volcanic light and heat.... [W]hen, at long intervals, the altars to patriotism, to friendship, to the ties of kindred, are reared in our familiar fields, then the first glow, the flames come up as if from the inexhaustible burning heart of the earth; the primal fires break through the granite dust in which our souls are set. (95–96)

Love of country ("patriotism"), family ("the ties of kindred"), and friendship (of the sort that might become "a lifelong affair") all have the capacity to bring out the naturalized "heart of the earth," in a landscape rendered indistinguishable through metaphor from the body of the New Englander whose nature appears to be granite and is, underneath, "volcanic."

In this extended metaphor of volcanic heat formed and energized across geological time, we have an expansion of temporal awareness and a claim made to the unmarried woman's intimate sensations thought on a global scale. Alongside this we have human history limited to the history of Europe and the colonized new world that Jewett's narrator associates with the Bowden family members by way of historical allusions. "We might have been a company of ancient Greeks," she asserts (100). In *Pointed Firs*, a transnational, transtemporal white European inheritance has come down to the contemporary unmarried New England daughter rendering her various passions seemingly natural ones that accord with various histories.

In alluding to European history and specifically Greek culture, Jewett clarifies other historical and literary allusions she has made throughout the novel that link Mrs. Todd to western European and colonial New England traditions of dissent. Mrs. Todd mounts "a gray rock, and stood there grand and architectural, like a *caryatide*," and at another moment, she "might have been Antigone alone on the Theban plain" (30, 49). These allusions align Mrs. Todd's body with the European past and with female forms of rebellion while also forming part of the project of what Scott Bravmann has called "the manufacture of a mythical 'Greek' past" for gays and lesbians since at least the early 1880s.[78] These allusions to democracy, transhistorical queer pasts, and former empires work together with those in the Bowden reunion chapters to alert us to the possibility that when the narrator tells us she "felt like an adopted Bowden" (99), she is feeling not just part of a parochial nativist group, but part of a larger, transhistorical democratic and dissenting community. Geological time and the life of sensation meet political time and the life of affiliation in *Pointed Firs*; the narrator's unfolding intimate history with Mrs. Todd reaches yet another climax at the reunion, one both sensual and intellectual. The unmarried women in this novel belong to and through simultaneous histories.

But there is another time Jewett's narrator understands as sedimented in the soil, transformed into plants, scenting the breeze, and incorporating itself into and onto the unmarried woman's body by way of material things: colonial New England time. As Ammons argues in "Jewett's Witches," *Pointed Firs* consistently suggests Mrs. Todd is witchlike; a similar observation could be made of a number of regionalist texts that portray exceptional women—Freeman's "A Church Mouse" and Alice Brown's "At Sudleigh Fair" among them. This is one way that the New England regionalists link queer women to colonial New England history.[79] Other traces of colonial New England history are everywhere apparent at the reunion and not solely in the "tiny trophies from 'exotic' foreign ports" that Ammons notices.[80] The colonial is in the desserts that Mrs. Todd and the narrator ingest: celebrants eat "an American pie," which "is far to be preferred to its humble ancestor, the English tart," not to mention "a model of the old [colonial] Bowden house made of durable gingerbread, with all the windows and doors in the right places, and sprigs of genuine lilac set at the front" (108). The colonial is manifest in the Bowden homestead itself, which "stood, low-storied and broad-roofed, in its green fields as if it were a motherly brown hen waiting for the flock that came straying toward it from every direction" (97). And even the very soil of the place contains fragments of the bodies of white New England women from the colonial era to the novel's present: on the Bowden homestead "most of the home graves were those of women" (98).

What we have in *Pointed Firs* is not a colonial revivalism only and easily reducible to the fetishizing of things or the articulation of a white supremacist nationalism, but one thought in tandem and variously intersecting with other histories: of geology, of democracy, of an unfolding intimacy of uncertain duration between unmarried women that refuses even to be contained between the covers of *Pointed Firs*. Jewett returned her readers again and again to Dunnet Landing and to the narrator's unfolding history with Mrs. Todd in the stories that came one after another in the years following the publication of *Pointed Firs*.[81] What Jewett offers, then, is a historicity that claims belonging for unmarried white New England women's embodied intimacies within various spatiotemporal registers, that writes a range of pleasurable, mobile relations into and on the record.

3

Out of the China Closet

In the period between 1865 and 1915, collecting antique china became a popular pastime in the United States, one centered in New England. China collecting had long been an adored hobby among the elite of England, from the porcelain craze of the early eighteenth century to the Aesthetes' obsession with old blue in the second half of the nineteenth. Early collectors in England bought new and old china at public auctions of East India Company imports or from fashionable shops in London, and those in France had the option of the flea market.[1] When, for the first time, a craze for antique china took hold in the United States, collectors bought pieces from similar sources: metropolitan shops and estate auctions. There was, however, a more time-consuming, engaging mode of collecting antiques. The collectors known as china hunters, who were generally more interested in the ceramics used in early America—Staffordshire, Liverpool, Delft, Chinese porcelain, and more—shunned the direct form of shopping in urban antique stores. These colonial revivalists preferred to collect by traveling the countryside, knocking on the doors of strangers' houses, and convincing the inhabitants to sell their valuable crockery.[2] Coastal New England in particular proved a treasure trove of valuable antique ceramic imports from China and Europe thanks to the region's participation in international trade at the turn into the nineteenth century. All manner of valuable pitchers and bowls might be found in the homes of once-distinguished trading families as well as across classes in the homes of anyone with sailor ancestors. This abundance of antiques attested to New England's cosmopolitan colonial and early national past.

In recent years, as scholars' interest in material culture has blossomed, studies of china collecting and collections have expanded beyond the fields of art history and museum studies, but they have tended to remain focused on Europe, especially England. When it comes to china collecting in the United States, scholars have emphasized male collectors of Asian art such as Henry Francis du Pont, John D. Rockefeller, and William and Henry Walters.[3] Women, however, were significant players in china-collecting culture in the late nineteenth century. In fact, women's domestic china collecting constituted a regionalist cultural practice, one focused on New England history.

Women dominated china hunting in late nineteenth-century U.S. culture, or to put it as the *New York Times* did in May 1893, "Women Collectors [are] More Numerous Than Men."[4] Virginia Huntington Robie, in her *By-Paths in Collecting*, reiterated this idea: "Not that all china collectors are women, far from it, but in this country the larger portion is undoubtedly composed of the 'unpunctual sex.'"[5] It was women, moreover, who authored the two earliest and most influential antique china-hunting guides of the era: Annie Trumbull Slosson's *The China Hunters Club* (1878) and Alice Morse Earle's *China Collecting in America* (1892). In the main, their field was New England, their mode regionalist.[6] At the turn into the twentieth century about ten more guides to antique china collecting in the United States were published, most of them by women.[7]

Late nineteenth-century china-hunting guides confirm that a productive overlap existed between literary regionalism, domestic tourism, and colonial revivalism. We see this first in terms of Slosson's and Earle's own careers: after publishing *The China Hunters Club*, which was a hybrid of regionalist fiction and informational text, Slosson became a well-known regionalist short story writer.[8] Earle, meanwhile, published on china collecting early in her career and then went on to become an author of popular colonial American histories, studies that "supplemented traditional archival sources with material evidence."[9] Yet I do not categorize china collecting as a New England regionalist practice only because of these two authors' professional biographies. China collecting was a New England regionalist project in that antique collecting and the texts written about it contributed to the larger movement to represent New England as a uniquely historical region and mobile New England daughters as perfectly suited to the engaging act of recollecting its past.

China collecting offers an ideal site for teasing out how literary and economic practices were bound up with women's claims to cosmopolitan mobility and the erotic freedoms and fantasies such mobility supposedly engendered. Christopher Castiglia has traced how in the periods before the Civil War "fantasy itself became an object of ridicule, characterized as wasteful, impractical, and self-indulgent, the opposite of productive (and reproductive) self-management and civic-mindedness" in U.S. culture.[10] China-hunting guides were, I argue, textual performance spaces, ones in which women interpreted, archived, and elaborated on embodied practices, including their generation of fantasies in the field of rural New England. Such fantasizing proved central both to the act of history making and to china hunting's exquisite delight. The few who have written about Earle or china-collecting women have overlooked how the imaginative, interior aspects of china collecting were perceived as practices of the body in the world, ones that defied notions of a clear boundary between the fictive and the real.[11] Consider Robie who, in one of her guides to antiquing, waxed poetic about how a Bristol teapot bought while on the china hunt was bound to conjure up the "real Mary Wilkins [Freeman] characters" encountered during its acquisition.[12] The history of the modern woman china collector's exploits was valuable in part because of the intimate type of consumerist contact and imaginative conjure it enabled. At the same time, regionalist fiction sometimes took as its subject china hunting based on real-life practices, as in Freeman's 1901 novella *The Jamesons*. This work's protagonist, the tourist Mrs. Boardman Jameson who summers in provincial Massachusetts, fills her china closet with "a very queer assortment of dishes"; "they [the Jameson women] had simply ransacked the neighborhood for forsaken bits of crockery-ware," the narrator relates.[13] Mrs. Jameson's obsession with old china forms part of her broader colonial revivalist fervor, one that results in her finding an old book in her attic proving the town's centennial is that year. Inspired by her discovery, Mrs. Jameson plans and orchestrates a centennial celebration of impressive proportions.

When women, usually in pairs, took to New England's dusty roads to track down old Liverpool pitchers and Staffordshire plates, they modified century-old discourses about white women's relationship to consumerism and labor by modifying how china collecting, gender, fantasy, and eroticism were constellated. Intimacy with china, it seemed, might even go so far as to disrupt the normative script that cast women into marriage. Women china hunters in late nineteenth-century New England portrayed themselves as ideal collector-citizens and as daring, obsessed connoisseurs who indulged in the queerly valenced sensual pleasures of the hunt. Far from being perverse, excessive, and monstrous, which was how male commentators often portrayed the desires of eighteenth-century English china-maniacal women, these New England collectors were savvy, bold, masculine, and familiar with erotic joy. Hot on the trail of heirlooms not (yet) their own, they represented themselves and their collector characters as released from the strictures of the domestic space thought as a sort of china closet in which the fragile, hyperfeminine woman dwelled. Driven by fantasies of rescuing ceramics from the confines of the cupboards, attics, and barns of rural New England, the china hunters, like C. Alice Baker in her recollections and like Freeman, Rose Terry Cooke, and Sarah Orne Jewett in their regionalist fictions, rewrote modern unmarried women in relation to and by way of history.

Grandaddy's Gender-Bending Girl

China-hunting women in late nineteenth-century New England represented themselves as historically minded and adventurous. In this, they distanced themselves from the debased, hypersexualized figure of the eighteenth century, the china-maniacal English woman, without sacrificing the erotic sensitivies or drive thought to characterize that figure. From the 1675 restoration comedy *The Country Wife*, in which the playwright William Wycherley exploits "the metaphoric potential of 'china' in relation to a randy sexuality," to Alexander Pope's use of porcelain as a figure for the hymen in *The Rape of the Lock*, ceramics have operated as a cultural site through which to theorize white women as desiring subjects and posit their bodies as fragile, sexual commodities.[14] In contrast to white women's conventional relationship to china (either oversexed in their excessive consumption or objectified as ceramic objects themselves) stood the studious male collector of eighteenth-century English and French tradition, one not taken in by fads but who exercised taste, one who pursued collecting as a "highly individual and often authenticity-based . . . creative, self-producing, order-making activity."[15] This enlightened male figure demonstrated his membership in "the Republic of Taste" by being rational and moderate, traits that fitted him for citizenship in the political realm.[16]

Throughout *The China Hunters Club* and *China Collecting in America*, Slosson and Earle represent china-hunting women as having inherited a range of masculine characteristics from adoptive forefathers, ones that emphasize their own fitness as women collectors and citizens. In fact, aside from the history of women in ceramics offered early in Slosson's guide, which establishes the seriousness and scope (versus the silly sensuousness) of women potters and collectors of the past, Slosson and Earle consistently link late nineteenth-century china-hunting women to male collectors of the past and present.[17] This may be, in part, because earlier in the nineteenth century men had dominated collecting. In New England, the practice had roots in the soil of early patriotism. It was largely the impulse to archive a distinctly local and national history that motivated the founding of early U.S. institutions dedicated to preservation such as the Massachusetts Historical Society (MHS), the American Antiquarian Society, and the New-York Historical Society. The Northeast led this preservation movement: Maine, Rhode Island, New Hampshire, Pennsylvania, and Connecticut all established such institutions in the 1820s, and other states, including western ones, soon followed suit. Women, however, were not permitted to join these societies.[18] Yet, part of the colonial revival mission in the late nineteenth century was to continue to ameliorate what one *Good Housekeeping* contributor represented as a national crisis in preservation: "Until the year 1876, when our Centennial exposition brought about a mania for collecting antiquities, we were, as a nation, given to vandalism; to destroying, by not taking means to preserve old papers, manuscripts and books; to obliterating landmarks and letting buildings of historical interest go to decay."[19]

China-hunting guides portray white women's propensity for historic preservation, history making, and citizenship by way of these constructed male lineages while reveling in the women-specific erotic potential of the hunt. For although china collecting had been a masculine pursuit, it was, at the same time, aligned with femininity. Take, for instance, the cultural stereotype of the effeminate male collector, the china-loving fop, which originated in eighteenth-century English culture. Similar ideas about china collecting as an inherently feminine pursuit persisted in the late nineteenth-century United States: "There must always remain . . . something peculiarly womany, if not womanly, about china collecting," maintained the *New York Times*.[20] The apparent tension between the masculine-coded, often sexualized aggression of the china "hunt" and the "womany" if not "womanly" aspects of china collecting made it a practice by way of which women could rethink traditional sex-gender roles and heteronormative proscriptions. Earle, for instance, frames the entirety of *China Collecting in America* by aligning her unnamed narrator, a figure for Earle herself, with a transhistorical community of male collectors, including those deemed effete, whose interest in old china involves, at its foundation, playing with, on, and through the binaries of the sex-gender system, on seeming and celebrating queerness.

China Collecting in America begins with a lengthy evocation of Charles Lamb and ends by asserting Earle's figurative kinship with Horace Walpole and Oscar Wilde. Here is how Earle opens her guide:

> My dearly loved friend, Charles Lamb, wrote, in his "Essays of Elia," "I have an almost feminine partiality for old china. When I go to see any great house, I inquire first for the china-closet, and next for the picture-gallery. I have no repugnance for those little lawless azure-tinted grotesques that, under the notion of men and women, float about uncircumscribed by any element, in that world before perspective—a china teacup." In that partiality for old china I humbly join, and it is of the search through New England for such dear china loves, and of the gathered treasures of those happy china hunts, that I write.[21]

In this passage, Earle's narrator and the eighteenth-century Englishman Lamb are intimates—"dearly loved friend[s]"—even though they lived at different times; they share a china-loving camaraderie across gender difference. Earle seems to want to put pressure on the very boundary that marks that difference: Lamb's is an "almost feminine partiality for old china," and Earle depicts herself time and again as coveting male roles. At one point in *China Collecting in America*, she wishes she could be a peddler, one of the "peaceful joys . . . forbidden to me, not because of lack of inclination or capacity, but—thrice bitter thought—because I am a woman," and at another, she figures herself a soldier in the battle for antique ceramics (18, 11). In the passage where Earle quotes Lamb, it is not only the china collector but the representation of gender as depicted on the actual china teacup that highlights indeterminate forms of gender identity. Lamb reiterates the language of freedom from stricture and, to a degree, expresses a cultural relativism in his account of the china teacup: the cup's figures are "lawless" and "uncircumscribed," specifically as regards their gender and its readability. The figures go "under the notion of men and women," which suggests that they are not clearly either.

We may have, both in Lamb and in Earle's use of Lamb, an example of what Thomas W. Kim argues made Oriental objects appeal to consumers in the nineteenth century: "The cultural capital to be gained by consuming Oriental objects resided quite specifically in the evocation of an aristocratic yet simpler past, a time characterized by effortless aesthetic cultivation rather than industrial, capitalist striving."[22] After all, Lamb figures the material space of the china teacup as temporal as well as geographical: "in that world *before* perspective." I would add, however, that here the idealized past of the Chinese accrues interest and value specifically as a time and place of gender indeterminacy. For Earle, there is also value in the intimacies to which such indeterminacy situated in an imperialist framework might give way. Lamb does not assert that he loves the china teacup or the "lawless . . . grotesques" it depicts, but he does link his "almost feminine partiality for china" and his decided lack of "repugnance" for figures that "go under the notion of men and women." Earle takes Lamb's largely tentative, negatively framed articulation of admiration for china and refigures it as love, china love for Lamb himself ("my dearly loved friend") as well as for china objects and the "lawless . . . grotesques" that are complexly gendered (those "dear china loves"). As I will discuss in further detail later in this chapter, the potentially alienating and exotic aspects of sexual liminality condense a racial otherness, the cultural products of China, and the gender-specific materiality of china, the ceramic so often taken to symbolize white women's bodies in Western thought.

The literature of china hunting depicts women as blending and bending gender traits, both those traditionally aligned with women and femininity—social adaptability, interpersonal dynamism, and domestic know-how—and those traditionally aligned with men and masculinity—physical and social mobility, economic savvy, a keen sense of adventure, erotic agency, and militarism.[23] Women china collectors herein reformulate the figure of the modern New England daughter, imagining that she could best contribute to the project of history making not through traditional feminine means—reproductive and domestic work (thus largely replicating that which already existed)—but by way of collecting and preserving history. As Slosson makes clear in *The China Hunters Club*, owning antique china could constitute a route to reinscribing traditional gender roles as is the case with one character, Victoria, who is the stereotypical, domesticated Victorian American woman. "Fond of old china," Victoria "goes, with well-filled purse, to the bric-a-brac [*sic*] shops of New York, Boston, and Philadelphia," where she "buys Chinese vases, warranted a thousand years old, yet fresh and bright as any modern reproduction," along with Dresden and Sèvres.[24] Even though she travels to rural New England with her china-hunting companion, an unnamed china hunter, Victoria refuses to take any part in pressuring rural people to sell their heirlooms. Victoria remains immobile, properly enshrined in a domestic space, namely "by the cheerful wood fire in the tavern parlor," while Slosson's spunky unnamed hunter purposefully travels hither and yon in pursuit of antiques (216). Part of what is hinted at here is a division of labor between Victoria, who stays home like a wife, and the unnamed hunter whose mobility takes her into the public sphere—along the roads—like a husband.

Slosson and Earle represent cosmopolitan women as ideal collectors, as implicitly better at acquiring and safeguarding the nation's ceramic treasures than men because they possess both feminine- and masculine-coded characteristics. Slosson builds this very argument about women's collecting edge into the structure of her account. *The China Hunters Club* consists of scenes from the meetings of a co-ed china-collecting club, which allows for both explicit and implicit comparisons to be made between male and female collectors. The early chapter "A Cow-Shaped Cream Pot" demonstrates that the rural old maid, Cousin Eunice, is the best steward of ceramic objects and the sentimental family histories they supposedly preserve; in "Daisy Farm Letters" the active, successful china hunter is Ethelberta who, boarding in New England for the summer and using her social wiles to find china, writes letters to her isolated cousin "Walter" summering at "Lonesome Lake." "Aunt Charry's Boarder" features the urban woman china collector Jane Forsythe who functions as a cultural translator between a rural woman and an urban china-collecting man who is proving incapable on the hunt, and in "What the Children Knew," young Daisy proves herself a much more adept collector than her male counterpart, the young Benny: in response to an old woman who yells at him and from whom he hoped to buy some china, Benny reports, "I had half a mind to shy a stone at her head, the mean old catamaran!" (237). Physical violence as a response to frustration gets reiterated in *The China Hunters Club*'s final chapter wherein two men argue over the origins of a vase and end up breaking it and breaking up the club.[25]

Writing more than a decade after Slosson, Earle depicted masculine traits in even more positive terms than did Slosson.[26] Again, Earle figures herself a soldier: "I never hear the words 'old china' but my heart is moved, more than 'with sound of a trumpet.' I breathe the battle afar and hurry to the fray, to return at times victorious with dainty trophies of war, and sometimes, alas, empty-handed, with the hanging head of sore disappointment and defeat" (11). Yet even given the increasingly combative relationships between country and city people and between competing collectors (especially ones involving the new professional antique dealers who had just entered the mix), Earle, like Slosson, implies women collectors' superiority over men, the latter of whom she represents "only to express my abhorrence, my condemnation" of their collecting tactics (26).[27] The examples of male collectors Earle offers—the pair who lie, the duplicitous antique salesman who sells worthless modern objects at an auction of "rare old colonial furniture and family china"—demonstrate modern men's immorality (35). *China Collecting in America* encourages readers to focus on Earle as authentic, ethical, and expert.

Time and again, china-collecting characters claim broadly conceived regional and national male ancestors as their forefathers. In this, their collecting disrupts assumptions about biological inheritance as the sole basis on which one might lay claim to an identity as ideal citizen just as it historicizes and thus legitimizes their assertions of masculine traits, ones imagined as their regional right. There are only a few references to literal genealogy in the works of Slosson—Jane Forsythe, the spunky trickster-collector of "Aunt Charry's Boarder" is "'Lyddy Burton's darter,' and a lineal descendant of 'old Major Johnny,'" and the unnamed hunter along the roads recounts what an honest china collector her father was (167, 232). Earle makes little mention of china-collecting women who have inherited their collecting propensities from family members aside from the narrator wondering if her own Uncle Royal, who bought a set of Crown Derby, "was china-mad" (380). Instead, Slosson and Earle imagine for their women characters adoptive male precursors that manifest themselves in fantastical ways to the collectors as they hunt for china. China collecting enabled gendered fantasies of belonging, ones that sought to legitimate women's economic aggression.

For Slosson, the predecessor of the contemporary female collector is the classic New England Yankee man. Slosson's unnamed hunter along the roads, for instance, adores "forcing [her] way into pantry or garret, coaxing, threatening, wheedling, dazing the inmates into disposing of quaint old crockeries" (214). These masculine-coded behaviors are legitimatized by her fantastical encounter with an aged, even ghostly, manifestation of old-style white New England manhood: the sixty-year-old Billy M'Kay. Billy is less meant to represent an actual person than the imaginative product of the hunter's physical contact with an antique, one that guides and historicizes her aggressive collecting. While hunting alone, the narrator comes upon a man who claims that the dingy coin in his pocket is an "old ancient relict" more than five hundred years old (221). Demonstrating the breadth of her collecting knowledge, the unnamed narrator identifies the piece as "a Spanish pistareen of 1805" (221). "While I held it [the old coin] in my hand," the china hunter writes, "there appeared upon the scene a new character" (221). The new character, Billy M'Kay, seems to manifest out of thin air, conjured by the narrator's physical contact with the coin. Billy is himself retro and fantastical. According to the unnamed narrator, Billy seemed like a character straight out of Harriet Beecher Stowe's *Oldtown Folks*, a novel set in early nineteenth-century Massachusetts; Billy was "Sam [Lawson] himself" (222). In Stowe, Lawson is an unproductive "do-nothing" whose presence defies conventional notions about male productivity but nonetheless provides the essential and erotically overtoned "lubricating power" for the "work, thrift, and industry [that] are such an incessant steampower in Yankee life."[28] In Billy M'Kay, however, Slosson fuses the productivity of the Yankee—the "typical 'brother Jonathan'"—to the seemingly indulgent excesses of the china hunt: Billy spends the entire day helping the china hunter in her quest for old crockery rather than working in a traditional way (221).

This unnamed china hunter of Slosson's, by the time of M'Kay's appearance, has already proved herself capable on the hunt, but the appearance of Billy gives her acquisitive acts a history, making clear that her collecting forms part of a larger New England tradition. It is literally and figuratively the stereotypical, historic Yankee in whose footsteps this bold woman collector follows, by whose curiosity and acquisitiveness she is pulled along. "He would run into a house," the narrator explains, "actually dragging me after him, throw open closets with scarcely a word of explanation, pull down dishes, and pile them up around me" (223). The precedent of Billy, himself a replica of a historical fantasy generated by a New England woman—Stowe—justifies the narrator's penetration of rural homes in the name of china hunting. Billy, in turn, demonstrates his unqualified approval of the narrator's collecting as well as of the intimacy imagined between the two by referring to her as "you old thing" as he gives her a "gentle shove" (223). In the affectionate "you old thing," Billy asserts the unnamed narrator's compatibility with history and suggests terms for her unique intimacy with objects: herself an old thing like an antique platter or the old coin, or even like the ghostly Yankee character of Billy himself, the unnamed hunter belongs among odd, aged valuables.

In *China Collecting in America,* Earle does not write into existence fictionalized hunters but employs the first-person point of view, constructing herself as an ideal china hunter.[29] She links herself to important men of the past, emphasizing all the while how gender strictures should be loosened to allow for a celebration of women's so-called masculine traits. Her recollections of historic men throughout *China Collecting in America* are creative, relying on a combination of Earle's vast knowledge of china and her own perception of herself as a capable New England daughter. Most striking, perhaps, is how consistently Earle links herself to the most prominent of U.S. forefathers, George Washington. Earle portrays the first president as having, as she does, "decided opinions and tastes about table-furnishings," and she acts on behalf of her nation, as she claims Washington did, by way of that interest (247). Washington, however, does not emerge as a straightforwardly masculine figure in Earle's guide. Instead, Washington, like Lamb before him, figures in Earle's text as a gender-bending precursor of sorts, one reimagined in the present as a fantastical construction, a double of Earle herself.

Many pieces of china produced in the early national period featured portraits of Washington. The Washington pitcher, of which this image is one of a host of examples, was quite popular (figure 11). At one point in *China Collecting in America,* Earle discovers a Washington pitcher that gives visual form to a complexly gendered version of Washington that echoes the version of herself presented in the text. Earle comes upon this particular Washington pitcher in a lighthouse, and she identifies it "only by its shape . . . [as] Liverpool ware" (381). Though it is "painfully covered with an ignominious shell of decalcomania and scrap-book pictures," she buys the pitcher. "Oh, the delight I felt," Earle's narrator confides, "when I reached home and scraped off Pauline Hall's smirking and high-colored countenance, and saw with a

FIGURE 11 George Washington pitcher. Earthenware, transfer-printed, ca. 1813–15. The Metropolitan Museum of Art, Gift of Mrs. Eleanor G. Sargent, 1980.

thrill of friendly recognition the black-lined face of my own solemn and immaculate Washington surmounting her full-blown, rosy shoulders and scarlet and gold bodice" (381).

In this example, Earle sees a pitcher that appears to have images of modern femininity on its surface: the body of Pauline Hall, a popular vaudeville actress who toured the nation and sometimes performed in trouser roles.[30] But once Earle gets her hands on the pitcher, a pitcher she recognizes as valuable even though it is sealed in the external images of contemporary culture, she reveals that it signifies contemporary mobile, performative womanhood and a gender-bending scenario of cross-generational drag. Earle could have easily represented this scene as justifying a virulent antimodernism, as suggesting all perceived to be wrong with late nineteenth-century culture: the serious realm of the political, our ancestors, and national history itself all concealed under the chaotic melee of popular, emasculating cultural images. Yet that is not the spirit of Earle's account. Instead, in the Washington pitcher story, Earle offers material evidence of what her collecting labors yield: an image of the past meeting the present on the material body of the Liverpool pitcher, and that moment of meeting, of melding if you will, is one in which Washington's most striking feature—his head—"surmounts" the curvaceous contemporary woman's body. The place where the past meets the present in china collecting opens a space for a sort of re-seeing of gender relationship, one that turns the cross-dressed Washington pitcher into a mirror image of Earle herself. Like Washington's, Earle's is a cosmopolitan, china-loving, adventure- and military-enthused head atop a woman's body.[31] She, moreover, has herself performed an act of keen penetration, one replicated in the image of Washington's head on and under Hall's form: Earle pushed into the lighthouse and then under the surface of the pitcher to recast Washington, the object, herself, and history.

Hot for Heirlooms

In the archive of china-collecting literature, the New England daughters who hunt are not indoors but in the field and far from home, hot on the trail of pitchers and plates, and apparently unconcerned with participation in the heteroerotic economy (flirting, marriage, sodalities of any kind aside from relations with old china).[32] In not reiterating a progress narrative that had as its climax marriage but fantasizing instead about a diverse series of cravings and penetrations, women's china hunting was decidedly sensual. Rather than eventually taking the white New England daughter out of circulation and hoarding her in the domestic space as marriage was to do, women's china collectors imagined the white New England daughter as endlessly mobile, her collecting having no clear end point and thus enabling a continuous series of dreams and sensations. The act of rescuing and being pleasured by old New England things provided yet another way for the unmarried daughters of New England to rewrite themselves as central to the modern history-making project while representing their alternative affinities as rooted in familiar regional, national, and imperial histories. Multiple and multiclimaxed, predicated on fantasies of china even more so than on scenes of its actual acquisition, the eroticism in literature by china-hunting women fluctuates between and sometimes simultaneously figures as masturbatory and queer. Reading the eroticism of china collecting depends, in part, on understanding how consistently ceramics have been aligned with the white female body and its racialized sexuality.

Mary Wilkins Freeman's regionalist story "The Willow-Ware" draws on this tradition of understanding antique china as a symbol for white women's sexualized bodies, bodies implicitly theorized as historic and the source of material pleasures. "The Willow-Ware" portrays china out of place (i.e., out of the closet) as china in circulation just as the young woman out of her domestic enclosure (i.e., out of the colonial house) is both in modernity and sexual with the potential to generate the present and future by way of her fertile, desiring body. Adeline Weaver, the young, unmarried white protagonist of "The Willow-Ware," lives with her maiden aunts in the old family mansion and, "fastened . . . by thongs of duty to age and conservatism, pulls hard at her leash."[33] Adeline yearns to remove herself from the painfully predictable and asynchronic experience of living as a genteel old maid at eighteen years of age, a state in which, according to the implied metaphor in the quotation above, her animal nature is chained. Adeline's "revolt" involves leaving the family's colonial mansion, the domestic space associated with restrained, repetitive spinster time, and entering what is thought to be the childish chronometry of same-sex intimacy between girls; freedom for the body and its urges means putting herself into affective circulation among peers who walk with "their arms around each others' waists" "sucking sticks of candy like children" (147, 159). Breaking with tea time and spinster time and initiating new sensual experiences with candy and girls leads to falling in love. While "sucking the sweeties," the girls see the minister's nephew, whom Adeline immediately recognizes as "the man of her dreams" (157, 158). She returns home and, a rage building in her over tea, works herself up to her most extensive rebellion yet: the theft of her family's willowware china.

Adeline's absconding with the willowware, a symbol of her own white, virginal body as treasured heirloom, brings with it autoerotic pleasure, and though it leads eventually to Adeline's domestication in the form of marriage, we are able to glimpse for a moment china's imagined relationship to alternative erotic forms. As soon as Adeline hides the stolen willowware under the boards of the family's summer house in the backyard, she is covered in blushes and "was conscious of a mad exhilaration which was entrancing" (165). She then promptly disrobes: "She took off her gown, put on a loose white wrapper, and lay down on a couch" (165). Rebellion is climactic and ceramic for this unmarried young woman as she occupies, for only an afternoon, the space between the compulsive repetitions of spinster time and, to borrow a concept from Elizabeth Freeman, the temporality of chrononormativity. Contact with antique china in Mary Wilkins Freeman's text functions as a means by which white daughters assert their independent personhood outside of marriage, an independence aligned with being single and in material relationship to one's own desiring body as well as to history in the form of antiques.

From its implied metaphor of the dog pulling at its leash to its use of willowware in particular, Freeman's story suggests that Adeline's oh-so-brief autoerotic rebellion on the way to heterosexual circulation and the denouement of marriage is not an exceptional, but, rather, a common one. Willowware, according to Earle, with whose writings Freeman was familiar, was the most abundant type of china found by china collectors hunting for antiques in New England, to the point where collectors began refusing to buy it (130). "The Willow-Ware," then, tells the story of a young woman with the potential to rebel against restrictive forms of gendered and sexualized time who ends up being reinscribed in the colonial home and within the marriage bond. Her story is typical rather than unique. But what if a woman were to elongate the time of china caressing and erotic independence? What if an affluent New England daughter were to remain mobile and single, continually cultivating sensual relationships to antique ceramics and the histories sedimented therein?

China-hunting women portrayed in their guides a complexly historical engagement of antiques that ended not in marriage but extended across durations and involved a multiplicity of pleasures. Quite consistently the china-collecting guides dismiss as provincial the notion that antique china is valuable in its ability to mark and preserve stories of nuclear heteronormative familial generation and inheritance (i.e., that china has sentimental value). China hunting, instead, constitutes an intimate historicism that recognizes china's role in larger regional, national, and imperial histories. The aggressive, desirous female hunter yearns for erotic contact with the only-fantasized-about china pitcher or bowl, but it is not necessarily acquisition that fulfills the hunter's desires. The intimacies forged between the china hunter and those from whom the hunter collects have the potential to take on sensual dimensions, and the mere thought of the china itself might send the hunter into an ecstatic state. Imagining an eroticism removed from heterosexual sex, the china collector's desires once again come to look masturbatory and queer. Because china has long figured as a symbol of the leisured white female with its white body and hoped-for embellishments, when women represent their cravings for china it is not entirely clear whether they are writing of erotic intimacy with an object, with one another's female bodies, or with their own female selves.[34] That it is variously one, some, and all is what gives the china-hunting guides their often breathless quality.

Collectors themselves differently theorized the erotic dimension of the china hunt. Robert and Elizabeth Shackleton in *The Charm of the Antique*, written in 1914, explain,

> No matter how much one's affectionate liking for an antique treasure deepens and strengthens with length of possession, there is never anything quite like the thrill that comes with the very moment of acquisition, that moment of ecstasy when the collector first holds, and holds as his own, something that he has longed for. The acquisition may be the unexpected good fortune of a happy moment, or it may be a triumph following the hope and desire of years; but no matter how it comes, it comes as one of the most delightful of sensations, a sensation that cannot in the least be understood by one who has never begun to collect.[35]

In the Shackletons' telling, the china collector gets to feel it all and feel exceptional at the same time. The Shackletons assert that the relation between the antique and its owner is alive and ongoing—it "deepens and strengthens with length of possession." Yet most valued is the temporally terse "moment of ecstasy" that is simultaneous to the "moment of acquisition," which it seems fair to read as a sort of sexual climax: it "comes." The structure of china collecting is polygamous, anticipating Jean Baudrillard's claim that "there is something of the harem about collecting," though that means, by definition, that collecting is understood, once again, as predicated on heteronormative forms of desire and affiliation.[36] Somewhere between the emphasis on the moment of possession as climactic and the implied figure of marriage with the gendering of the collector as male, the multiclimactic aspect of women's china collecting and its emphasis on fantasy, autoerotic anticipation, lust, and sensory memory are lost. In the Shackletons' vision of antiquing, the collector may have many loves, but he "comes" with each only once and then settles down.

Rather than advocate sentimental family feeling or replicate the Shackletons' explicit theory of object desire fulfilled, Slosson and Earle multiply the histories antique objects are capable of narrating and the kinds of desire they are capable of eliciting in women. One of the women china hunters' goals, as implied by their writings, was to remove heirlooms from their places in a trajectory of heteroreproductive inheritance to center them, instead, in scenarios of exchange that throbbed with alternative forms of desire, ones implicitly linked to regional, national, and world histories. From such scenes, these antiques joined collections where they would, whenever dusted or displayed, engage the collector, rendering her a producer. As imagined by the china hunters, the antique object prompts the voicing of multiple narratives from across its life as an object; this uneven generation of histories may include the story of its production, the history of its journey to the Americas, the story or stories of past owners, the story of being sighted, sighed over, and purchased by the collector, the acts of resistance or savvy staged by its former owner upon the suggestion of its purchase, and the fantasies the collector has about its future before, during, and after its sale. The historicized antique object also engenders the collector's telling of those stories in various orders and unevenly across time. These overlapping performances do not end in Shackleton-like scenes of a onetime wedding night with the virginal and uxorial porcelain body but take the form of ongoing relations.

Writing a mere decade before china collectors in the United States took to antiquing in greater numbers, Karl Marx laments in *Capital* of how in the process of the commodity being reduced to "human labour in the abstract," "all its [the commodity's] sensuous characteristics are extinguished."[37] Arguably, the antique, as an already existent almost-art-object retains a handcrafted sensuousness to which the china hunters add their labor, rendering china hunting, at least in part, a critique of industrialization. Susan Stewart, in her theorizing of collecting, appears to disagree, asserting that the collection "says that the world is given; we are inheritors, not producers, of value here."[38] "We 'luck into' the collection," she insists.[39] The labor of the consumer in collecting is, for Stewart, "a labor of total magic, a fantastic labor which operates through the manipulation of abstraction rather than through concrete or material means."[40] Slosson and Earle, however, take their readers to scenes wherein collectors plan, knock on doors, drink countless cups of water, climb and fall through a chicken house roof, invent tales, and, in some instances, return again and again to the same houses to continue working valuable ceramics out of rural residents' hands. Far from being the product of luck, china hunting was repetitive, sweaty, and often trying. The china hunters, in theory and practice, more closely anticipate Pierre Bourdieu in his claim that "the consumer helps to produce the product he consumes, by a labour of identification and decoding which, in the case of a work of art, may

Out of the China Closet 105

constitute the whole of the consumption and gratification, and which requires time and dispositions acquired over time."[41] These questions of labor and production inflect china hunting's sometimes erotic themes. In Slosson's and Earle's tellings, the original human labor expended to produce the antique object is revitalized and added to by way of the china collector's variously repetitive, frustrating, and deeply pleasurable labors. These women imagined themselves as producing a range of things other than commodities or children—pleasure, history, fantasy, narrative, class distinction, and china guides—by way of their relations with antiques.

The chapter from Slosson's *The China Hunters Club* entitled "A China Craze" provides a rich example of the temporal complexity of china fantasies as well as of how the erotics of china hunting did not only involve the hunter and the object hunted but also involved the New Englanders from whom the hunters tried to purchase antiques. After all, before the collected object could even be acquired (an event not often depicted in women's china hunting guides), the collector had to form some sort of relationship, perhaps even an intimacy, with the person who owned the antique. This rich triangulation of desire was often shot through with historical significance in terms not only of the future of the valuable antique but also of the relationship between rural and urban spaces, between (often) women, and between members of different classes. One example is an instance from Alice Van Leer Carrick's antiquing guide wherein a woman china hunter's "whole collecting heart went out to" a Staffordshire platter she found "and [whose] modest tentative offer [for it] soon reached immoderation."[42] In the end, this covetous collector, at the platter owner's request, shed and exchanged the skirt she was wearing for the dish. In this example, the rural woman's strong desire for what is presumably a high-quality, modern skirt is as strong as the collector's desire for the antique. The intimate relations that constituted china collecting involved a dyadic desire between collector and antique and an unevenly triangulated, even multiply proliferated desire, felt and negotiated among the collector, the person collected from, and the coveted object.

Slosson's "A China Craze," which even in its title evokes ceramic love as irrational, serves as an object lesson in such triangulations. Depicting Miss Jane Norton's story of "an adventure of my own" hunting for china, the chapter is framed by same-sex desire between young women: Jane's boarding school roommate, Ellen Bates, has been pining away for Jane (117). Ellen, in a letter, invites Jane to visit her in rural Littlefield, reminding her of how she left "poor weeping me" on graduation and has been begged "again and again" by Ellen to "have pity on my loneliness, and come to my quiet home" (117). Ellen's longing for Jane forms part of a more broadly conceived history, one that refers back to the founding of the United States. Ellen writes of trying to get Jane to visit, pointing out, "This is Centennial year, and I shall try a hundredth time" (117). The implication is that Ellen has been yearning for Jane for what seems like the length of the United States' life; there is unfinished business between these young, unmarried women (as between the country and the city where each lives respectively). This quotation also ties their intimacy to the colonial moment, a moment Ellen yearns for and that Jane associates with backwardness: Littlefield, in Jane's account, is so restrictive (a little field) that it resembles a tomb. Rejecting rural New England as well as same-sex intimacy in the familiar terms of anachronism—Jane calls Littlefield "old," "primitive," and a place she does not want to "bury myself"—she goes nonetheless, for as a resident of the cosmopolitan town of Littleville Jane understands that Littlefield is an unexplored field for china hunting (117).

Armed with an oversimplified view of the provincial outskirt as aligned with history in a distinctly pathological way that recalls nineteenth-century notions about the spinster as unproductive, Jane sets out. "Sighing for new worlds to conquer, new pantries to plunder," Jane imagines her engagement of rural New Englanders will involve a clean assertion of power, one reliant on the assumed superiority of modernity thought as masculine and capable of subordinating and penetrating the so-called primitive place (118). Jane, for instance, recounts how on the ride from the train station to Mrs. Bates's house in Littlefield, they "passed an ancient farm-house, [and] I spied in the window a broken cup, and, like turkey-cock at sight of scarlet rag, I woke to action" (119). By way of this simile, Jane's gaze figures as a sort of eroticized look. Likening herself to a male turkey, Jane suggests her body or some part of it is phallic—a wattle that gets engorged on arousal. Jane's plan to straightforwardly swoop in and penetrate rural cupboards to possess Bow and Bristol china, however, does not go forward so simply.

"A China Craze" foregrounds the experience Jane has trying to get Ellen's mother, Mrs. Bates, to show and give or sell her valuable old china. (Ellen, it turns out, never makes an appearance at the house.

Having been called away unexpectedly to nurse a sick uncle, Ellen cannot serve as a mediator between her mother and Jane. It is the wild misunderstandings and delusions of both Mrs. Bates and Jane that make this one of the funniest chapters of *The China Hunters Club*.) Jane has a wildly sensual time at the Bates home, vacillating between frustration, excitement, fulfillment, and fear. During the day, Jane, trying to play the part of substitute daughter, patiently probes Mrs. Bates for information about porcelain and is paid in kind by the old woman's detailed descriptions of valuable Bow, Chelsea, and Bristol china. Far from experiencing ecstasy in the form of possessing china as the Shackletons describe Jane climaxes by way of fantasies about Mrs. Bates's china, specifically her "old bowl," which it is hard not to read euphemistically. Consider Jane's response to Mrs. Bates's description of this antique Bow bowl: "A longing desire to be alone seized me irresistibly. I cannot remember how I managed it, but in a few moments I found myself in my own chamber. Sinking into a chair, I breathed out one word: 'Bow!' and subsided. My recollections of the next half hour are very misty" (126).

Viscerally transported at the mere suggestion that such a valuable antique could be in the Bates home, Jane retreats into private to climax. In addition to being rapt by the erotic urges of her own body—the only sound Jane utters is the word-moan of pleasure: "Bow"—Jane loses her awareness of time; ecstasy here muddies time's distinctness. As we shall soon see, that collapsing of, or inability to account for, time's passage is precisely what happens for Mrs. Bates as well. We can only imagine for ourselves what happened in that "very misty" half hour that Jane cannot recollect, and thus we as readers are brought into Jane's chamber, potentially rapt as well by what we imagine. It is the cross-generational friction over the body of a third term—the antique object—that gives way to Jane's solitary and multiple pleasures, pleasures centered on the fantastical generations and possible valuables of the older New England woman.

Mrs. Bates, it turns out, owns no china at all. The entire time she spends with Jane she moves in and out of a clear sense of what is real and what is not. Most of her descriptions of the wondrous ceramics she owns are her own misty recollections of details from a book of ceramics Ellen recently read aloud to her. Just as she cannot clearly differentiate between the real and the fictional, Mrs. Bates has a hard time knowing what time she occupies. Far from an easily penetrated other, Mrs. Bates has strong desires and fantasies of her own, ones that also carry an erotic charge. She yearns, for instance, to be in relationship again with a host of women and one man from her past and variously misrecognizes Jane as "'Miss Mosely,' 'Susan,' and 'Aunt Ann,'" and, later, "'Lisha" (123, 124). Mrs. Bates herself assumes the role of penetrator when she tries repeatedly to enter Jane's chamber at night. The first night Jane is in Littlefield, Mrs. Bates tries to get into Jane's bed chamber three times. The second night, Mrs. Bates insists on sleeping with Jane, and Jane agrees, hoping to, like a daughter, get into Mrs. Bates's good graces. But, as Jane puts it, "what a night!" (130). Mrs. Bates urges Jane to cross-generational dress to look like "Aunt Ann," and thus makes Jane perform the role of an older woman (130). Later, Jane wakes to Mrs. Bates holding a bowl to her lips and pressing her to imbibe a "nauseous mixture" that Jane's "fevered brain thought . . . poison," but which turns out to be tea (130). The Bow bowl description over which Jane climaxed earlier in the day morphs, at least in Jane's mind, into this other bowl, which, a figure for any of the receptive cavities of the female form, Mrs. Bates forces upon Jane at night.

Jane's own erotic obsessions and fantasies about china end up being revealed as akin to the fantastical notions of an older form of New England womanhood, one encapsulated in the almost ghostly character of Mrs. Bates. Jane may play surrogate daughter and try to keep intact the generational difference between herself and Mrs. Bates by the light of day, but her venture to Littlefield disrupts her own sense of temporal linearity, giving way to dark and confusing nights. Mrs. Bates is not just a dotty old woman, one distraught by the absence of her daughter, Ellen, but a representative of historical womanhood, its erotic fantasies and its draw. Significantly, Jane is not willing to leave Littlefield, so strong is the pull of Mrs. Bates's fantastic bowls. She reaches her limit only when Mrs. Bates douses her with water in the middle of the last night, a kind of emission that appears to put out Jane's fire. The historical and queer temporality Mrs. Bates occupies renders her spectral: she is "ghostly in her white night garb, and with long gray hair hanging loosely about her tall form" (125). In the end, it seems as if Jane and Mrs. Bates are just as alike as they are different: they both seek pleasure by way of china bowls, and that pleasure involves erotically charged manipulations and performances of other moments in time, including their phallic penetrations and fantastic ejaculations. By the end of the story, Jane's notion of the ease with which she would, in her modern superiority, penetrate the older rural woman's house and mine it for its riches has been abandoned. Jane discovers that a much more textured, disorienting erotic pertains to the china hunt by way of its requisite encounter with gender in history. At the story's end, Ellen offers Jane an early Worcester saucer-shaped dish "in lieu of the wonders dear mama did *not* show you" (136), but Jane never looks at it without "remembering the bright hopes, the eager expectance, the exultant emotions, I found, but lost so cruelly, in my visit to Littlefield" (136).

The Imperial Imagination

Underwriting the eroticism of Littlefield for Jane Norton is, in part, its exoticism. Not only is it, in her words, an "out-of-the-world place," "primitive," and "as old as the hills," but two black characters, rare in New England regionalist writings, a young boy named Romulus and his mother, Almiry, live in the Bates house as servants, and they are the ones who guide Jane into and eventually escort her out of the household.[43] Across the archive of china-collecting literature, rural New England often becomes a foreign-seeming space, and in this it resembles another place of consumption, the turn-of-the-century department store. William Leach has explained that department stores decorated their interiors as Japanese gardens, "mosques, temples, or desert oases."[44] In Slosson, engaging rural strangers who, though apparently white, spoke dialect and often resisted friendly overtures, traveling through unfamiliar country climes in the heat of August, "the air sweet and spicy," lusting after never-before-seen "Oriental" treasures that may not, ultimately, be found, all of these aspects of china hunting made it look a lot like imperialist adventuring (119). China collectors explicitly imagined themselves as moderns seeking out material objects that attested both to Great Britain's and the early United States' imperial prowess while yearning for the virginal, white bodies of old porcelain in whose figurative embrace lay new, intimate claims to historicity, queerness, generation, and belonging.

The very word "china," as Vimalin Rujivacharakul observes, has come to signify "porcelains produced in China, *as well as* in other world regions; it thus designates not a binary between East and West, but a complex history of global interrelation.[45] Embodied engagement of imported goods had a particular history in New England. According to the historian James Lindgren, the display of exotic artifacts at the

East Indian Marine Society (EIMS), founded in Salem in 1799, drew and "titillated" both the men and women among its two thousand yearly visitors.[46] According to the early nineteenth-century diaries of young women who visited the museum, they "wandered almost breathlessly around the hall," "gazed with delight and wonder," finding the museum to have "a mysterious attraction."[47] Lindgren's sources, from which these quotations are drawn, hint that women were not necessarily any less apt to fantasize about imperial adventure than their male counterparts. The distinctive yen among women visitors to partake and even initiate sexualized adventures of empire is further suggested by the fact that by the late 1830s, the EIMS museum superintendent "had to encase a mannequin of a fully dressed mandarin behind glass since it had suffered from 'excessive handleing [*sic*] by visitors.' . . . 'A habit to which the females are very much addicted.'"[48] By the time that the nineteenth-century women china collectors were working, the dynamic space of rural New England had become another potentially exotic landscape in which to pursue intimately imperial fantasies. The EIMS by the 1890s was, according to Earle, no longer interesting, having changed in the 1880s from being the museum of objects "queerer then than now" with "old-time glamour" and "unstudied grace" to a modern, well-catalogued museum (409, 411).

In *China Collecting in America*, as in Slosson's "A China Craze," the imperial aspects of the hunt get reconfigured as temporally complex. Earle, in the final chapters of *China Collecting in America*, theorizes two different sorts of histories to which the china hunt gives way: china memories and china dreams. China memories are the sensory responses pieces in a collector's collection trigger in her body: "Fair country sights does my old china bring to my eyes; soft country sounds does it bring to my ears . . . .When I found that old yellow Wedgwood dish in the country tavern, it was filled with tiny fragrant wild strawberries—I smell, nay, I taste them still" (377). China memories are historical but refer to the tangible and the real; they link the present and the past by way of sensory experiences. China dreams, by contrast, are the product of the imagination, "children of an idle brain" (377). Posited as productive—children—but of the unproductive mind rather than the systems of the maternal body, china dreams are fanciful. "Every cup, every jar in our china ingatherings, has the charm of fantasy," Earle writes, "visions of past life and beauty, though only imagined" (376). Based not in the experienced, but in the "very haze of uncertainty," china dreams link the dreamed-of past to the hoped-for future (376).

In both these china-hunting guides—*The China Hunters Club* and *China Collecting in America*—narrating the hunt itself is part of a dream, a crafted fancy, in which the unmarried china hunter assumes the role of desiring imperialist within her own inner dialogue. When about to get a glimpse of a rural woman's china cabinet, Ethelberta of Slosson's "Daisy Farm Letters" confesses: "In what a state of excitement I watched the opening of that [rural corner cupboard] door. What discoveries was I about to make? I understood the feelings of Cesnola and felt a keen sympathy with Schliemann" (72–73). Luigi Palma di Cesnola was a prominent nineteenth-century collector who directed excavations in Cyprus. He oversaw the exhumation of tens of thousands of objects, most of which were sold to the Metropolitan Museum of Art in New York, of which he became director in 1877. Heinrich Schliemann was a German amateur archaeologist and wealthy importer who made a fortune off the California Gold rush and was thought of as one of the nineteenth century's true adventurers. Among his feats were the excavations at Troy in 1870 and the discoveries of preclassical Greek objects there and at Mycenae. Dashing, daring, and decidedly cosmopolitan, Schliemann and Cesnola were also wealthy businessmen who knew how to manipulate the market and wield power.[49] The kinship to these contemporary figures that Ethelberta imagines arises from her encounter with the unsophisticated rural aunty whose mode of treasuring objects for their sentimental cache does not mesh with the urban tourist's way of perceiving value. China hunting was not only a practice of historic preservation aimed at the consolidation of cultural capital but itself an elaborate performance through which unmarried New England daughters imaginatively linked themselves to the imperial projects of the regional past and global present by way of affective consumption.

The china-collecting guides demonstrate, too, how a specifically imperialist class logic leads to the racialization of lower-class people, including white New Englanders, and verifies that the china hunter has a cosmopolitan understanding of global world history tied to eroticism. At one point in *China Collecting in America*, Earle indulges in one such historical reverie, a fantasy of colonial china purchasing:

How truly Oriental that old Canton china must have been
to Boston and Providence and Salem dames when they had

tiptoed down on the rough old wharf in wooden clogs or velvet-tipped golo-shoes, their fair faces covered with black velvet masks if the weather waxed cold or the wind blew east; when they had seen the great weather-beaten ship, with its stained sails and blackened ropes and cables—the ship that had brought the fragile porcelain cargo to port—the Lively Prudence, the Lively Peggy, the Lively Sally, and Lively Molly, or any of the dozen great ships named by Yankee shipmasters and shipowners for the lively young women of their acquaintance. They had been on board the Indiaman, perhaps, and smelt its bilge-water and its travelled stale ship-smells; had watched the strange picturesque foreign sailors, barefooted and earringed, as they brought the packages and spread out the boxes on deck, or carried in their brawny arms the great crates on Scarlett's or Rowe's Wharf, and with their bronzed tattooed hands took out the precious porcelain from its rice-straw packing and rice-paper wrapping. (186)

This passage reveals the ways in which imperial commerce shaped Earle's view of china consumption as a sexualized gendered act that reinforced ideas about leisure class New England women's pristine whiteness while presenting a historical precedent for those women having rich commercial and erotic lives. The feminine dames with "fair faces" that Earle envisions and with whom she empathizes must cope with the "rough old wharf" and encounter the sights and sounds of the masculinized foreign ship: the *Indiaman*. The ship has been transformed, it seems, over the duration of its journey: it is "weather beaten," its sails "stained," its ropes "blanched," its smells "stale," its sailors' hands "bronzed and tattooed." White surfaces get darker over time, darker surfaces bleach over time; racial distinctions muddy, making all the more difficult the readability of surfaces.

And while Earle amps up the scene's eroticism by way of the *Indiaman*'s sailors' decided contrast to the white dames—the women wear clogs or golo-shoes, whereas the sailors are barefooted; the dames' faces are covered with black masks, their fair bodies hidden under dresses, whereas the sailors are exposed, bronzed, brawny, and tattooed—the most intimate encounter, the one toward which the passage moves us, is that between the dames and the china. The Anglo woman here meets the Oriental object—what Earle calls "truly Oriental" china—which it turns out is the mirror of her own white erotic potential kept under wraps and soon to be revealed.

China collectors, however, did not just think the rural outskirt was exotic, its people a threat to preservation. In the popular discourse of the era, another threat to antique china resided in the urban home in the form of immigrant labor.

> Sing a song of breakage—a closet deep and wide—
> Cracked and broken dishes setting side by side,
>
> ....
>
> Sing a song of Bridget—of Mary Ann—of Kate—
> The coming, going, restless tide, who form the family fate.
> Heaps of sea-washed wreckage strewn along the shore
> Tell of devastating storms when the fury's o'er.⁵⁰

In these lines from the poem "The China-Closet," it is specifically Irish immigrant women who destroyed valuables that, like "grandma's blue-sprigged china," were to be passed on to future generations.⁵¹ Immigrant women and rural New England women are both, in china-hunting guides, aligned with modernity—as lovers of new things—and perceived as physical threats to the preservation of the regional past. Earle, for instance, reports being afire with "wounded indignation" when she sees "mugs and pitchers . . . battered, nicked, and handle-less, despitefully used to hold herb-teas, soft-soap, horse-liniment, or tooth-brushes" (163). On one occasion, she looks on as a "Washington pitcher, noseless and fairly crenated with nicks," is used to carry hot water to the henhouse, and, on another, she spots a different Washington pitcher used to store "a villainous-looking purple-black liquid compound which the owner explained was 'Pa's hair-restorer'" (163). Part of the underlying problem with using antiques in this way, at least according to Earle, is that it demonstrates a troubling lack of not only aesthetic sense, but historical awareness.

We might say that china collecting became, in the late nineteenth century a new, alternative form of shopping for the well-educated, adventurous white woman, one that distinguished her from other late nineteenth-century women, among them middle-class women entering public marketplaces as consumers, rural women opening their homes and hearts to the entré of the public marketplace in the form of the new mail-order catalogue, and immigrant women working in urban households. China collecting was coincident and in implicit dialogue with the apparent passing of regional specificity as marked by the rise of centralizing economic forces such as national magazines, transatlantic transportation systems, chain department stores, and mail-order retailers.[52] Amid increased nationalization and mass marketing, Northeasterners' labor-intensive (or should we call it leisured-labor-intensive) collecting affirmed cosmopolitan regional difference as opposed to modern nationalism by advocating local forms of consumption.[53] At the same time, china collecting shored up the hunters' cultural capital. Having the same domestic effects in your home as other women might be considered fashionable by some, but to cosmopolitan white women it represented the limitation and conformity characteristic of industrialization.[54] As the interior design guru Clarence Cook pointed out in 1877, "There never were 'sets' known till modern manufacturers began to take a trade view of life in all its phases."[55] In defiance of uniformity, Cook advised women to "make a heroinic strike for freedom" by buying pieces of old Worcester, Wedgwood, Spode, or Devonshire and building collections of china based on harmony and singularity.[56] For the preservation advocate Charles Eliot Norton, "newness [was] equivalent to uniformity," and it was only in the buying and restoring of old things like old houses and china, that individualism could be reintroduced to American life.[57] And we must not forget that this was the age in which decorating the home came to be understood as an expression of a woman's personal identity.[58] One way individualism could supposedly be demonstrated was by way of chinaware.

The dead ends, loops, and historical dreams of china hunting constituted an alternative temporal space, one rife with feelings and implicitly opposed to another form of production for women—childbearing, which followed from pursuing heteronormative desire and marriage. China hunting encouraged prospective hunting women to engage their bodies' urges, itches, senses, and yearnings, tying these to and offering them as potential alternatives to other forms of sexualized labor. Certainly, when the young china hunter Jane Norton retreats to the parlor to spend a dizzying half hour after hearing the mother of an old girlfriend describe her china bowl, when Earle's narrator transports herself in daydream to an eighteenth-century scene of colonial dames receiving into their hands virginal china pieces straight off a ship at port in Salem's harbor, we have before us sexually sensuous relations engendered in the encounter with antique objects. By way of these practices, New England daughters produced china collections, china writings, regional and national histories, and evidence of their own abilities as laborers in the field of preservation.

Part of the mixed-up time of china collecting, too, was the set of historical social relations felt in and on the collector's body. Tracking, finding, and perhaps buying a piece of old china involved new social relations with china owners in the present as well as new, imagined intimacies with people from the past, whether it be George Washington or a young rural woman's sea captain grandfather. When the china hunter awakened the antique that had theoretically been asleep, hoarded in the cabinet or attic, that act could resurrect a host of ghosts with which the contemporary collector might be in relation by way of shared or kin labors: the potter(s) and painter(s) who created the vessel, or perhaps the colonial or early American citizens (mostly men) who sought out, bought, and brought home the china in the first instance. The woman china collector, by way of her labor as well as by way of an imperial economic inheritance, entered a historical tradition of male workers. Through fantasy and dream, the china-hunting woman participated in a transhistorical imagination; her membership in this genealogy of dreamers required a laborious intimate historicism, in this case the intellectual, creative labor that constituted the pleasurable pursuit of pitchers and plates.

4
Spectral Fusions, Modernist Times

The work of New England regionalism, on which the first three chapters of this book have focused, was taken up by a group that included women from two generations: members of the first generation were born in and around 1830—C. Alice Baker, Susan Minot Lane, Rose Terry Cooke, and Annie Trumbull Slosson—and members of the second were born in and around 1850—Sarah Orne Jewett, Mary Wilkins Freeman, and Alice Morse Earle. In this chapter, I explore how rather than passing from the scene, which is how most accounts of literary history represent it, regionalism was taken up by members of an even later generation of women writers born in the 1860s, women who produced work through the first decades of the twentieth century. Each of these writers authored fiction that consistently alludes to colonial New England history and makes use of colonial revival practices in an effort to rethink women's radical acts in relationship to modern time. These New England writers—Charlotte Perkins Gilman, Alice Brown, and Pauline Elizabeth Hopkins—either are rarely read as engaging the regionalist mode or are rarely read at all, as in the case of Brown.

As figures within literary history, Gilman, Brown, and Hopkins, uncannily like the haunted female characters in their fiction, have tended not to have clearly delineated roles to inhabit. Gilman, while consistently read as a feminist, gets cast variously as a realist and a naturalist, though never as a New England regionalist, while some interpret her later work as anticipating modernism.[1] Charlotte Rich, for instance, contends that "Gilman's novels ... share feminist concerns that later reemerge ... in the work of such female Modernist novelists as Gertrude Stein and Virginia Woolf."[2] Brown, meanwhile, has been almost entirely overlooked by scholars even though she enjoyed a successful career first as a writer of regionalist short stories and then as a significant contributor to modernist American drama. Across genres, Brown emphasizes the figure of the unmarried woman. Pauline

Elizabeth Hopkins, perhaps one of the most written-about African American women novelists, has been overlooked in another way: read as part of an activist tradition in African American letters, she has been categorized as a writer of romances rather than of realism, naturalism, or modernism. But when Thadious M. Davis delineates the central work of black women modernists as the staging of a "dialogue between the past and the present as a way of approaching futurity," she may as well be describing Hopkins, too.[3] Hopkins's use of intimate historicism demonstrates how the practice could be deployed to do the work of black feminist racial uplift in an age of white supremacism rather than used to assert white women's claims to Anglo-Norman belonging, as was often the case within New England regionalism.

Gilman, Brown, and Hopkins all felt deeply connected to New England and its history, a history they alluded to consistently in their writings. Gilman was born into an established New England family, the Beechers. Even though she lived in California for much of her life (often among relocated New Englanders as when she resided in Pasadena), she wrote of herself as being "a Connecticutter by birth," and her works consistently feature New England women.[4] Brown was born in New Hampshire and lived in Boston where she and her partner Louise Imogen Guiney helped bridge the gap between the Beacon Hill set, which included established authors such as Jewett, and the bohemian crowd.[5] (Guiney once wrote to her close friend and cousin, the queer aesthete Fred Holland Day, "A. [Alice] is a capital companion, a perfect 'mother' to me, and *almost* as much of a bohemian as you are.")[6] Hopkins was born in Portland, Maine, and lived in Boston where she formed part of that city's influential African American community.[7] A stage performer, playwright, magazine editor, novelist, and more, Hopkins remained unmarried throughout her life, dedicating herself to the work of making history.

Just as important as their identifying with New England and its communities is the fact that these three women writers thought carefully about the regional past and engaged their culture's ongoing colonial revivalism. In Gilman's short story "The Yellow Wall-Paper," the colonial mansion of New England is the setting for the protagonist's encounter with gender history. Antiques, old houses, and colonial costumes also animate the landscape of Brown's New England short stories. And in the magazine novel *Hagar's Daughter*, Hopkins not only "critiques plantation mythology" but also takes up her era's

New England–dominated colonial revivalism through references to heirloom china and colonial dames.[8] Gilman, Brown, and Hopkins all use colonial revivalism toward the same end: to explore women's alienation, the ways in which women have been prohibited from entering modern time, and how they might assert themselves as agents to recalibrate the terms of historical belonging. Exploring the "disjuncture between modern and premodern temporalities" characteristic of American modernism specifically as that disjuncture manifests itself for women, these authors posit feminist action, including resisting or critiquing marriage, through what I call spectral fusions.[9]

The New England regionalists whose cultural productions I examined in this volume's first three chapters explored women characters' as well as their own complex relationship to history through various means: the performing of male-dominated scenarios of history, the use of historical allusions, and sensual encounters with colonial objects—all activities that involved considerable gender play and sensual abundance. Specters have reared their heads throughout: from C. Alice Baker's assertion that the "ghosts of unburied shades [the colonial women taken captive] . . . had wandered, restless, haunting my whole life" to Slosson's representation of Mrs. Bates as a frightening and desirous ghost.[10] Yet, in these instances, the female self is implicitly theorized as something that remains distinct from, even if in complex relationship to, the ghost. In these earlier examples from New England regionalism, the contemporary woman may feel herself proximate or drawn to the ghostly foremother, and she may even house that specter, but she remains distinguishable from her; the two do not fuse together. In this way, Baker's and Slosson's hauntings take a shape that looks a lot like what Judith Butler, building on Freudian psychoanalysis, calls melancholic incorporation and understands as operating on a broad social scale.[11] In Butler's reading of Freud, "there is no final breaking of the attachment [between the ego and the object of desire]. There is, rather, the incorporation of the attachment *as* identification. . . . Insofar as identification is the psychic preserve of the object and such identifications come to form the ego, the lost object continues to haunt and inhabit the ego as one of its constitutive identifications."[12]

The generation of New England women writers on whose works I focus in this chapter, however, portrayed hauntings differently. Though practitioners of intimate historicism interested in the uses to which colonial object matter might be put, Gilman, Brown, and Hopkins represent encounters with ghosts as leading to late nineteenth-century women's recognition of their own spectrality. Herein the object of desire seems a form of selfhood rendered impossible; contemporary women in these accounts do not incorporate the lost object of desire, for the possible-but-unrealized self is what they have lost and never been. Women are ghosts. Contemporaries of Freud, these authors offer feminist critiques of women's identities and identifications in modern time. The hauntings they portray resemble those theorized by Avery Gordon in that they give way to a "transformative recognition," a "structure of feeling" that results in the identification of the ghost not only as a "social figure," as Gordon has it, but as a particularly gendered, racialized social figure located within overlapping regional, national, and global histories.[13] As we will see in the conclusion of this chapter in which I return to Elizabeth Bishop Perkins, the colonial revivalist and aspiring writer with whom I began this book, examining the modern underpinnings of such spectral fusions shifts our view onto what have long been dismissed as the eccentric habits of unmarried women, rendering visible how those habits form part of a larger, distinctly modern project to constellate temporal dissonance, gender difference, and history.

These texts by Gilman, Brown, and Hopkins are also unique in that the ghost does not just show up. Instead, throughout this fiction, women who find themselves faced with threats to their independence invite communion with ghosts either through occupying colonial habitations or donning colonial habits. It is by way of these activities that Gilman's, Brown's, and Hopkins's women characters become, either temporarily or permanently, the ghostly foremother, an inhabiting of gender identity and a breaking with temporal linearity (or the revelation of an already existing break) that reorients the body and how it might live in the world. Such spectral fusions do not quite constitute instances of what Elizabeth Freeman calls temporal drag, wherein "some bodies, by registering on their very surface the co-presence of several historically contingent events, social movements, and/or collective pleasures . . . [might] articulate . . . a kind of *temporal* transitivity."[14] Dressing like the dead or occupying colonial spaces alter the body's surface and the body's orientation, changing its relationship to the material world and, in the process, modifying not only its conscious life but its material form and thus what it might do.[15]

A central use to which the ghost has been put in literature, particularly within the African American literary tradition, has been to remember and work through the trauma of slavery and its violent legacies, as in Toni Morrison's *Beloved*. In calling forth the specter, Gilman, Brown, and Hopkins evoke the trauma of being women and, in the case of Hopkins, the trauma of black women's enslavement, yet they sustain a focus, too, on what Dana Luciano has called the specter's ability to index "pleasure, inventiveness, [and] radical departures not just from the norm but also the known."[16] Spectral fusions concern the past, yet they are focused primarily on a radical rejection of temporal linearity and a recognition of continuity throughout time, a hopeful recognition made possible by the pain of living as a woman in the present. In featuring a female protagonist who realizes that she is indistinguishable from the ghosts of the women who came before her, Gilman critiques women's position as backward and thus anticipates by a century Judith Bennett's claim that women's history has been "a history of *change without transformation.*"[17] Becoming the dead mother, in Brown, solves the present pain of Lucy Ann Cummings who chose loving and living with her mother over marriage but, on her mother's death, is pressured to assimilate herself into a heteronormative family formation; Brown's spectral fusions launch young women into another lifetime, that of unmarried independence with its attendant range of queer erotic forms.[18] In Hopkins, becoming the ghost of powerful and rebellious women of the past lays bare that the revolution against colonial subjugation continues for black women in the United States at the turn into the twentieth century even though their lived era historically occurs long after the American Revolution and the Civil War.

Part of my project here is to reconsider the dominant narrative wherein regionalism gets extinguished by a male-dominated naturalism before the so-called modernist turn. The argument that has linked New England women regionalists to the stereotype of the pathological spinster as atavistic and lacking echoes throughout a century of literary criticism and has helped relegate regionalism to a minor cultural space between 1865 and 1915, even between 1865 and 1900. Henry James's private reflection, "I hate 'old New England stories'!—which are lean and pale and poor and ugly," was echoed by the naturalists' various figurations of realism and regionalism as limited, womanly, and, like old colonial things, of the past.[19] Frank Norris wrote, "Realism is minute, it is the drama of a broken teacup"; Theodore Dreiser insisted that "a big city is not a little teacup to be seasoned by old maids"; Sinclair Lewis labeled realism "tea-table gentility"; and George Santayana positioned the "American Intellect" against the "American Will," associating the former with "the American woman," "genteel tradition," and the "colonial mansion," in contrast to the masculine and virile modern skyscraper.[20] In many ways, the naturalists proffered deft readings of regionalism in their figurative expressions: if porcelain teacups, as we learned in chapter 3, symbolize the white female body and its many passions, then the work of members of the New England regionalist group was very much concerned with the teacup, a surface on which whiteness, unmarried status, materiality, eroticism, historicity, and imperial dreams condensed. Yet this long-standing representation of regionalism as pathologically female, genteel, and quaint orients it *in opposition to* modernity and, by extension, to modernism. By definition, the quaint cannot be avant-garde, and so if any aspect of regionalism persisted through the modernist turn, it would be impossible to see it if working with the terms set forth by the naturalists' deeply biased theories of gendered literary history.

The tradition of understanding regionalism as itself the lacking, even grotesque, spinster of U.S. literary history has not been entirely undone in more recent scholarship. According to Donna Campbell's influential account, regionalism (a term she uses interchangeably with "local color literature") had little staying power when faced with the energetic assaults of naturalism, the movement that supposedly supplanted it.[21] In Campbell's analysis, the story is one of conflict and defeat: "The rhetoric employed by the writers of the time suggests not a transition but rather a genteelly pitched battle between the two, a conflict ended by the successful subversion and banishment of local color fiction."[22] While Campbell makes a significant intervention in emphasizing the importance of the regionalists, even pointing to a few ways in which the naturalists shared some of the regionalists' concerns, in the end, her study focuses on the naturalists' fevered response to regionalism, rendering her depiction of the battle one-sided. The main role regionalism ends up playing in Campbell's telling is to provide something against which a young generation of men (and Edith Wharton) reacted to usher in literary progress.[23] Jennifer Fleissner's provocative reading of late nineteenth-century U.S. literature, meanwhile, productively blurs the boundaries among realism, regionalism, and naturalism. In her reading of women regionalists, which she focuses on Mary Wilkins Freeman, Fleissner reads Freeman's women as examples of obsessional domesticity.[24] Borrowing from Fred Lewis Pattee, Fleissner notes that Freeman depicts "'a type of womanhood often so individual and so peculiar in its tragic problems as to be classifiable as unique,'" which, said another way, means that Freeman, like the naturalists, depicted characters with a kind of "'grotesque impossibility.'"[25] Fleissner, apparently agreeing with Pattee's representations of Freeman's characters as grotesques or near grotesques, posits that to place these characters at center stage "is to suggest that they perhaps can pose a particular kind of challenge to modernity itself."[26] Yet here, once again, the non-normative, "obsessional" woman challenges the modern rather than being of its very fiber. In repeating Pattee's masculinist characterization of Freeman's queer women—women with a range of differently articulated passions who commit themselves to serial enterprises such as creating quilts and distilling essences as opposed to having, nursing, and raising children—Fleissner runs the risk of repeating the powerful cultural narrative that certain alternative lives for women may be of modernity but bordering on the pathological.

In trying to tease out a kinship between New England regionalism and modernism in works written before 1914, I knowingly seek to trouble progressive, period-bound notions of literary history.[27] I remain attuned to how women writers who associated themselves with New England continued to live and produce texts in the regionalist mode into the modernist moment and how some of their early productions were themselves modernist even if published before the supposed watershed date of 1914.[28] I want to posit, too, that my recollection of regionalism in relation to literary history is only possible at this moment because of how I have redefined New England regionalism as an interdisciplinary historicist movement, one that enabled intimate historicism for a range of women cultural producers, particularly those interested in queer modalities. Without having first considered the myriad desires articulated in the work of the New England regionalists, it would not have been possible to recognize how Gilman, Brown, and Hopkins explored modern notions of selfhood and gender by way of intimate historicism.

Becoming Colonial

In February 1890, Charlotte Perkins Gilman donned a colonial gown and attended a "'Colonial Tea' at Mrs. Grangers" in Pasadena, California.[29] She therein participated in a popular form of historical performance

FIGURE 12 The Perkins-Davidson colonial garden party, York, Maine. Photograph, 1899. Courtesy of the Museums of Old York Collections, York, Maine.

known as "colonial fancy dressing," which was a form of generational cross-dressing. Organizations such as the Daughters of the American Revolution (DAR) and ladies' church societies regularly put on colonial teas as fund-raisers, and many articles in middle-class journals outlined how to host them. One such article published in the widely circulated *Ladies' Home Journal* in 1895 assures readers that colonial costumes are in such demand that one need only contact one of the "leading pattern stores" for specific sewing instructions.[30] At these teas, guests and hosts would don colonial-period fancy dress and, in addition to sipping tea and hot chocolate, might dine on "such eatables as Boston brown bread, Washington pie, crullers, and doughnuts."[31] Whether large in scale like the "Martha Washington Reception" in Woonsocket, Rhode Island, which attracted more than two thousand participants, or modest in scale versions among friends, like the colonial garden party Mary Sowles Perkins and Elizabeth Burleigh Davidson hosted as a fundraiser in 1899 in York, Maine, these events encouraged fancy-dressing participants to take on the identities of their colonial counterparts and thus to think historically and collectively for an afternoon (figure 12).[32]

Gilman's attendance at Mrs. Granger's colonial tea seems to have inaugurated a productive intellectual period during which Gilman gave much thought to colonial America in relation to modern American women. Just a little more than a week after attending the tea, Gilman and her best friend Grace Ellery Channing Stetson began work on a "Colonial play" eventually titled "In the Name of the King! A Colonial Romance."[33] Depicting women's radical political action in colonial Salem, Massachusetts, during a period of witchcraft trials, Gilman and Stetson's play posits the aristocratic, white colonist Lady Dolly Herrisford as the ideal proto-citizen. Mere days after starting work on the colonial play, Gilman returned to her short story "The Giant Wistaria," adding to it an opening scene set in colonial New England.[34] This story highlights the continuities between an unnamed colonial woman who got pregnant out of wedlock and a late nineteenth-century woman tourist to New England, the young Mrs. Jenny, whose sexual urges her doctor husband tries to control. These works of Gilman's colonial revival paved the way for the writing of her most famous story; within just a few months of completing the manuscript of "In the Name of the King!" and sending "The Giant Wistaria" off to the publisher, Gilman took the fusion between the New England woman of the past and the modern woman of the present, as well as the queer, racialized aspects of that fusion, to new heights in "The Yellow Wall-Paper."

Reading "The Yellow Wall-Paper" as engaging her era's colonial revivalism complements and adds to recent scholarship exploring the racial aspects of Gilman's feminism. After all, putting on the old dresses of the dead not only "expressed a decidedly genteel interpretation of the past" but also echoed the racist claims to national belonging like those made by the DAR.[35] As Alys Eve Weinbaum observes, it has been the scholarship on Gilman's nonfiction writings as opposed to the scholarship on Gilman's fiction that has explored the racist and nativist aspects of her theories.[36] Although scholars have begun to consider these issues in Gilman's imaginative works—most notably Weinbaum in her analysis of *Herland* and Jennifer S. Tuttle and Dana Seitler in their respective examinations of *The Crux*—to date, no one has satisfactorily accounted for how fully these issues shaped Gilman's "The Yellow Wall-Paper." Susan S. Lanser, the first critic to question Gilman's story's "status as a universal woman's text" and to insist on its placement "within the 'psychic geography' of Anglo-America at the turn of the century," made a significant intervention within Gilman scholarship by arguing that the yellow wallpaper alluded to racist, nativist panic in 1890s America, yellow being associated with the Chinese.[37] My focus on Gilman's engagement of the colonial revival, however, results in new and very different conclusions about what the wallpaper and its yellow color signify as well as about how Gilman figured white racial identity and national belonging in this important early feminist work of fiction.

"The Yellow Wall-Paper" takes the form of a woman's diary. In it the narrator relays how she, her husband, and their infant son are living in a colonial mansion for the summer and that her husband, a doctor, has dictated that she occupy the top-level room of the house. The narrator, who is, at her husband's prescription, on the rest cure, which means not working, sleeping a lot, and ingesting special medicines and meats, becomes interested in and then obsessed with the yellow wallpaper that decorates her room. In the end, the narrator appears to have gone insane: she believes she has helped free a woman/women trapped in the wallpaper, that in fact she is that selfsame woman/women.

That there are many old things in "The Yellow Wall-Paper"—the "colonial mansion," the "old-fashioned chintz hangings," "the riotous old-fashioned flowers"—has gone largely unremarked by critics.[38] I want to posit, however, that the wallpaper's yellow color reveals its age: it is an old document in a colonial house that tells an unwritten story of gender injustice repeated across time, one that cannot be read in any traditional way but that must be felt with the body.[39] In the airy but eerie environment of the "nursery at the top of [this] house," the narrator of "The Yellow Wall-Paper" finds herself surrounded by this historical source (168). Thus "The Yellow Wall-Paper" invokes and reformulates an influential literary work about colonial America, Nathaniel Hawthorne's *The Scarlet Letter*. Much like Hawthorne's narrator in "The Custom-House," who finds a package wrapped in a "piece of ancient yellow parchment" and is guided by a "ghostly hand," the narrator of "The Yellow Wall-Paper" stumbles on a piece of yellow paper in an upper story room that appears haunted.[40] Yet Gilman's aged paper, much like her account of one unnamed modern woman's historical intimacy with the past, differs from Hawthorne's in that the discovered primary source of colonial history is a nonliterary, nonlinear one acted upon by an anonymous collective of ghostly women whose lingering presence draws her to try to read their history—and thus leads her to understand her own.

It is no coincidence that both Hawthorne's and Gilman's narrators find their old yellow papers on the upper floors of colonial New England buildings. For late nineteenth- and early twentieth-century

Americans who read "The Yellow Wall-Paper," the attic most immediately would have figured as a space rife with historical and particularly Anglo-American associations.[41] During the colonial revival, Americans ransacked attics looking for unclaimed material treasures that had witnessed the unfolding of national history as well as for evidence of connections to colonial ancestors.[42] Accordingly, the upper levels of colonial-era structures were often written about in gendered terms that emphasized late nineteenth-century anxieties about racial purity and the sexual purity on which it depended. One 1891 contributor to the *New England Magazine* (which published both "The Giant Wistaria" and "The Yellow Wall-Paper") writes, "Where the family changes, the attic loses its stately lineage and becomes the preying ground of all vandals."[43] Articulating the popular sentiment that the virginal attics of New England's colonial homes were valuable as testimonies to Anglo-American history, this writer reassures readers that the attic they are about to explore in prose "has known but one family" and thus is "the pure type."[44]

Like other attic artifacts, Gilman's unscrolled yellow parchment constitutes a primary historical document that tells a story of the Anglo-American past. When the narrator of "The Yellow Wall-Paper" first arrives in her "haunted house," however, she assumes that history unfolds along a progressive trajectory, following a "natural" course much like humans grow up over time, but the material evidence she keeps encountering suggests a story of repetition, not progress. Initially she insists, "It [the room] was nursery first and then playroom and gymnasium" (168). Continuing to imagine the inhabitants of the room maturing, the narrator concludes that it may have also been used as a "boys' school" (168). In this passage, the narrator identifies the progression of human life—from infant to boy—as distinctly male, which implies, in turn, that linear advancement in history is a male experience. But as the reader and the narrator soon realize, this room's function as a prison—it even has bars on the windows and "rings and things in the walls"—has remained unchanged over time and attests to the physical and temporal immobilization of women (168).

Early on in "The Yellow Wall-Paper," the narrator likewise misreads herself as belonging to the modern time of the democratic nation-state. Over the course of the story, however, she realizes that she cannot discriminate between herself and the woman in the wallpaper not because they are part of an essential woman writ large, but because in the time that has elapsed between past women's experiences in this room and her own nothing about women's condition in the United States has changed. Later details about the room—the bed "is nailed down" and "fairly gnawed," and the wallpaper has been stripped off precisely to the height that the narrator can reach—suggest that the narrator is the double of at least one past inhabitant (172, 181). The wallpaper-as-document attests that a history of female imprisonment and temporal stasis is the basis of New England and national history.

In "The Yellow Wall-Paper," the narrator is being held back physically and temporally. As John, her husband, says when the narrator suggests renovating this colonial house so that she may live in it more comfortably, "Really, dear, I don't care to renovate the house just for a three months' rental" (169). He, like the other controlling husbands of Gilman's fiction, is invested in maintaining the status quo, in keeping what has been passed down—features of the colonial mansion— intact. The moment when the narrator fully realizes her temporally backward condition is, ironically, the passage that has confirmed for many readers that she has regressed into insanity, demonstrating the power of the fantastical or seemingly crazed to political critique, to consciousness even.[45] "I really have discovered something at last," the narrator writes, "The front pattern *does* move—and no wonder! The woman behind shakes it! Sometimes I think there are a great many women behind, and sometimes only one" (178). The term "behind" in this passage indicates a physical as well as temporal position, anticipating the claim that Gilman would go on, in her best-selling study *Women and Economics*, to develop: society has undertaken the "absurd effort to make a race with one sex a million years *behind* the other."[46] That the narrator uses the present tense of "come" when she wonders "if they all come out of that wall-paper as I did," also suggests that being behind is the ongoing condition of white women in the United States (181). The historical experiences of the colonial house's ghostly women persist in the experience of the modern Anglo-American woman as embodied outside of and within the wallpaper.

We have in Gilman's narrator's recognition of her self as contiguous with the ghostly foremothers who have been residing in this prison-like space since colonial times, orienting their bodies to it, a spectral fusion *par excellence*. The sense of the past as the present expands in "The Yellow Wall-Paper" to include the narrator's own body, and, as we will soon see of Alice Brown's regionalist tales, the recognition of the self in the ghostly other engenders a set of nonreproductive pleasures. It seems important that Gilman's narrator lies awake beside her husband in bed each night not making conjugal contact with him but thinking, instead, about the wallpaper: "John was asleep and I hated to waken him, so I kept still and watched the moonlight on that undulating wallpaper till I felt creepy" (174). By the story's final scene, the narrator's nursery room looks to have transformed into a figurative womb and thus the wallpaper an interior tissue. The narrator, tied to the bed by a rope resembling an umbilical cord, is happily confined to the space: "Here I can creep smoothly on the floor, and my shoulder just fits in that long smooch around the wall" (182). In Gilman's time, smooch meant both "to sully, dirty" and, in New England, it "signifie[d] to foul or blacken with something produced by combustion or other like substance"; the word would soon come to mean "to kiss," but in its noun form it means "smear."[47] We certainly could say that the narrator has become infantlike, but she also "creep[s]" through the womb-like space, rubbing its surfaces, which looks like masturbatory action and recalls her feeling "creepy" while lying alongside John. The sensation of creeping recalls a crucial scene in "The Giant Wistaria" in which Gilman also explores the queer pleasures of colonial hauntings. It is worth taking a brief detour back to "The Giant Wistaria," which, again, Gilman was writing just a few months before "The Yellow Wall-Paper," to apprehend the sensuality of spectral fusions in Gilman's more famous text.

In "The Giant Wistaria," the young, married Mrs. Jenny sees an old colonial mansion in rural New England and immediately desires to live in it. She says to her husband, "O, George . . . what a lovely house! I am sure it's haunted! Let us get that house to live in this summer!"[48] The month of June finds Jenny and George leasing the mansion and sitting with two other couples on its porch admiring the wisteria vine that has grown up over the house's side. But instead of bringing these young urbanites mild weather, picturesque environs, and stereotypical encounters with old New England, their tourism brings them into contact with a grisly tale of female sexual expression and colonial violence. Gilman prefaces the story about the haunted colonial mansion of modern New England with a narrative set in the same house more than a century earlier. This prefatory scene depicts a wealthy eighteenth-century immigrant, Samuel Dwining, who plans to punish his daughter (who remains unnamed in the story) for her errant sexuality by leaving her bastard infant in the colony, taking her back to

England, and forcing her to marry a cousin she abhors. As readers, we have limited knowledge of the young woman, but we are led to believe that it is her skeleton and the body of her infant that are uncovered at the end of the tale and that she is the one who haunts Jenny the night before the workmen discover her bones among the wisteria roots. The spectral fusion of "The Giant Wistaria" occurs between the unnamed, murdered colonial daughter and the vine, the latter of which seems to Jenny, the other women, and Gilman's readers to have human features: it has both a "trunk" and "arms" and is an agent that "had once climbed" and now "held" the house's pillars (156). In fact, the very matter that constitutes the Dwining daughter's body has been resurrected as her cells have fed the wisteria vine over the decades.

When Jenny narrates the scene of having been haunted by what she and readers believe is the unnamed colonial daughter's ghost, the specter takes the form of the vine, and Jenny's body expands to appear indistinguishable from the colonial mansion. "The moonlight came through in my three great windows in three white squares on the black old floor," Jenny relates, "and those fingery wistaria leaves we were talking of last night just seemed to crawl all over them. And—O, girls, you know that dreadful well in the cellar?" (158–59). As in "The Yellow Wall-Paper," here a female narrator projects her own body onto the materiality of the colonial house. In this passage, the phrase "my three great windows" signifies that the windows belong to Jenny's room (though she shares it with George, and so "our" would appear to be the accurate pronoun), but the use of "my" also makes it sound as if Jenny *is* the house and that the windows form part of that self. The "fingery wistaria leaves" that "crawl all over" Jenny's windows suggests a sensual, sexual touching (158). That Jenny then transports her female readers/listeners—"O, girls"—breathlessly to the well, a figure that unmistakably stands for female genitalia, at the end of her account, seems to repeat a sort of climax. The wisteria's sensual movements retain their stimulating power over time, affecting Jenny's body when she narrates the story: "It makes me creep to think of it even now," she tells her listeners (158).[49] In this example, sexual ecstasy is imagined as occurring among women across time, both between the colonial era and the present and among modern women in the present time as registered by Jenny's ecstatic "O, girls" and the repetition of her arousal.

As George lies in bed beside his wife, much like John of "The Yellow Wall-Paper," he does not participate in or understand her excited state but wants to render impotent her sensual, historicized experience of the colonial mansion's ghost. When Jenny gets that ecstatic, ghostly feeling, George, a doctor, gives her "bromide," which, unlike other readily available tranquilizers such as laudanum and alcohol was thought in the nineteenth century to be particularly effective as a sexual sedative (159).[50] Here we begin to discern the story's underlying critique of men who act to suppress female sexual desire. Such acts limit women by cutting them off from recognizing and experiencing intimacies with past American women and simultaneously forcing them to repress memories of their own sexual history. The bromide is so strong that Jenny, the next morning, at first cannot recollect that she was haunted.

As we have seen, the sensual "creeping" so central to "The Giant Wistaria" animates "The Yellow Wall-Paper" as well. Variants of the word occur multiple times in the final scene of "The Yellow Wall-Paper," linking the narrator to the women in the wallpaper: "There are so many of those creeping women, and they creep so fast," the narrator writes, and she remarks, "It is so pleasant to be out in this great room and creep around as I please!" (181). "Pleasant" and "I please" together foreground the pleasure the narrator takes in this form of mobility, this sensual historical redress. The narrator of "The Yellow Wall-Paper" has, at this point, recognized her oneness with the ghost; she is the women of the past embodied as the woman of the present, and it is her movements creeping and smooching that pleasure her and give her some semblance of power coded as sexual. This self-satisfying set of gestures looks both masturbatory and queer in that the narrator has fused with and so is the creeping women.

The last line of the story emphasizes the narrator's creeping, for John faints "and right across my path by the wall, so that I had to creep over him every time!" (182). The purport of this ending, the seemingly mad but powerful position of the narrator mounting her completely immobilized doctor husband, is well captured in the original illustration from *The New England Magazine* (figure 13).[51] The spatialization of gendered power within heteronormative culture that places women "behind" men gets reworked in this image as women coming up from behind and getting on top, pressing down on and possibly penetrating those men. The spectral fusion of the unnamed narrator and the women from across the colonial mansion's past in "The Yellow Wall-Paper" reconfigures the narrator's consciousness and her very body, changing its actions, its desires, and its pleasures. Becoming the

FIGURE 13 Joseph H. Hatfield, illustration for "The Yellow Wall-Paper. A Story." Published in the *New England Magazine* 11 (January 1892): 656.

ghost of the colonial New England past gives way to reconfigurations of power and time thought along the axis of history.

Gilman's narrator's position at the story's end may be triumphant in its recognition of the temporal arrest of women as well as suggestive in its exploration of masturbation and queer sex between women as a means of satisfying oneself and thereby temporarily overpowering men. (In 1890–91, Gilman continued cultivating same-sex intimacies, including sexual relations, with women: her friendship with Grace Stetson, whom Gilman confessed in late 1890 she wanted to marry, persisted, and in early 1891 Gilman fell in love with Adeline E. ["Delle"] Knapp.)[52] Yet, ultimately, "The Yellow Wall-Paper" does not separate alternative erotic forms from the backwardness that Gilman so wanted women to leave behind; spectral fusions and queer sensations may be part of how to catch up to men, but that is not the trajectory on which Gilman imagines her ideal woman remaining.[53]

Getting on the Ghost

Alice Brown entered the literary scene in the mid-1890s with her two collections of regionalist short stories, *Meadow-Grass: Tales of New England Life* and *Tiverton Tales*, and she was a contributor to William Dean Howells's collaborative novel project, *The Whole Family*, which ended up blending features of realism and modernism.[54] Almost entirely overlooked by scholars, Brown's regionalist enterprise may seem, at first glance, belated, coming as it did at just the moment some nineteenth-century writers were promising the end of regionalism as a mode.[55] Yet Brown had a successful career as a writer of fiction and plays, which she published through the first three decades of the twentieth century. Years before Eugene O'Neill gave form to the repressed desires and drives of New England men and women in plays such as *Desire Under the Elms* (1924), Brown won the prestigious Winthrop Ames prize for her play about these same themes—*Children of Earth: A Play of New England* (1915); yet Brown staged such yearnings with an emphasis on the unmarried protagonist Mary Ellen Barstow and her immigrant, alcoholic foil, Jane Hale. It is not an exaggeration to say that Brown was one of the most well-respected early modernist playwrights in the United States: she was one of only two U.S. writers whose work was consistently produced by Maurice Browne's Little Theatre in Chicago, one of the primary venues associated with the Little Theatre Movement, which played a key part in modernist drama's development.[56] Brown's one-act play *Joint Owners in Spain* was not only a hit at Browne's theater but was so often produced in little theaters throughout the United States that, according to one scholar, Brown often said that its royalties "bought, if not all her bread, the 'butter and jam.'"[57] I think it no coincidence that *Joint Owners in Spain* was based on a regionalist short story of the same title published as part of Brown's first regionalist collection, *Meadow-Grass*. In those stories, as in the ones from *Tiverton Tales* that I analyze here, we see laid bare a broad range of erotic impulses, queer characters, and spectral fusions that seek to give form to the temporal dissonance of modernism, from extended mother love to adultery and from same-sex intimacies to orgiastic encounters with ghosts. Of Brown's modern woman characters, one of most memorable lives in a queer modality and communes with ghosts as a way to keep intact her maidenly independence: Dilly Joyce, the protagonist of the short stories "At Sudleigh Fair" and "A Last Assembling."

Brown's first story about Dilly, "At Sudleigh Fair," follows the tradition within New England regionalism of aligning rebellious women with witchcraft while linking those same characters to alternative sociosexual desires. "At Sudleigh Fair" depicts the middle-aged Dilly as a "queer little woman," and Brown's invocation of racial markers in her description of Dilly seems an example of how "the structures and methodologies that drove dominant ideologies of race [in the nineteenth century] also fueled the pursuit of knowledge about the homosexual body."[58] Dilly has a "healthy coat of tan," is close friends with the Native American woman Nance Pete, and has "abnormally long and sinewy arms" (192, 282). Her skin and her social ties seem Indian, while the form of her arms marks a sexual orientation: "the 'attitude,' angle, and length of the arms were viewed medically as a sign of either femininity or masculinity," and long arms on women were sometimes read as marking sexual deviance and racial degeneration.[59] Yet even, or perhaps given, this racialized queerness, Dilly, in the end, embodies old American ideals of individuality—"she resembled her own house [a colonial homestead] to a striking degree"—and she proves better able than the minister to guide erring members of the village's next generation back onto the path of ethical conduct (192).[60]

"A Last Assembling," published in Brown's later short story collection *Tiverton Tales*, provides Dilly's intimate prehistory, which is to say it tells the story of how Dilly came to be "queer." In "A Last Assembling," Dilly is a fairly young unmarried woman who has been engaged to a man, Jethro Moore, for years. When the story begins, Jethro has finally made his fortune in Chicago and has written to let Dilly know that he is on his way back to Tiverton to marry her. The night of Jethro's return, after they have spent the afternoon together, Dilly sneaks back to her family's colonial homestead for what she thinks is a final goodbye. But in the house she is visited by a host of Joyce family ghosts, ghosts of those ancestors who led alternative lives. After a night of sensual spectral fusions, Dilly tells Jethro she will not marry him and will remain single in her colonial home.

Dilly's nighttime experience in the colonial house is deeply sensual and demonstrates how spectral pleasures and colonial houses might support the single life. As Dilly is lying alone in a neighbor's bed, "the old house," in which "since colonial times" her family had lived, "called on her to come."[61] Dilly responds to the call, and on entering the colonial dwelling, "she drew forward her father's chair, and sat down in it, with luxurious abandonment, to rest. Her mother's little cricket was by her side, and she put her feet on it and exhaled a long sigh of content" (167). Dilly's overt expressions of peace and release constitute a performance that cites and radically revises those staged by her parents and by her fiancé: the day before Jethro had sat in this same "great chair" of father's, and Dilly had responded "with a start, as if it were an omen" (158). With the colonial home as her performance space, Dilly rehearses and thus revises the tableau of patriarchal domesticity by using her body as a bridge to connect the two gendered antiques—the father's great chair and the mother's diminutive stool. Her physical form in this scene replaces the uneven power relations and the eroto-racial inscription of heteronormative coupling with the figure of the single New England daughter who is free and will remain free to draw on the legacies of her queer ancestors.

Dilly's performance on the stage of the colonial homestead rescripts history, rendering the unmarried daughter's body a mutable, sensual site for a reaffiliation with whiteness understood as tied not to genetic reproduction by way of marriage and childbearing but to the work of cross-generational communion with disaffiliated specters who are related to her by blood and so conceptualized as, at least in part, always already in her body. In the precise moment that Dilly takes the place of the patriarch in this domestic scenario, she looks at "the dark cavern which was the fireplace," and suddenly she experiences "completed bliss, as if it [the fireplace] were alight and she could watch the dancing flames" (168). The revisionist performance of the solitary unmarried woman, instead of bringing to the domestic scene frigidity, coincides with the colonial homestead's womb-like fireplace seeming licked by flames and with Dilly achieving what looks like an orgasm ("completed bliss"). By means of the ecstatic self-pleasuring inherent to replacing the heterosexual dyad (the mother and father) with the solitary self, Dilly suddenly becomes "aware that the Joyces [their ghosts] were all about her," engaging her sensually: those "sweet" ancestors "drowned her will, and drew her [Dilly] to themselves" (168, 166).

In the extended communion of what is a specter-filled, orgiastic night, Dilly comes to know all the disgraced, abused Joyces of the past in and through the sensations of her own temporarily ghostly body: the colonial shoemaker who, torn between his pacifist beliefs and his patriotic yearning to shed blood in the early years of the Revolution, committed suicide; the woman left on her wedding day whom people said wasted away but who Dilly comes to understand as "a woman serene and glad" (169). Far from the typical Revolutionary war heroes or brave and frugal good wives of late nineteenth-century colonial revival discourse, far from her own normative parents, these Joyces induct Dilly into an alternative historical narrative of the misunderstood and disaffiliated, remaking her notion of family and belonging.

Getting it on with these ghosts curtails Dilly's prospective membership in the national collective imagined as progressive and heteroreproductive (marriage to Jethro) and welds her instead to a historical regional family imagined as haunting, haunted, and queer.

Dilly's queer character is inherited not at her actual birth so much as in the womb-centered scene of her engaging in a new kind of erotic labor, one just as saturated with racial consequence as her being born or giving birth to a child might have been. The experience of rebirth heats Dilly up and fuses her not to the nation or even to her environment but to a broadly conceived space and time that includes entire worlds: Dilly, the narrator tells us, "held herself remote from personal intimacies; but all the fine, invisible bonds of race and family took hold of her like irresistible factors, and welded her to the universe anew" (153). Taken "hold of," or rapt, by factors "irresistible" in a sexualized embrace, Dilly transitions from the solitude of the young "old" maid into a queer and historicized form of belonging contiguous with white New England dissent construed not just as regional, national, or global but as universal in scope. The domestic, supposedly confining space of the house is, in Brown's story, the space by way of which Dilly comes to understand her own corporeal relation to queerness thanks to these ostracized ancestors. It is the colonial homestead that calls on Dilly "to come" and that provides her with an externalized, cavernous womb-like space in which to nourish dreams of fire, holding her and the ghosts of history with whom Dilly enjoys intimacy in its history-rich embrace.

Spectral fusions and the queer sensations involved in them, rather than signifying, as they did for Gilman, the pathologies of women's backward place in time, mark, in Brown's fiction, the arrival of solutions to the problem of being pressured to conform to membership in a heteronormative nuclear family. Brown portrays Dilly Joyce both as queer and as a full fledged member of a transhistorical community of white dissenters, all of whom belong to New England history and its variously imagined traditions of dissent. Such a tradition of dissent leads to socio-sexual freedom. Being rapt by these "sweet" ancestors within the dynamic walls of the homestead allows Dilly to refuse Jethro, which she does first thing in the morning: "She [Dilly] looked in his [Jethro's] eyes with a long, bright farewell glance, and turned away. She had left behind her something which was very fine and beautiful; but she could not mourn. And all that morning, about the house, she sang little snatches of song, and was content. The Joyces had done their work, and she was doing hers" (174). Meditating on the temporal dimension of Dilly's choice, Brown pivots her readers on the play between not mourning the elected loss of the husband-to-be and the unfolding of the future encapsulated in the new "morning" of Dilly's life as an independent, queer New England daughter. Heteronormative coupling here gets objectified as a luxury item—something fixed, "fine and beautiful"—but living single in the colonial house means living in the forward-oriented temporal space of early day. Committed to citizen-being rather than citizen-making, the latter an activity based on the labors of heterosexual sex, childbirth, and the material and affective cultivation of children in lieu of the individuated self, "A Last Assembling" unyokes female patriotism from heterosexual reproduction. In the end, through her character Dilly Joyce, Brown imagines queer collaboration with a community of specters as generative, pleasurable, and offering an alternative to marriage and maternity for women, one involving not Virginia Woolf's modernist vision of a room of one's own but an entire colonial house.

"A Last Assembling" depicts a temporary spectral fusion; it is an account of how the colonial home and its ghosts might support the unmarried state and house pleasure for the unmarried New England daughter. In another story from *Tiverton Tales*, "The Way of Peace," Brown explores the possibility of spectral fusion becoming a permanent state. Lucy Ann Cummings, the unmarried New England daughter in "The Way of Peace," before the time the story tracks, gave up a proposal of marriage "to stay at home with her mother . . . the path she loved" (181). When her mother dies, Lucy Ann fuses herself with the mother, resurrecting the mother in bodily form through costuming and self-presentation. Right after her mother's death, Lucy Ann "caught sight of herself in the glass. 'Oh, my!' breathed Lucy Ann. Low as they were, the words held a fullness of joy" (177–78). Lucy Ann's exhaled expression of pleasure is over the fact that she sees in her own face the face of her now-dead mother. Excited by the presence of the ghost in her own cellular organization, which has aged before its time, Lucy Ann cuts and curls her hair so as to look just like the dead mother and dons her mother's dress, which still carries a distinctive smell.

This act of mother-loving self-transformation makes possible a new set of pleasures for Lucy Ann: "It was done, and Lucy Ann looked at herself with a smile all suffused by love and longing. She was not herself any more; she had gone back a generation, and chosen a warmer niche. She could have kissed her face in the glass, it was so like that other dearer one. She did finger the little curls, with a reminiscent passion, not daring to think of the darkness where the others had been shut; and, at that instant, she felt very rich" (178). The desired one, for Lucy Ann, is the mother, but in putting on the garb of the ghost, crafting her hair, her face, to look even more like the mother, Lucy Ann transforms her own body into its own erotic object. That Lucy Ann's glance at herself-as-the-mother is "all suffused by love and longing" coincides with the "warmth," "passion," and richness she feels in this moment of physical satisfaction. Her longing, moreover, looks forward just as it looks back and will be ongoing, it seems, over the duration of Lucy Ann's life.

Beth Fisken asserts, in her discussion of different works by Brown that they explore "other means of connection than conjugal, [how] generation can be imaginative as well as genetic."[62] In "The Way of Peace," the unmarried woman, Lucy Ann, undertakes acts of generation that are both imaginative and genetic, if we can call cross-generational, intrafamilial fusion genetic. It is this genetic aspect that challenges the boundary between the living and the dead, the child and the mother, ultimately disrupting a supposedly natural linearity, reconstituting time as well as the structure of "worlds." After Lucy Ann's transformation, "she [Lucy Ann] did not seem to herself altogether alive, nor was her mother dead. They had been fused, by some wonderful alchemy; and instead of being worlds apart, they were at one" (179–80). "At one" here marks the becoming one of Lucy Ann and her mother as well as their inhabiting a singular time and place. Brown's narrator elaborates on this unified time-space in terms that, again, defy historical sequence. After her fusion with the mother is complete, Lucy Ann "went downstairs, hushed and tremulous . . . and there she stayed, in a pleasant dream, not of the future, and not even of the past, but face to face with a recognition of wonderful possibilities" (179). This space of the dream cannot be located in the past or the future and thus demands a whole new configuration in terms of generation, both acts of creation and how people are organized according to temporal sequence. Power over her mobility, her affective and erotic life, and her material space is one of the "wonderful possibilities" Lucy Ann goes on to bring into existence by way of her self-authored transformation.

Alice Brown's stories foreground the pleasures of spectral fusions pursued largely in response to the threat of being forced to become part of a nuclear family. (Much of the conflict in "The Way of Peace" stems from the fact that both of Lucy Ann's brothers want her to stay with them and their families whereas she wants to live alone as her mother in her own old house.) Brown's unmarried women characters turn back to fuse and commune with ancestors who may not have been valued in the past: the suicide, the abused wife, the supposedly morbid spinster, the ailing mother, yet these are the figures that give the female protagonists energy, the ones through whom the latter change their permeable selves and perform acts of sociosexual defiance. If Gilman's "The Yellow Wall-Paper" imagines women prohibited from modern time and yearning to reenter it to escape the primitive dis-ease of temporal backwardness, Brown's women characters posit a mode of modernity rich in queer sensation, temporal dissonance, and intimate historicism.

Dreaming of Colonial Dames

Pauline Elizabeth Hopkins was another influential woman writer working at the turn of the twentieth century who identified with New England, and she used intimate historicism to reimagine the terms of African American women's historical belonging. In Hopkins's fiction, as in the works of Gilman and Brown, modern women fuse with their ghostly foremothers, transforming their bodies and lives in the process. Variously optimistic and despairing, these corporeal metamorphoses change the course of history while revealing that only through historical knowledge felt on the black woman's body might her possible futures be imagined. In Hopkins, we see New England regionalism's genealogical and non-genealogical bases of racial belonging for unmarried women—C. Alice Baker's notion of dissenting blood and Freeman's historical allusions—activated for black women in a world-historical frame. As Hopkins scholars have consistently noted, she understood history making, the recollecting of the past in the present, as central to her intellectual life. Hazel V. Carby concludes that all Hopkins's writings "testified to an aspect of black presence in history," while C. K. Doreski asserts that Hopkins worked across discourses "to shape a rhetorical self to counter the absence of a reliable race history."[63] Hopkins's historicism, moreover, formed part of a broader cultural renaissance in African American history writing.[64] Hopkins's magazine novel *Hagar's Daughter* provides an object lesson in how her intimate historicism proceeded.

Hopkins was an influential editor, novelist, feminist, and activist. In her early adult life, she also worked as a performer: a noted soprano and actress in the 1870s, she wrote at least three plays, among them *The Slaves' Escape; or, The Underground Railroad*, which toured nationally under the title *Peculiar Sam*.[65] At the turn into the twentieth century, Hopkins expanded her literary repertoire and became a visible race activist, writing novels and serving as the editor of and a major contributor to the *Colored American Magazine*, "the most widely distributed Afro-American periodical before 1909."[66] The *Colored American Magazine*, in which three of Hopkins's novels and most of her other writings appeared, was decidedly cosmopolitan: by 1903, "the staff considered that the journal was 'not only National but International in character.'"[67] Hopkins's fiction, likewise, melded the regional, the national, and the international in its depiction of interrelated histories of slavery in the Americas. By her fourth and final novel, *Of One Blood; or, The Hidden Self*, Hopkins had embraced a pan-Africanism modernist in scope. Hopkins's works, like Gilman's and Brown's, represent the alienation and temporal dissonance unique to modernism as constitutive of women's lives. Hopkins engaged the specific theories of psychology offered in William James's influential 1890 essay "The Hidden Self," a work thought to have laid the foundations for modernist writers' experimentation with stream of consciousness.[68] In her international vision of history, her untiring dedication to social justice, the model she provided for black women editors of modernist magazines such as Jessie Fauset, and her characterization of the alienation of black women in a white supremacist culture as one of temporal dissonance, Hopkins brought regionalism's intimate historicism into the modernist moment.[69]

Building on the work of Eric Sundquist, who explores how Hopkins contests dominant historical discourses of the Old South, and blending it with Carby's and Lois Brown's recognition of Hopkins's investments in New England, I argue that in *Hagar's Daughter*, Hopkins invoked colonial New England history as an important precedent, encouraging her readers to see how revolt against an imperial force is a necessary and ongoing action undertaken by black women.[70] Mikko Tuhkanen has argued that *Hagar's Daughter* constitutes a "passing narrative" and that "such collective passing renders the future only an echo of the past, immobilizing the nation in uncanny repetitions of its disastrous history."[71] While I agree that this repetition may well characterize the histories of Jewel and Aurelia, two young mixed-race characters of the novel, Hagar and Venus, I contend, offer another mode of bodying forth black history. In *Hagar's Daughter*, black daughters of all regions of the United States regardless of skin color may call on a New England–based legacy of revolutionary activism, a foundation for belonging they may claim as the basis for a not-yet-realized dream of gendered racial justice. The mixed-race character Hagar, through her engagement of colonial antiques and her fantasies about colonial times, temporarily resists marriage and its concomitant objectification. Yet ultimately she cannot break with the colonial mansion as a historical figuration of domesticity and its promises of white gendered belonging. Hagar and Jewel both get pulled into marriage's limiting sphere. Only Venus Johnson manages to don the dress of New England revolutionaries, remain unmarried, contest male authorship of history, and, as Carby has it, evolve "into a heroine of the story."[72]

Public, national history frames *Hagar's Daughter*, which opens at the moment of the South's succession, a breaking down of white familial ties on the national stage paralleled in the private history of the Ensons, a white slaveholding family from Maryland. Early in the novel, Ellis Enson, a successful plantation owner and slaveholder, marries the beautiful white daughter of the adjacent plantation, Hagar Sargeant, and they have a daughter. Hagar, it seems, understands herself as white, but it turns out that she has repressed the knowledge of having been a slave in childhood. Through the evil plots of St. Clair Enson, Ellis's younger brother, and his slave-trader friend, Walker, Hagar is "proven" to be black and taken to the capital to be sold. In a recasting of William Wells Brown's influential novel *Clotel*, Hagar throws herself and her infant daughter into the Potomac to escape life in slavery.[73]

The novel then jumps ahead twenty years to Washington, D.C., where we encounter the same characters who, in various new identities, form elite white society in the post-Reconstruction era. Hagar (now passing as the white woman Estelle Bowen) is the brilliant wife of the Western politician and millionaire Senator Bowen and the stepmother of the lovely young Jewel Bowen. The two villains, St. Clair Enson now living under the alias General Benson and Walker masquerading as Major Madison, plot to get their hands on Jewel's inheritance by having her marry Benson. They arrange for Jewel's abduction to Enson Hall, the now dilapidated colonial mansion where Hagar and Ellis once lived before her history was known. Venus, Jewel's African American maid, cross-dresses and rescues Jewel. But when Jewel learns that she is the biological daughter of Hagar and thus mixed-race, she is rejected by her new husband, the New Englander Cuthbert Sumner. Herein history repeats itself, for Ellis Enson also rejected Hagar when he learned she was black, but Jewel is more fully objectified than Hagar, much as her name suggests; she is a white woman without a history. In the end, Jewel dies, Hagar and Ellis Enson reunite, living out their days in the colonial mansion, and Venus remains unmarried but with the prospect of marriage, and moves to New England.

The first scene in which we are introduced to Hagar, Hopkins explores the disjunction between how this young woman is framed as domestic (when viewed through the eyes of the white slaveholder and to-be suitor, Ellis Enson) and how she imagines her own life unfolding (when viewed by way of Hagar's interior thoughts). Here is how we first see Hagar: "Hagar stood at the window contemplating the scene before her. It was her duty to wash the heirlooms of colonial china and silver. From their bath they were dried only by her dainty fingers, and carefully replaced in the corner cupboard. Not for the world would she have dropped one of these treasures. . . . Not the royal jewels of Victoria were ever more carefully guarded than these family heirlooms."[74]

The sort of independent, historically mindful housekeeping Hagar models was most famously linked to northeastern New England womanhood in the works of Harriet Beecher Stowe, from the unmarried New Englander Ophelia's "exemplary New England domestic economy" to ideal unmarried New England women like Grace Seymour of *Pink and White Tyranny* who not only keeps house for her brother but cares for its colonial and Revolutionary-era American furnishings.[75] Antique objects and their proper care were understood to play a key role in the health of the modern home. As Stowe indicates in her *House and Home Papers* and cultural commentators like Clarence Cook, the author of the influential *The House Beautiful*, expressed, this ideal, northern, middle-class housekeeper performed patriotic, implicitly nativist work by way of her careful treatment of domestic effects. For Stowe, "the mistresses of American families . . . have the duties of missionaries imposed upon them by that class from which our supply of domestic servants is drawn," while for the more vicious Cook, servants should not handle the family heirlooms for the Irish have "destroyed the domesticity of [American] . . . homes."[76] It is into this discourse about Anglo-American women's domestic labor as a form of belonging that Hopkins inserts Hagar, who perfectly fulfills the northern, middle-class domestic ideal while being a black daughter.

Crucially, however, in *Hagar's Daughter*, a text that in its very title announces an interest in women's racial genealogies, Hopkins insists that a colonial-revival historical sensibility, often considered by whites as a racially exclusive legacy, both frames how Ellis and the reader perceive Hagar and how she perceives herself. The image of Hagar that Hopkins paints, which is specifically aestheticized by Ellis—on seeing her framed by the window he exclaims, "A fairer vision was never seen"—also calls on the popular colonial revival image of the young woman safeguarding a sexualized white colonial legacy as in Joseph DeCamp's oil painting *The Blue Cup* (figure 14) (34). DeCamp's work reiterates a classic construction of the ideal Anglo-American housewife as white, fertile, turned toward the future of the new day, and able to tend properly to the antique china teapots and plates placed in her care. Here, the ability to preserve the nation's history is linked to an aesthetic of fertility and white reproduction.

Like the woman of *The Blue Cup*, Hagar safeguards the antiques that attest to the Sargeant family's long residency in America. It was, after all, families who dated their arrival back to the colonial period and mostly those who were affluent who boasted such treasures. And those treasures testify, as items circulated within the larger British Empire, to a specifically Anglo-American racial legacy and economic prowess. Hagar's own white, dainty body, with its fertile, "rosy, dimpled arms," is further linked to history in that it appears to guarantee Ellis a future based on Anglophilic fantasies of racially pure heterosexual reproduction and a gendered division of labor (34).

But just as it locates the white-but-soon-to-be-black Hagar in a fantasy of heterosexual reproduction borne out of confinement in the domestic sphere, this image of Hagar laboring to wash the domestic effects also suggests the backward-looking idealization of women's value as bound to objectification and domestic servitude. When Hopkins represents Hagar as an ideal housewife and tender keeper of familial heirlooms, she implies that a black daughter can perform the same material and reproductive work, the same historical work, as a white one. Hopkins also suggests that framing black and white women according to this static, supposedly transhistorical domestic ideal does not allow them to realize their potential as historical actors. In other words, there may be other historical work the black and white daughters

FIGURE 14 Joseph Rodefer DeCamp, *The Blue Cup*, 1909. Oil on canvas, 49 7/8 x 41 1/8 inches. Museum of Fine Arts, Boston. Gift of Edwin S. Webster, Lawrence J. Webster, and Mrs. Mary S. Sampson in memory of their father, Frank G. Webster, 33.532. Photograph ©2015 Museum of Fine Arts, Boston.

of America could and should perform. Ellis's fantasy depends on Hagar as passionless and static—framed by the window like an object of sorts, or a mere image. That Hagar might represent the possibility of the black daughter as idealized virgin and proto-wife would have been significant given that black women were consistently aligned with sexual promiscuity. As Ann duCille has argued, "For early black women writers, literary passionlessness negated a negative: it endowed virtue to the historically virtueless."[77] *Hagar's Daughter* simultaneously depicts Hagar as virginal and static and allows readers to see her as desiring and mobile.

That Hagar "wash[ing] the heirlooms of colonial china and silver" suggests more than appropriate domestic duties and family feeling becomes apparent once we gain access to her thoughts. When she cares for the china, like the china hunters discussed in chapter 3, Hagar handles erotically charged, racialized objects that signify her own sexual "treasures" (33). The porcelain of paste-based china—regardless of whether it is decorated with blue, brown, or another color—is, at its foundation, white or cream, signifying an interrelated sexual and racial purity. Whether characterized by receptive curves or jointlike angles, china had been aligned with the white female body since the eighteenth century in British cultural discourse.[78] The silver Hagar washes, meanwhile, complicates the color-based racialization of the cared-for heirlooms. Silver, if tarnished, becomes dark gray, blackened even, and, when polished, a reflective gray, a color that brings together black and white. Hopkins aligns these objects with female reproduction, sexuality, and state power just as she aligns them with Hagar's complexly racial body: "Not the royal jewels of Victoria were ever more carefully guarded," she writes (33). These differently racialized but similarly sexualized treasures also elicit sensual feelings in Hagar as she cleans and caresses them. They were, we are told, "dried only by her dainty fingers," an activity during which she "was filled with a delicious excitement" and "felt a physical exhilaration" (33). Her washing of these treasures transforms the scene from one of Ellis observing and consuming the unwed woman as love object to one of an unmarried woman actively pleasuring herself. It is Ellis's own trespass onto Sargeant land that threatens to undo the pleasurable, multivalent potential of Hagar's self-caress, to reposition Hagar as a static, sexual treasure bound to a single racial identity and its inheritances: first adored white wife, later rejected black slave.

When we are introduced to Hagar, she occupies the in-between space on a supposedly progressive life trajectory: the time after her father's death and before marriage. But we soon glimpse her not as fixed by the aestheticizing frame of domesticity, but as mobile, a dreamer of intimately historicist dreams.[79] After we, alongside Ellis, look at Hagar through the window, we learn that Hagar fantasizes about a life very different from "the housekeeping and churchgoing which stretched before her," one that, again, references colonial women's history:

> She always lamented at this season of the year the lost privileges of the house of Sargeant, when their right of way led directly from the house to the shining waters of the bay. There was a path that led to the water still, but it was across the land of their neighbor Enson. Sometimes Hagar would trespass; would cross the parklike stretch of pasture . . . and sit on the edge of the remnant of a wharf, by which ran a small, rapid river, an arm of Chesapeake Bay. . . . There she would dream of life before the Revolution, and in these dreams participate in the joys of the colonial dames. (33)

By the water's edge, Hagar meditates on the affective alternatives felt by colonial women of the dominant class (upper-class dames rather than lower- and middle-class good wives) before the consolidation of an exclusionary U.S. nationhood, a consolidation often imagined by women writers to have its parallel in the social form (and social death) of marriage. And it is Hagar's washing of the china and silver, the pleasurable caressing of the material objects that belong to her wealthy, white family, that leads to the reader learning of her inner thoughts, which is to say, her personhood is expressed in the form of fantasy, access to which we gain by way of glimpsing her autoerotic fingering of heirlooms. She is, in this scene, a daughter who owns and dreams not a slave girl or wife-to-be. The text challenges readers, giving them first the male slaveholder's frame, making a queer reading secondary, necessarily contestatory, illegal even, in its trespass. Will we acknowledge Hagar's interior, historically embedded, potentially radical life, or will we imprison her in the frame of the windows of the colonial mansion as Enson goes on to do?[80]

Another young woman of *Hagar's Daughter*, Jewel, the affluent, seemingly white daughter of Senator Bowen, grapples with her identity in relation to the past by way of a colonial revival frame as well. Later in *Hagar's Daughter*, Hopkins returns us to the colonial mansion, this time Enson Hall, where Jewel finds herself imprisoned in an uncanny rescripting of "The Yellow Wall-Paper." Like the narrator of "The Yellow Wall-Paper," the newly wed Jewel ends up immobilized in a room in Enson Hall where "the windows were barred" and from which she "looked out upon extensive gardens" where "the once well-kept walks were overgrown with weeds" (214). Jewel also experiences an insomnia so pronounced that it leads to "her eyes wander[ing] aimlessly" "up and down the sides of the room," causing her to sometimes feel "that she was losing her mind" (214). Just when we learn that Jewel's Gothic immobilization may be threatening her sanity, Hopkins's narrator tells us, "presently, a painting fixed into the wall arrested her attention. It was the portrait of an impossible wood nymph, but so faded that its beauty—if it had once possessed any—was entirely gone" (214). Like the narrator of "The Yellow Wall-Paper," Jewel persistently examines her prison decór, a project that eventually leads her to discover an image of womanhood that must be destroyed for her to achieve freedom. In "The Yellow Wall-Paper," the image on the colonial wall is of white American women immobilized temporally, a reflection of the narrator's own location "behind" modernity; in *Hagar's Daughter* the image of white femininity is superhuman, an unattainable, aesthetic vision of woman persisting across time.[81] But this ideal is faint, so old that Jewel cannot discern whether it is ugly or beautiful, white or black.

Just as Gilman's narrator must rip and smooch off the wallpaper once she recognizes a kinship with her imprisoned white foremothers, so Jewel must penetrate the canvas of this art object: she cuts it and thus symbolically destroys the two-dimensional figuration of femininity that she herself is thought to embody, revealing in its place a transhistorical network of biracial ties. When Jewel passes over the threshold that she discovers behind the "portrait" and moves into the "dark passage" within the wall, she is moving into the black (and back) passages of American history, into the hitherto concealed habitations of her figurative and literal black ancestors who were enslaved within and moved behind the walls of colonial mansions (215). As Eugenia DeLamotte puts it, the "idealized nymph separates the white Jewel from her African American past."[82] Tuhkanen elaborates on this point, arguing that "the dark space [of the passage] opens for Jewel as a redemptive, liberatory conduit," but what Tuhkanen leaves unexamined is the fact that access to the back passage of the colonial mansion in and of itself does not suffice.[83] Jewel ultimately cannot escape on her own; she is trapped in the colonial mansion and must rely on Venus Johnson for her rescue.

What sets Hopkins's exploration of the colonial mansion apart from Gilman's is that Hopkins does imagine an escape for her heroine, a means by which the "lavishly supplied" white woman might progress into modernity and, in so doing, advance herself as a black woman in history (214). For Hopkins, however, the white (soon to learn she is biracial) Jewel cannot find her own way out of the colonial mansion and the intertwined ideologies of racial and gender discrimination that it has come to represent; the legacies passed down across generations to white women are not enough to undo the powerful mythologies of the Old South wielded by self-interested white men like General Benson. These myths, in addition to idealizing slavery, keep white women temporally arrested. Living in two rooms on the upper floor of the colonial mansion, Jewel experiences time as repetitive: the "monotonous interval of time passed" for Jewel "one day . . . the record of another" (214). Part of the problem of domesticity (taken to its Gothic extreme in Jewel's imprisonment) is its repetitive nature. Jewel's position as a prisoner, after all, is not that different from what Hagar's would have been if she had stayed married: "the calm routine, the housekeeping and churchgoing which stretched before her"; "Oh, for a break in the humdrum recurral of the same events day after day" (34). In *Hagar's Daughter*, the Southern colonial mansion after the failure of Reconstruction serves as a literal and symbolic tool used to turn back time and return the South to a state of sociopolitical tyranny against African Americans and women all under the guise of tradition.

In the complex love plot of *Hagar's Daughter*, it turns out to be not a man who saves the beautiful Jewel from her imprisonment in the plantation house of white supremacy but the adventurous, analytical, unmarried black daughter, Venus Johnson. Venus carries out the rescue by cross-dressing, taking on the fictive persona of Billy, the supposed grandson of the Civil War veteran Uncle William Henry, who is a federal agent in disguise. In the scene in which Venus-as-Billy approaches Enson Hall and discovers Jewel and Aunt Hetty within, Venus is represented by Hopkins's narrator as having undergone a complete transformation along gender lines. Rather than a costumed woman, Venus is referred to only as "Billy," "the lad," "the boy," and "he" (233–34). Her drag act, however, is more than the cross-dressing that would be used so often in detective fiction.[84] Venus uses her body to perform a multiplicity of spectral fusions and thus to lay claim to various legacies of heroism linked to the north and New England in particular, legacies that render her a "black daughter of the Revolution" trying to throw off the yoke of ongoing colonial tyranny.[85]

Venus's cross-dressing connects her to black military service in the Civil War, the history of black women's resistance to the colonizing force of chattel slavery, and Revolutionary-era New England history. Her heroism suggests that black women continue to make history as soldiers in the ongoing battle for equality and citizenship. The references to the Civil War and Venus's inheritance of the spirit of that conflict constitute the most explicit of the three historical allusions. In naming Venus's male persona Billy, Hopkins suggests that Venus is the offspring of Uncle William himself. That she is his grandson is part of the ruse, but the use of names has larger implications. It suggests that the young black woman of Hopkins's era may adoptively inherit the courage of black soldiers, the loyalty of Union patriots. This also comes across in the language of the passage wherein Uncle William transmits responsibility for the mission to Venus-as-Billy: he "waved a handkerchief three times, nailed it to the side of the hut and retired" (233). The use of "retired" here communicates that Uncle William went to bed, or at least back into the hut to keep an eye on the villainous Isaac, but it also opens up a space for Venus to demonstrate a new generation's militaristic activism as equal to and replacing traditions of black male military and federal civil service.

Cross-dressing would have also reminded Hopkins's readers about the many narratives of black women fleeing from slavery, whether in literature by writers such as William Wells Brown and Harriet Jacobs or in privately circulated stories of slavery and escapes from it. Like countless antebellum and Civil War–era characters—fictive and real— Venus battles to end the imperial tyranny of white supremacism that was ongoing in Hopkins's era. Hopkins thus portrays Venus as reenacting the radical transvestism of a host of ancestors, female and male, regardless of her literal genealogical ties to such figures.

Venus's cross-dressing is also radical in its alluding to a contested figure in U.S. history, one aligned with both African American women's history and white New England women's history in the late nineteenth century: Deborah Sampson. A popular cultural figure, Sampson (later, she married and took the last name Gannett) was a transvestite soldier in the Continental Army, a heroic woman claimed by both white and black nineteenth-century communities as a Revolutionary-era foremother. Sampson would have been known to Hopkins, who was an avid reader of history. The first mention of Sampson within black histories occurred in William C. Nell's groundbreaking book *Colored Patriots*, and Hopkins knew of Nell's work through her stepfather, William Hopkins, who was a member of Boston's co-ed Histrionic Club beginning in 1858, when Nell served as the club's manager.[86] Nell references Sampson in his history: "Lemuel Burr (grandson of Seymour), a resident of Boston, often speaks of their [Jeremy Jonah's and Seymour Burr's] reminiscences of Deborah Gannett."[87] Nell then replicates the Massachusetts court resolution of 1791 to award Sampson a soldier's pension. More strident in its claim to Sampson as black foremother was Mrs. Gertrude E. H. Bustill Mossell's volume of black women's history, *The Work of the Afro-American Woman* (1894). Mossell goes into greater detail about Sampson as an Afro-American woman: "It is also on record that Deborah Gannet [*sic*], who had enlisted during the Revolutionary war in Captain Wells' company, under the name of Robert Shurtliffe, serving from May, 1782, until October 23, 1783, discharged the duties of her office and at the same time, preserved inviolate the virtue of her sex, and was granted therefore a pension of thirty-four pounds."[88] Mossell's work, according to Lois Brown, "provided for Hopkins an invaluable model of scholarship and strategic historical assessment, and Hopkins enthusiastically applied it in her writings."[89] That Hopkins would allude to Sampson, even obliquely, was, like her proclamation in 1905 that she was a "black daughter of the revolution," a bold critique of the racist agendas of organizations such as the DAR. After all, one of the most active DAR chapters in the United States at the turn of the twentieth century was the Deborah Sampson Chapter chartered in 1897, which comprised many suburban towns surrounding Boston where Hopkins lived.

That black and white communities both included Sampson in their racial histories is not surprising given the lack of clarity about Sampson's own race. Daughter of an impoverished Massachusetts family, Sampson was placed into indentured service by her mother after her father abandoned them. At the age of seventeen, her indenture over, Sampson determined to travel and so, on the sly, bought material, men's shoes, and a man's hat with money she had earned from selling eggs in order to get herself a man's suit. Once outfitted as a man, Sampson left the farm on which she was working and hid in the woods, avoiding all townspeople. Not knowing where to go but unwilling to give up her "masquerade," she enlisted in the Continental Army under the wittily chosen name Robert Shurtliff. Sampson successfully served as a soldier, being specifically commended for leading a dangerous raid on a Tory house, and she developed a reputation as being a favorite with women. Sampson acted nobly and her sex remained undetected for about eleven months, until a doctor, examining her for brain fever, went to check her heart and discovered that she had breasts. In the end, Sampson was discharged honorably and eventually awarded a life pension that converted into a widow's pension for her widower, Benjamin Gannett.[90] According to one historian, Sampson's brother Nehemiah Sampson was listed in the records of the Continental Army as "molatto [*sic*]."[91]

Venus, during the time in which she acts as a sort of transvestite military hero, becomes myriad women of the past, those known and unknown to recorded history. Her actions are a layering and consolidation of many historical moments in one act of radical spectral fusion. It is this haunting, one staged outside of and in recognition of the colonial mansion as a prison and ideological structure reinforcing racist notions of womanhood that, of those staged in *Hagar's Daughter*, has the best chance of changing history. Venus's role in the rescue modifies history insofar as it provides a new narrative of the past, one that Hopkins represents as also capable of promoting intimacies between women. Once Venus, Jewel, and Aunt Hetty return to Washington, Mrs. Bowen (who unbeknownst to all but herself is Hagar) invites over all the women concerned with Jewel's rescue. Hopkins's narrator tells us that at this celebration: "Again and again Venus was called upon to repeat the story of her adventures" (240). The repetition of this history appears, moreover, to be performed at Mrs. Bowen's/Hagar's request. Hopkins writes, "'Yes, Mis' Bowen,' she [Venus] said for the twentieth time, 'when I peeked in through that window and saw Miss Jewel an' gran sitting there talkin',' I was plum crazy for a minute'" (240). As in Gilman's and Brown's fiction, insanity, the unbelievable, fantasies, and dreams are the result of the experience of becoming a ghost, if even for a short time.

BY WAY OF CONCLUSION, I want to return briefly to Elizabeth Bishop Perkins, the colonial revivalist and aspiring writer with whom I began this book. Perkins, I argue in the introduction, typifies how colonial revivalism and literary regionalism were intertwined at the turn into the twentieth century, and yet, though she knew Jewett, she was not a member of the regionalist group proper. Instead, she, like Gilman, Brown, and Hopkins, lived throughout the modernist age (she died in 1952 when about seventy-three), pursuing an intimate historicism all the while. When we look back at her unpublished work "'Almaqui'" in light of the spectral fusions of Gilman, Brown, and Hopkins, its plot of a young, unmarried woman who has erotic fantasies about an old house for years and realizes at the story's end that she is both an unmarried schoolteacher living in the modern city and a ghost from an unspecified

FIGURE 15 Elizabeth Bishop Perkins in colonial dress on porch, ca. 1930. Photograph. Courtesy of the Museums of Old York Collections, York, Maine.

past haunting a colonial mansion seems less surprising and more of the persistent regionalist-into-modernist moment. When read alongside Gilman's colonial fancy dressing at Mrs. Granger's colonial tea party, Lucy Ann's becoming of the beloved mother in Brown's "The Way of Peace," and Venus Johnson's radical historical act of transvestism in *Hagar's Daughter*, Perkins's own dressing up in colonial costume also seems less startling. Perkins's colonial dressing was sometimes public. In figure 12, for example, at her mother's colonial garden party fundraiser, she stands in the back, middle right alone with the big bonnet, an awkward part of a co-ed group of modern colonials whose bodies in formation seem to support rather than defy heteronormative notions of history. But more often Perkins's colonial dressing was private. In figure 1, for example, the young Perkins in brilliant white colonial costume boldly descending the stairs is in motion and getting on the ghost in an act of self-possession. Her spectral fusion takes center stage. Importantly, figure 1 is only one image of a handful remaining in the archive of Perkins wearing colonial garb. In fact, she practiced historical fancy dressing throughout adulthood (figure 15). Taken together, these photographs of Perkins's spectral fusions with colonial women map the unfolding of a life that embraced temporal dissonance across time well into the twentieth century.

I propose that the problem of orienting Perkins forms part of the wide-reaching dilemma created by existing accounts of literary history. In traditional narratives of the ultimately sequential emergence and passing of literary movements, American literary regionalism gave way to or died with the coming of naturalism and, soon after it, modernism. Yet did it pass entirely? Women throughout New England and the nation continued to restore colonial houses, collect china, and write "New England" stories long after 1915, variously calling on and reworking the intimate historicism of prior generations. And in one form or another, many people in the twenty-first century continue to value the experience of putting their bodies in the history-rich spaces that women of the past assembled, be it the Elizabeth Bishop Perkins house in York, which still receives visitors, or C. Alice Baker's Frary house in Deerfield, which does as well. Across the material spaces that constitute our archives, the New England regionalists and the many writers, artists, and collectors who have followed their precedent in one way or another have insisted on the role of textual and material recollections by women living in a queer modality as central to history.

Epilogue

The Intimate Historicism of Late Twentieth-Century Feminist Criticism

I have argued in this book that a range of late nineteenth-century women intellectuals—fiction writers, historians, visual artists, and collectors—were fascinated by questions of gender and history. These women rethought the figure of the modern unmarried daughter in distinctly historical terms while exploring the various desires engendered by her intimacies with people, objects, and spaces from the past. In this epilogue, I want to relate a series of recognitions regarding how the intimate historicism practiced by the New England regionalists resonates with the historicism pursued by the generation of feminist literary scholars whose work began in the 1970s and 1980s and who turned their attention to U.S. women writers. Attentive to history and seeking to collaboratively build new canons, intellectuals such as Judith Fetterley, Marjorie Pryse, and Hazel V. Carby not only recovered and wrote about nineteenth-century women as part of a larger project of presentist activism; they also read themselves across temporalities, variously yearning for and with their scholarly subjects. In proposing as much, my purpose is twofold: I hope to begin rethinking the late twentieth-century period in U.S. women's intellectual history and to outline the ways in which forms of historicism not only are compatible with but have productively grounded queer and feminist practices across time.

A COMMITMENT TO thinking historically and aligning feminist scholarship with histories of women's intellectual endeavor and resistance lay at the heart of much feminist work of the 1970s and 1980s, despite later accusations about feminist critics' failure to historicize.[1] The Combahee River Collective (CRC), a group of black feminists and lesbians that began meeting in the early 1970s, affirm early in their "Statement" *"we find our origins in the historical reality* of Afro-American women's continuous life-and-death struggle for survival and liberation."[2] The very name of this group, which included Barbara Smith, Akasha Gloria Hull (Gloria T. Hull), and Cheryl Clarke as members, marked a black feminist activism rooted in nineteenth-century radicalism: the Combahee River Raid was the military effort of 150 Union soldiers led by Harriet Tubman in which she directed Union ships away from Confederate torpedoes set along the river, enabling the rescue of about 800 fugitive slaves.[3] It is important to note that the CRC not only imagined itself as extending an activism based in history and thinking historically but also strove to use its members' "skills in writing, printing, and publishing" to "gather together a collection of Black feminist writing."[4] This effort eventually took the form of the anthology *All the Women Are White, All the Blacks Are Men, But Some of Us Are Brave*, edited by Smith and Hull along with Patricia Bell Scott, which collected new work in black women's studies, helping to constitute it as a field, while revising history in the form of the literary canon by bringing together and disseminating syllabi for black women's studies courses.[5]

Self-aware engagements of history also grounded the efforts of white feminists like Joanne Dobson, Karen Dandurand, and Martha Ackmann who decided, in 1983, to propose a "New Journal on Nineteenth-Century American Women Writers."[6] This venture became *Legacy*, first a newsletter and then (and still) a peer-reviewed journal dedicated to research on early U.S. women writers. From the creation of *Legacy* sprung the New England Nineteenth-Century American Women Writers study group, which also supported the work of early feminist literary critics and historians of nineteenth-century U.S. culture.[7] It is fair to call the extensive recovery work of this cohort of intellectuals—the proposing and overseeing of Rutgers's American Women Writers series, the editing of and scholarly writings on a wide range of women authors and women-authored texts—another form of recollection, one pursued with a clear sense of collective action in mind. These women, like the members of the CRC, had a sense of themselves as a feminist group, and they, too, gathered the primary source materials, the materials from earlier moments and their own moment, that helped recalibrate their own (and our) self-understanding as intellectual women. They also supported one another socially and intellectually and, through the Society for the Study of American Women

Writers, still offer various forms of mentoring and support to feminist scholars. As the historian Mary Kelley emphasizes in her contribution to a forum on *Legacy*'s past and future for the journal's twenty-fifth anniversary issue, "Our historicist emphasis is one of our strengths."[8]

Looking back over this feminist literary criticism, we see how women scholars foregrounded history and archival research in particular as central to their endeavors. The case of Sarah Orne Jewett serves as an object lesson in the distinct attention to history emphasized across feminist scholarship in literary studies. The article that brought Jewett and her work into view for feminist academics was Josephine Donovan's "The Unpublished Love Poems of Sarah Orne Jewett" (1976). Donovan's exploration of Jewett's desire for women as expressed in private poems turned readers' attention to the archive and to the need for more feminist historicist research. (That the article was published in a special issue of *Frontiers* dedicated to lesbian history meant it was doubly framed by queer history.) Donovan contests the dominant image of Jewett as a passionless "spinster," claiming it resulted from a faulty research method, a failure to thoroughly engage available archives: "These poems have been available to researchers for more than forty years: none has chosen to pay them any attention."[9] Along the same lines, Fetterley wrote in the introduction to her anthology, *Provisions: A Reader from Nineteenth-Century American Women* (1983), of the "cavalier approach to facts" taken by male critics "when the subject is mid-nineteenth-century women writers."[10] In other words, feminist critics felt that earlier and predominantly male scholars had made unfounded assumptions about women writers, had failed to think historically or employ historical records in their accounts.[11]

Importantly, it was not only in traditional archives such as Harvard's Houghton Library, which houses the Sarah Orne Jewett Papers, that these feminist literary scholars undertook their research. As with the New England regionalists whose desires for intimacy with the past were often felt in and through material spaces, the very labor of doing history in new, sometimes unexpected places gave way to complex meditations on the relationship between past and present. In early issues of *Legacy*, for example, we see the elaboration of what might count as research on women's writing. The inaugural number begins with an essay on the significance of diaries as a form of women's writing and includes a call for information about women writers' houses that results in four later articles advocating for the integration of on-site and material culture research. In one of these articles, Cheryl B. Torsney's "In Anticipation of the Fiftieth Anniversary of Woolson House," readers have manifested before them a Gothic scene primed for the arrival of Woolson's ghost, one that resonates with the specter-friendly stages found in the history writing of C. Alice Baker. Torsney writes of her visit that she found Woolson's papers

> locked behind an iron gate in a small alcove of the house. It was covered with dust and mostly hidden by cardboard book boxes, stacked four high. Tins of boric acid were scattered liberally around the area to prevent the cockroaches from eating the books, to little avail. Dust covered the glass cases that display, among other memorabilia, the now tarnished silver bell Woolson is said to have rung in the minutes preceding her suicide. . . . I found that much of the collection—including the manuscripts of Woolson's novels held by the house—was missing.[12]

In researching the papers of Alice Dunbar-Nelson, which were held privately by Pauline A. Young, one of Dunbar-Nelson's relatives, Akasha Gloria Hull, had to navigate a different sort of material and interpersonal archival terrain. Hull offers, first, a physical description of the collection: "There in the small cottage where she lived was a trove of precious information—manuscript boxes of letters, diaries, and journals; scrapbooks on tables; two unpublished novels and drafts of published works in file folders; clippings and pictures under beds and bookshelves."[13] And then there is the interpersonal dimension of Hull's work; from making herself "a bit of a nuisance" to access the collection to negotiating the inclusion of evidence of Dunbar-Nelson's romantic relationships with women, Hull pursued a research that involved becoming intimate with Young, a black woman of an older generation.[14] Out of the meeting place of an embodied feminist activism and historicist attention to an overlooked body of books, manuscripts, diaries, and old houses, feminist scholars began to develop an intimate historicism, one that implicitly theorized the relationship between scholars and their subjects, as I will soon explore.

It is important to note that the revival of interest in women's history and historical analyses was not exclusively the purview of those feminists writing nonfiction and doing academic research in literary studies. As was the case with New England regionalism in the late nineteenth century, the intimate historicism of 1970s and 1980s feminist criticism crossed disciplinary boundaries; it shaped and was shaped by work in creative writing, material culture, and the discipline of history. For instance, the earliest syllabus on "African-American Literature and Black Women Writers" collected in *But Some of Us Are Brave* was from Alice Walker's Fall 1972 course at the University of Massachusetts, Boston. Walker, as both a creative writer and an essayist, helped bring new attention to the question of what method to use to recognize women's intellectual endeavors and artistry throughout a historical record generated in an era in which "it was a punishable crime for a black person to read or write."[15] Walker answers this question by proposing that we look to the material productions of ordinary black women: the quilts, the songs, the gardens.[16]

The quilt, in fact, became exemplary in the 1980s as a material object that might tell history and be produced in the present as a way to reconnect with the past. By 1980 there was enough interest in quilts as a material art, a creative practice, and a legitimate topic for research that the journal of the American Quilt study group, *Uncoverings*, was founded. In the first volume, essays on rural quilting styles, contemporary quilts, African American women's quilts, and archiving quilts are set side by side, giving a sense of the richness of this area of inquiry. Yet, as Lorre M. Weidlich noted in 1994, that publication originally drew primarily from a nonscholarly group of writers; the academic community of quilt scholars were part of folklore studies and published their work in established academic venues.[17] As in the late nineteenth century, so-called amateurism was central to women's history making in this era. For many academic feminists, too, from the literary scholar Elaine Hedges's focus on quilting as an African American art form to the historian Laurel Thatcher Ulrich's use of a Mormon quilt from 1857 as the basis for her presidential address to the American Historical Association in 2010, analyzing, collecting, and creating quilts has proven a powerful way to engage personally with the history of gender and sexuality.[18]

Throughout the 1970s and 1980s feminist intellectual movement we see emerging the recognition that a range of sensations and queer desires might be engendered by history's ghosts.[19] Now-classic feminist works such as Maxine Hong Kingston's *The Woman Warrior: Memoirs of a Girlhood among Ghosts* (1976) and Toni Morrison's *Beloved* (1987) explore intimate historicism, variously linking the pain of the present and the past, making both central to contemporary women's creative acts. These feminist works push past Gothic literary convention in their insistence on the historical specificity of art's production. Morrison, for example, opens *Beloved* with an emphasis on history and women's labor—her own. She begins the foreword with "In 1983 I lost my job—or left it."[20] The freedom of being a writer full time, the conditions of her labor as a black woman, led her to meditate on the meanings of freedom for black women *in a present context*. "In the eighties," Morrison writes, "the debate was still roiling: equal pay, equal treatment, access to professions, schools . . . and choice without stigma. To marry or not. To have children or not. Inevitably these thoughts led me to the different history of black women in this country."[21] The apparition called forth by this act of historical analysis is Beloved, a black daughter, who, as Morrison was thinking of all this, "walked out of the water, climbed the rocks, and leaned against the gazebo. Nice hat."[22] Beloved's many desires mix up times, and Morrison talks to her—"Nice hat"—across and in time. This queer encounter involves, like so many others before it, an alternative form of women's generative labor. Morrison's intimate engagement of her body's feelings in history ("I began to feel an edginess") and her knowledge of history (the story of Margaret Garner) coalesce in a writerly practice that challenges time's linear unfolding and reorients gender identifications: Morrison writes, "I *husband* that moment on the pier, the deceptive river, the instant awareness of possibility, the loud heart kicking, the solitude, the danger. And the girl with the nice hat. Then the focus."[23]

The model of cross-temporal engagement rooted in analytical meditation and manifestation practiced and articulated by Morrison is only one of an unpredictable set of possibilities. I want to end things by recognizing the diversity of relationships between the scholar and her subjects imagined by feminists through intimate historicism. Judith Fetterley, reflecting on the relationship she developed with early nineteenth-century women writers in her anthology *Provisions*, recounts how turning her attention to overlooked women of the past resulted in a professional crisis. Fetterley theorizes that she became so overwhelmed by the "long history of denigration and contempt" for women writers that she discontinued the work at one point, unsure of the value of her labors.[24] She only took up the project again when she experienced the "major shock of recognition" that others were interested in learning about these women writers.[25] For Fetterley, her own intellectual productivity required a shift in approach, one she depicts as erotic and tied to gender: "I wanted my words [in *Provisions*] to serve as medium and instrument, not interference and armament.... I was no longer an antagonist, I was a lover.... The posture of a lover, especially when one is a woman loving women, is not the most conventional one for a critic to assume, nor is it particularly comfortable or safe."[26] The change Fetterley traces as being engendered by her editing of *Provisions* depends not on celebration (as we have been taught to expect of early feminists) but on fear: Fetterley emphasizes that she harbored "the fear that in choosing to work on the literature of nineteenth-century American women I had lost my voice and ... I had failed as an advocate for the writers and texts I had come to love."[27] Explicitly framed by her lesbianism, the intimate historicism of Fetterley's intellectual project, at least in her own account, enables the development of a new narrative, one that tracks how gendered positions might be troubled and changes the way histories unfold. In Fetterley's words, "in coming to know my past, I have begun to dream my future."[28]

Like Fetterley, Hull is one of many feminist critics from that generation who imagined herself in close relationship to queer women of the past. In "Researching Alice Dunbar-Nelson: A Personal and Literary Perspective," Hull recounts the experience of discovering and working through the large archive of Dunbar-Nelson's papers that she found by word of mouth. In addition to exploring the "charged and catalytic" relationship between herself and the owner of the papers, Hull characterizes the relationship between herself and the ghost of Dunbar-Nelson as one of complex self-recognition and peace.[29] "Alice herself has not deigned to trouble me," Hull concludes, "which I take as a sign that all is well between us."[30] Not being haunted is, here, a mode of relationship too, one Hull prefers to the non-responsiveness she perceives as characterizing another of her scholarly subjects, the Harlem Renaissance poet and playwright Angelina Weld Grimké. "Grimké lived a buried life," Hull asserts; "We research and resurrect—but have to struggle to find and connect with her, for she had no spirit left to send us."[31]

And, still, the ways of imagining intimacy with women of the past proliferate. Barbara Smith, in "Toward a Black Feminist Criticism," mourns what she portrays as the haunting *absence* of knowledge about black feminist and black lesbian experience: "I finally want to express how much easier both my waking and my sleeping hours would be if there were one book in existence that would tell me something specific about my life.... When such a book exists then each of us will not only know better how to live, but how to dream."³² And even when the ongoing relationship between scholar and scholarly subject is not explicitly reflected on, as is the case with Sandra Zagarell's writings on Jewett, intimate historicism may be at play. Working toward a reading of Jewett that explicates her writings in terms of gender, class, and race, Zagarell has come back to these stories again and again with an affectionate openness to new readings, new possibilities.³³ Such returns register the sense that the intellectual and affective work is not complete, perhaps never will be. It is in these returns that we catch sight of yet another way in which women writers of the past may resist intimacy or, as Heather Love puts it, how they may "turn their backs on us."³⁴

THIS EPILOGUE HAS been speculative in spirit. I have wanted to explore how the intimate historicism practiced by the New England regionalists has been taken up in our time. And I have been, all along, practicing a sort of intimate historicism, too, at least that is how I understand my method and purpose. Crucially, however, I do not see intimate historicism as a form of recovery work. On the one hand, recovery connotes possession—one recovers some*thing* lost—and on the other, it can also mean "the restoration of a person to a healthy or normal condition."³⁵ The historicism in which I am interested is neither about control nor about becoming well. I reject the notion that I (as a woman scholar) or the subjects whose cultural productions are taken up in this book (also women) were somehow lacking, unhealthy, or incomplete in advance of my work, though that notion has long been central to critiques of, and even responses authored by, feminist critics. And, to be honest, I do not feel personally restored or made healthy by my scholarly acts, nor do I imagine that my scholarly subjects are somehow finally made complete by my intellectual endeavors here. So although I am indebted to the recovery work of the 1970s and 1980s, and to notions of a recuperative, singular past of the sort that Fetterley asserts in *Provisions*, I want to reconceive the recovery model itself along the lines of what Love, building on the work of Michel Foucault as well as Louise Fradenburg and Carla Freccero, has called "a mode of historiography that recognizes the inevitability of a 'play of recognitions,' but that also sees these recognitions not as consoling but as shattering."³⁶ But even this does not quite capture it, for I cannot help but wonder why such recognitions must be either consoling or shattering. What seems of the utmost importance, instead, is not to name *in* *advance* the affects and effects of such recognitions but to hold open a space for their accompanying sensations and illuminations to be complicated, contradictory, and hitherto unimaginable. Recognition, in its emphasis on knowledge and on remaking knowledge, in its imagining as possible that we may engage in "the mental process of identifying something that has been known before," better captures my sense of intimate historicism's possibility.[37] Herein the energy of the scholarly subject's desire and resistance is kept in view, the uncertainty of the scholarly project foregrounded.

Such distinctions between recovery and recognition are important because they prompt us to think through the relationship among historicist, feminist, and queer methodologies. Almost as soon as feminist literary criticism gained some traction in the last quarter of the twentieth century, it began being critiqued, and those critiques often relied on assessments of approach. Feminist scholarship was deemed by many as not sufficiently objective and, in particular, as somehow inherently opposed to historicism. To borrow the language of one influential new historicist, Richard Brodhead, feminist literary criticism of the 1980s tended "to repeat the autonomy fantasies of the nineteenth-century ideology of separate spheres."[38] "This criticism has tended to forget," he continues, "that no culture is ever specified by its gender dimension alone: that in *the real historical world* there has been no 'women's culture' but plural and divergent women's cultures."[39] Brodhead refers here to white feminist critics writing about a white woman writer: Jewett. Though Brodhead makes a number of important and characteristic claims, I want to focus on his assertion that feminist critics have historical amnesia, that feminists' "rescue plan" for nineteenth-century women writers involves merely fantasizing and celebrating rather than analyzing what he calls "*the real historical world*," as if those various acts are inherently incompatible with one another.[40] Brodhead assumes here a particular relationship between feminist critics and their scholarly subjects: one of objectification and an implicit feminization of the woman writer from the past as a damsel in distress. Brodhead denies feminist criticism's legitimacy by delimiting it as imagined, as not grounded in the "real," and as divorced from historicism, assertions that coalesce. The problem of feminist method as posed by scholars like Brodhead has long shaped subsequent work in American literary regionalist studies and American literature more generally. Historicism, for some, like Jennifer Fleissner, has become aligned with classification and objectification: "The moment they [women, persons of color, and other members of historically oppressed groups] display characteristics not conforming to absolute rationality and dignity, they seem inexorably reduced to pure objects, sheer victims of determining forces beyond their individual control."[41] Fleissner gestures toward an alternative approach when she suggests a practice whereby texts are acknowledged as living a practice, which would, in her words, allow "a place in which we find that, if we do reencounter ourselves or what matters to us, it is precisely as that which we do not already know."[42] I argue in this book that many women intellectuals have been desiring and enacting these reencounters variously and passionately all along.

Intimate historicism practiced by women across generations has been a rich enterprise variously felt as labor, fear, desire, ecstasy, and kinship, and it has been dismissed as unprofessional, incomplete, dominated by emotion, and unhistorical across the same span of time. It has dovetailed with and helped do the work of consolidating elite and racist notions of belonging, and it has been a practice by way of which queer and feminist desires and communities have come into being. It has a longer history than we may have realized, and it is ours to continue to collectively recognize and recollect—to critique, reassemble, and remember—by way of our own scholarly practices. We would do well not to cede history making as a central aspect of our endeavor to keep on imagining what has been and what might be.

Notes

ABBREVIATIONS

CAB   The C. Alice Baker Papers, Pocumtuck Valley Memorial Association Library

EBP   The Elizabeth Bishop Perkins Collection, Museums of Old York

ELC   The Emma Lewis Coleman Papers, Pocumtuck Valley Memorial Association Library

SML   The Susan Minot Lane Papers, Pocumtuck Valley Memorial Association Library

SOJC   The Sarah Orne Jewett Collection, Clifton Waller Barrett Library, University of Virginia

INTRODUCTION

1. Antebellum fiction such as Nathaniel Hawthorne's *The Scarlet Letter*, Catharine Maria Sedgwick's *Hope Leslie*, and Lydia Maria Child's *Hobomok* were all set in colonial times and coincided with the emergence of a handful of early nineteenth-century antique collectors determined to preserve the past by way of material culture, among them the Reverend William Bentley, Cummings Davis, Ben Perley Poore, and Anne Allen Ives. See Stillinger, *The Antiquers*, xii, 17, 22, 27; Michie, "'Bought ... of nobody.'"

2. On historical works set in colonial and Revolutionary times, see Seaton, "A Pedigree for a New Century," 278–79. On Wallace Nutting, see Denenberg, *Wallace Nutting*. For a thorough examination of SPNEA, especially the gender dynamics of its work, see Lindgren, *Preserving Historic New England*. The rise of the antique industry is treated in Stillinger and Fales, introduction.

3. Nissenbaum, "New England as Region," 46.

4. Conforti, *Imagining New England*, 205.

5. New England regionalism was distinct in that it was dominated by women, whereas literary regionalism in the South, West, and Midwest involved the work of many male authors, Charles Chesnutt, Bret Harte, Mark Twain, Edward Eggleston, and Hamlin Garland among them. Fetterley and Pryse, in *Writing Out of Place*, define regionalism as a U.S. women's literary tradition, one that has distinct "ideological underpinnings" (4). Importantly, however, New England writers dominate in Fetterley and Pryse's work: five out of the fourteen writers featured in their *American Women Regionalists* are New Englanders (Harriet Beecher Stowe, Rose Terry Cooke,

Mary Wilkins Freeman, Sarah Orne Jewett, and Celia Thaxter). Ammons and Rohy, meanwhile, offer a much broader definition of literary regionalism in *American Local Color Writing*. All these scholars seek to move away from what they see as the dominance of New England in accounts of literary history such as Brooks's *New England*, Westbrook's *Acres of Flint*, and Donovan's early and influential feminist study *New England Local Color Literature*. I purposefully return to New England as a distinct region because I am interested in the ongoing sectionalism of late nineteenth-century U.S. culture as well as in women-dominated cultural movements.

6. James, *The Bostonians*, 341.

7. Examples of articles offering advice on being and keeping summer boarders include Burrell, "Keeping Summer Boarders with Success"; Kate Upson Clark, "Keeping City Boarders"; Herrick, "Country Boarding"; and Hooker, "On Boarders and Boarding."

8. Following Jagose, I recognize queer as an open, contested adjective, just as I recognize that it is linked to gay, lesbian, and transgendered subjects. While I appreciate Rohy's use of the word "lesbian" to refer "to texts and figures before the 1880s [the decade when the concept of the lesbian entered medical discourse] ... as a strategic anachronism that can illuminate the continuities between nineteenth-century views of female deviance and twentieth-century notions of lesbian identity," I prefer "queer" because of its capaciousness, its ability to designate a range of desires, including ones that may not be part of twentieth-century notions of lesbian identity (Rohy, *Impossible Women*, 9).

9. Reverend J. Newton Perkins, Elizabeth's father and Mary's husband, rarely set foot in York, nor was his name mentioned in the documents related to the Perkins house. For all intents and purposes, theirs was an all-female household. Johnson, "Elizabeth Perkins House," 70.

10. Kevin D. Murphy, "The Politics of Preservation," 196; Nash, "Elizabeth Bishop Perkins," 189. Mary Sowles Perkins was encouraged to take on the project by William Dean Howells, a tourist-lover of York. For more on York as an elite vacation destination, see Dona Brown, *Inventing New England*, chapter 6.

11. Johnson, "Elizabeth Perkins House," 67.

12. In restoring the Perkins house, the Perkins women sought to create a usable contemporary version of the colonial past, one that served their modern needs. But that temporally messy, so-called amateur approach to colonial revivalism was castigated by men working in the emerging professions of architectural restoration and preservation. For example, wanting her York house to become a museum, Perkins contacted Appleton in 1924 to gauge SPNEA's interest. "Appleton," however, "informed her that in his opinion the original condition of the house had been too far altered ... but suggested that the house might be better preserved if it were let out to private organizations or 'men of letters' as a retreat or center for scholarship" (Johnson, "Elizabeth Perkins House," 68).

13. Perkins, "History of the Piscataqua Garden Club," 1, Piscataqua Garden Club Collection, Museums of Old York. The Piscataqua Garden Club included among its members Sarah Orne Jewett, Mrs. John Mead Howells (Howells's daughter-in-law), and Mrs. Edith Wendell, the wife of the Harvard literature professor Barrett

Wendell, demonstrating the cross-fertilization of tourism, colonial revivalism, and literary culture (Perkins, "History," 4, 10, 9).

14. Giffen, "Old York," 91.

15. "Piscataqua Garden Club Petition," Piscataqua Garden Club Collection, Museums of Old York.

16. Wood, *The New England Village*, 89. For more on the white village ideal in antebellum U.S. culture, see Conforti, *Imagining New England*, 125–30.

17. Kevin D. Murphy, "'Secure from All Intrusion,'" 190.

18. Ibid., 196; Johnson, "Elizabeth Perkins House," 67.

19. Kevin D. Murphy, "'Secure from All Intrusion,'" 198.

20. Perkins was very interested in performance. She "produced numerous plays, pageants, and films about old York," and one of her few published imaginative works is a short play starring an unmarried aspiring actress (Kevin D. Murphy, "'Secure from All Intrusion,'" 203).

21. Perkins, "The Codfish Ghost," Part IV, 2, 4, EBP.

22. Ibid., Part IV, 4, 5, EBP.

23. Perkins, "'Almaqui' The House in the Woods," 1, EBP, hereafter cited parenthetically in text by page number.

24. The kinship between New England literary regionalism and the colonial revival has gone largely unexplored. A few historians have suggested such connections. Nissenbaum, for instance, links New England's postbellum pastoralization in literature to the colonial revival. In a similar vein, Conforti, Wood, Truettner, and Stein all mention regionalist literary productions, particularly those of Harriet Beecher Stowe and Jewett, as exemplifying the nostalgic, romantic representations of old New England found in late nineteenth-century culture. In her account of the rise of domestic tourism, Dona Brown goes further to differentiate between Jewett's, Cooke's, and Edith Wharton's regionalist visions and that of dominant culture. In Brown's telling, these writers' "meticulously crafted observations were only a trickle in a flood of sentimental memoirs and tales of childhood memorializing the nostalgic features of the New England farm" (Brown, *Inventing New England*, 151). Brown implies that these women writers representing New England were up to something different than writers whose works constituted the purely nostalgic cultural mainstream.

Literary critics' attention to colonial revivalism as it relates to literary regionalism has been cursory at best. Zagarell, Ammons, and Bill Brown have noticed the "colonial exotica," as Ammons calls it ("Material Culture," 93), scattered across Jewett's *The Country of the Pointed Firs*, and Brown posits the post-Centennial era's interest in objects as part of the generalized context within which Jewett wrote. (Zagarell, "Troubling Regionalism," 641; Brown, *A Sense of Things*, 109–11).

25. In treating New England as a distinct section, I follow the lead of scholars such as Nissenbaum, Conforti, Wood, Murphy, Dona Brown, and the art historians William Truettner and Roger Stein working in the interdisciplinary field of New England studies.

26. For more on Boston marriages, see Faderman, *Surpassing the Love of Men*, 190–203; Smith-Rosenberg, *Disorderly Conduct*; McCullough, *Regions of Identity*,

chapters 1 and 2; and Cleves, *Charity and Sylvia*. For a more broadly conceived exploration of the range of forms same-sex eroticism between women took in the nineteenth century, see Vicinus, *Intimate Friends*; Diggs, "Romantic Friends or a 'Different Race of Creatures?'"; Lisa Moore, *Dangerous Intimacies*.

27. Roman, "A Closer Look," 127. See also Faderman, *Surpassing the Love of Men*, 190-203.

28. Fisken, "Within the Limits of Alice Brown's 'Dooryards,'" 22. See also "Miss Brown and Miss Guiney"; Blanchard, *Sarah Orne Jewett*, 221-22.

29. Earle was married to Henry Earle, a stockbroker, in 1873. They had four children, and Earle balanced her family life with an active career as a clubwoman and writer (Susan Reynolds Williams, *Alice Morse Earle*, 33). Slosson married a lawyer, Edward Slosson, in 1867 and was widowed in 1871. Her biographer, Edward Ifkovic, asserts that it was William Cowper Prime, the widower of Slosson's sister, who most influenced her life. Slosson and Prime traveled together and lived together at Prime's Gale Cottage in the White Mountains as well as in his New York home (Ifkovic, *Annie Trumbull Slosson*, 126, 132, 134-35).

30. Fetterley and Pryse, *American Women Regionalists*, 92.

31. Koppelman, "About 'Two Friends,'" 43; Reichardt, *A Web of Relationship*, 105.

32. Fetterley and Pryse, *American Women Regionalists*, 34.

33. Coviello, *Tomorrow's Parties*, 4.

34. Sedimented in this legacy of dissent we may have what Coviello more generally calls the "freedom" of early erotic forms (*Tomorrow's Parties*, 7).

35. Cather, preface, 9. Hereafter I refer to *The Country of the Pointed Firs* as *Pointed Firs*.

36. When Cather and Jewett met, Cather was on the cusp of deciding whether or not to begin living with her friend and colleague Edith Lewis. Blanchard, *Sarah Orne Jewett*, 357.

37. See Vicinus, *Independent Women*; Doan, introduction; Johns, "Some Reflections on the Spinster"; and Kent, *Making Girls into Women*.

38. I build here on the work of Kent who, in her reading of Stowe's *Oldtown Folks*, emphasizes the white spinster as a figure whose existence threatened the gender binary and foregrounded problems of production.

39. Foote, *Regional Fictions*, 15. Works of criticism wherein Jewett is representative of New England regionalism or women regionalists include Brodhead, *Cultures of Letters*; Pryse, "Sex, Class, and 'Category Crisis'"; McCullough, *Regions of Identity*; Lutz, *Cosmopolitan Vistas*; Joseph, *American Literary Regionalism in a Global Age*; and Fleissner, "Is Feminism a Historicism?" The one notable exception is Fetterley and Pryse, *Writing Out of Place*. In queer literary studies, meanwhile, Jewett has consistently played a central role; Love's *Feeling Backward*, Coviello's *Tomorrow's Parties*, and Rohy's *Anachronism and Its Others* are examples of books that dedicate a chapter to Jewett and Cather or Jewett herself.

40. My categorization of these women is necessarily misleading because many of them worked across forms and practices. There are, moreover, other regionalists whom I might have included in this study: the colonial home-renovating mother-daughter

team Emily and Elise Tyson; the photographer sisters Frances and Mary Allen; and the writer Celia Thaxter among them.

41. Many of the New England regionalists came to know one another through Mary Louise Booth and Harriet Prescott Spofford. Spofford included Fields, Jewett, and Cooke in her *Little Book of Friends*, itself a testimony to a community of artistic women in New England.

42. Freeman and Jewett exchanged letters in 1889 and, by the late 1899s, had met in person in what Freeman refers to as "my little reunions with you" (Freeman to Jewett, 16 March 1899, 223). Jewett, Freeman implies in an early letter, praised Freeman's mystical "Gentle Ghost," and Freeman, in turn, wrote to Jewett, "I never wrote any story equal to your 'White Heron.' I dont [*sic*] think I ever read a short story, unless I except Tolstoi's 'Two Deaths,' that so appealed to me. I would not have given up that bird any more than you would, if he had come first" (Freeman to Jewett, 12 August 1889, 97). A related critique of men surfaces in a letter from later that year: "I think your old Sea Captain in Harper's, is beautiful. You wrote him just right, I believe I like that kind of a man" (Freeman to Jewett, 10 December 1889, 99).

43. Blanchard, *Sarah Orne Jewett*, 221.

44. Lane mentions writing to Jewett in a letter to Baker (SML), and there are multiple letters from Jewett to Coleman and Baker in SOJC.

45. According to Hufnagel, all four women collaborated on this project ("Emma Lewis Coleman," 152). *"A Noble and Dignified Stream,"* the volume in which Hufnagel's research appears, represents this particular illustrated edition of *Deephaven* as published, but that appears not to have been the case (152, 181). The only extant copy is not a published novel but an unpublished version in the Sarah Orne Jewett Compositions and Other Papers, Houghton Library, Harvard University.

46. Kevin D. Murphy argues that the Tysons, through their renovation of Hamilton house, created a queer, heterotopic space like Perkins house. Murphy, "'Secure from All Intrusion.'" For more on Hamilton house, see Nylander, "Hamilton House."

47. Freeman to Coleman, 7 February 1891, 109.

48. Freeman to Baker, 2 March 1892, 136.

49. Freeman to Earle, 8 October 1894, 167.

50. Berlant, introduction, 3.

51. *Oxford English Dictionary Online*, s.v. "intimate," http://www.oed.com/view/Entry/98506, November 28, 2012.

52. I do not use the term "historiography" in the specific disciplinary sense, but in the broad sense suggested by its etymology: the writing of history. I want to clarify my use of the term "historicism" as well. I am not thinking here of historicism as the scientific notion of objective history making that emerged in the late nineteenth century, the later iterations of which have been vigorously critiqued by scholars, most famously Walter Benjamin in "Theses on the Philosophy of History." I am interested in emphasizing a less-definitive form of historicism, an interest in the past that might complicate or defy assumptions about the progressive march of history.

53. Taylor, *The Archive and the Repertoire*, 20.

54. Ibid.

55. In her diary entry for November 11, 1890, Gilman wrote, "Go to Colonial teaparty as Madame de Remusat in the evening—at Mrs. Dexters" (Gilman, *The Diaries*, 424).

56. For a rethinking of the archive and repertoire in terms of material culture and its relation to cultural texts, see Bernstein, *Racial Innocence*.

57. Fradenburg and Freccero, preface, viii; Freeman, *Time Binds*, 96.

58. Luciano, *Arranging Grief*, 3.

59. Brodhead, *Cultures of Letters*, 144; emphasis mine.

60. Gillman, "Regionalism and Nationalism in Jewett's *Country of the Pointed Firs*"; McCullough, *Regions of Identity*, 9; Zagarell, "Crosscurrents," 355; Foote, *Regional Fictions*, 4; Fleissner, *Women, Compulsion, Modernity*.

61. Nealon, *Foundlings*, 4; Jagose, *Inconsequence*; Freeman, *Time Binds*; Luciano, *Arranging Grief*, 9; Luciano, "Geological Fantasies," 287. Work on U.S. culture has also been in productive dialogue with that focused on the early modern period, from which my thinking has benefited, including Dinshaw, *Getting Medieval*; Traub, *The Renaissance of Lesbianism in Early Modern England*; Freccero, *Queer/Early/Modern*; Goldberg and Menon, "Queering History"; and Traub, "The New Unhistoricism in Queer Studies."

62. Foote, *Regional Fictions*, 5.

63. The role of young, white New England men in imperial ventures is everywhere apparent across New England regionalist fiction. Stowe's late novel *Pink and White Tyranny* has its ideal New England man, Walter Syndenham, seeking his fortune in far-away California; in Freeman's "A New England Nun," Louisa Ellis's unmarried artistry is made possible by Joe Daggett's remaining fourteen years in Australia to work; Alice Brown's story "A Last Assembling," from *Tiverton Tales*, is also based on its protagonist, Dilly Joyce, having gotten engaged to a man who spends years making his fortune in what was then the "west": Chicago. For a close consideration of how ideas about empire inflected U.S. literature and culture in the nineteenth century, see Kaplan, *The Anarchy of Empire in the Making of U.S. Culture*.

64. Kaplan, "Violent Belongings," 5.

65. With firmly rooted black communities, growing urban immigrant neighborhoods, and communities of native peoples, New England was by no stretch of the imagination an enclave of whites in the late nineteenth century. Much nineteenth-century literature, however, seems to reflect the assessment of one *Atlantic Monthly* contributor that in outlying parts of northern New England, "good stock" predominated and there was "not an Irishman, nor a German, nor an Italian, nor a negro [*sic*]" (Morgan, "The Problems of Rural New England," 583). For more on African Americans in New England in the nineteenth century, see Gatewood, *Aristocrats of Color*; Oliver and Horton, *Black Bostonians*; Lee, *Black Bangor*; and Guyette, *Discovering Black Vermont*.

This period also saw a continued influx of immigrants to New England. A town like Lawrence, Massachusetts, which Boston merchants built in 1845 and in which they "planted elms, laid out broad streets, and set aside many acres for a common and parks," all features of the white village ideal, could not retain the identity of a rural-capitalist oasis given the increased dependence on immigrant labor (Cole, *Immigrant City*, 19–20). Between 1848 and 1880, Lawrence went from having 3,750 American-born and 2,100 Irish residents to having the foreign born, including Irish, French Canadians, British, and German immigrants, constitute 74 percent of its population (Cole, *Immigrant City*, 24, 59). Other factory towns with colonial histories, such as Holyoke and Fall River, Massachusetts, "were already half foreign-born" by 1875 (Frisch, *Town into City*, 124).

66. Onuf, "Federalism, Republicanism, and the Origins of American Sectionalism," 25.

67. Conforti, *Imagining New England*.

68. Dickinson, *The Complete Poems*, Poem 285, lines 15–17.

69. These notions of freedom as an exclusively white inheritance were significantly complicated and challenged by Pauline Elizabeth Hopkins's claim that dissent was the legacy of "black daughters of the Revolution" (Hopkins, "Address," 355). I take this up in detail in chapter 4.

70. Brodhead, *Cultures of Letters*, 145–49.

71. Lutz, *Cosmopolitan Vistas*, 3.

72. In this, their worldview looks much more like what Edward Larkin defines as Crèvecœur's "cosmopolitan vision": "local identities engaging in free exchange across space and time" (Larkin, "The Cosmopolitan Revolution," 68).

73. Bonnie G. Smith in *The Gender of History* explores how Germaine de Staël theorized women's citizenship by way of a history that "espoused an erotic hermeneutic . . . [and] also positioned itself in a geographic and national extraterritoriality unusual for historical writing in the modern period" (31). For how Mary Wollstonecraft, Margaret Fuller, Abigail Adams, Lydia Maria Child, and others grappled with similar questions, see Smith as well as Teresa Anne Murphy, *Citizenship and the Origins of Women's History*.

74. Baker, *True Stories*; Jewett, *Pointed Firs*, 64.

75. Radical white women interested in alternative forms of affiliation and women's rights, such as Charlotte Perkins Gilman and Victoria Woodhull before her, were often also advocates of eugenics. On Gilman, see Weinbaum, *Wayward Reproductions*, especially chapter 2; Seitler, "Unnatural Selection." For a preliminary reassessment of Woodhull, see Carpenter, introduction.

76. Fetterley and Pryse, *Writing Out of Place*, 28, 28–29.

77. Boeckmann, *A Question of Character*, 4.

78. Howells, "The Southern States in Recent American Literature," 281.

79. Howells, "Editor's Study," 640. Howells was from Illinois but embraced the idea of New England as the cultural and personal "home" of people from the Midwest and the West. Howells, in fact, thought of New England as having disseminated its values across the nation. As he wrote in "Literary Boston Thirty Years Ago": "There was in those days very little good writing done beyond the borders of New England. . . . If the case is now different . . . still I do not think the South and West have yet trimmed the balance; and though perhaps the new writers now more

commonly appear in those quarters, I should not be so very sure that they are not still characterized by New England ideals and examples" (866–67).

80. Baker, *True Stories*, 208; Alice Brown, *Tiverton Tales*, 153; Jewett, *The Story of the Normans*, 29.

81. Kammen, *Mystic Chords of Memory*, 12.

82. Puar, *Terrorist Assemblages*, xii.

83. Ibid.

84. Roosevelt, "The Parasite Woman," 56.

85. Adams, *The Education of Henry Adams*, 447.

86. One notion about old maids, and those from New England in particular, was that they had, as a population, served consistently as supplement mother figures within heteronormative families. As one 1890 article insisted, many a New England family depended on the labor and loving dedication of a spinster aunt. This source quotes one "single woman" asserting "reverently, 'The children are my greatest comfort; they are all to me: father, mother, husband, and lover'" (Woods, "The Old Maid Mothers of New England").

87. Puar, *Terrorist Assemblages*, 4.

88. Ibid., xii.

89. Ibid., 35.

90. Benjamin, "Theses," 255.

91. Baker, *True Stories*, 222.

92. Sedgwick, "Paranoid Reading," 27.

CHAPTER 1

1. Hereafter referred to by the short title *True Stories* and cited parenthetically in text by page number.

2. Sheldon, *Tribute to C. Alice Baker*, 6. In the words of Jennie Arms Sheldon, Baker's friend and cousin-in-law, Lane and Baker "came together, and it was not long before the union was complete, as each chose the other for a life companion" (*Tribute*, 6). Baker and Lane themselves used the language of romantic love in their correspondence. In one letter, Lane writes of having left Baker to sail out: "I did not feel as if I could endure life longer and the sensation can only be counterbalanced by the delight of meeting. . . . I shall never never forget, my darling, seeing you cover your face with your hand as we pushed off, then, to see you rally and wave to my going. God bless you my own" (To C. Alice Baker, 19 May 1886, SML). And in a letter during that same trip from Lane to Baker, sentences regarding Baker's letters are crossed out, and only this portion of the letter remains legible: "They fill me with pain and anxiety about you. You suffer so because I do not write. . . . I feel I have done very wrong to try and see so much and that I have not given time enough to my writing. [Scribbling out of sections ends.] I think of you every moment and at every thing [*sic*] I see" (To C. Alice Baker, 20 June 1886, SML).

3. Sheldon, *Tribute to C. Alice Baker*, 6, 9.

4. Hufnagel, "Emma Lewis Coleman," 154.

5. Hereafter referred to by the short title *New England Captives*.

6. Coleman, "Concerning Frary House," 34, 40, ELC.

7. See the introduction to the present volume for a full discussion of intimate historicism.

8. Baker to an unnamed cousin, 22 July 1895, CAB. Baker dates the attack on Deerfield as taking place in 1703. She is using the date that, according to Haefeli and Sweeney, was based on the Julian calendar used by the English as opposed to the date based on the Gregorian calendar used by the French. Because the Julian calendar had the new year beginning on March 25 rather than January 1, the English often wrote dates between January 1 and March 25 as "1703/04." Baker follows the English dating, but I follow contemporary historians in using the Gregorian calendar date of 1704 (*Captors and Captives*, 295).

9. This photograph is not necessarily the exact one sent to Baker's cousin. It is, however, very possible that it is the same image, for this is the one photo of Baker's bedroom taken by Coleman to be found in the archive. It is in "Concerning Frary House," a typescript in ELC which has multiple photographs taped onto its pages.

10. Carter, "Picturing Rooms," 252.

11. Barthes, *Camera Lucida*, 31.

12. In addition to chapters on the colonial women and girls taken captive, *True Stories* includes chapters on key male figures who shaped the captives' experiences (John Sheldon, Father Muriel, Father Silver, and Hertel Rouville), the attack on Deerfield, Joseph-Octave Plessis, and Baker's own research ventures to Canada.

13. Haefeli and Sweeney, *Captors and Captives*, 1.

14. Sheldon, *Tribute to C. Alice Baker*, 10. Baker began her association with the Cambridge Women's Suffrage Association in 1874. Baker and Lane "believed that a woman had the sacred right to do whatever she was fitted by birth and training to do thoroughly and well" (Sheldon, *Tribute to C. Alice Baker*, 7).

15. Wheelwright's narrative is particularly important as a story of women's increased authority and public work as a result of captivity. As Emily Clark explains, "The spiritual underpinnings of the Ursuline educational project lay in a reimagining of the place of Mary in the celestial hierarchy and an expansion of the basis and scope of women's authority" (*Masterless Mistresses*, 2).

16. Haefeli and Sweeney, *Captors and Captives*, 285. Baker offers her readers a translation of the record of the marriage of Elizabeth Twatogwach and Ignace Shonatakakwani: "This 29th July 1715. I have married Ignace Shoentak8anni and Elizabeth T8atog8ach, both English, who wish to remain with the Christian Indians, not only renouncing their nation, but even wishing to live *en sauvages*, Ignace aged about twenty-three or twenty-four years,—Elizabeth about fifteen. Both were taken at Dierfile about thirteen years ago. [Signed] M. Quéré, prêtre S. S." (*True Stories*, 247).

Twatogwach was initially renamed Kanawkwa which, in Mohawk, "came to signify domestic animal as well as captive and slave" (Haefeli and Sweeney, *Captors and Captives*, 152). Baker spells Twatogwach, "T8atog8ach" and Shonatakakwani, "Shoentak8anni." Throughout this chapter, I have elected to call these captives by their Mohawk names and rely on the spellings used by modern scholars. For more on captives' naming and the stakes of using particular versions in our scholarship, see Newman, "Fulfilling the Name."

17. Kanenstenhawi was the daughter of Reverend John Williams, author of the eighteenth-century best-selling captivity narrative, *The Redeemed Captive*. Nineteenth-century publications on Kanenstenhawi include Champney, *Great-Grandmother's Girls in New France*, and Johnson, *An Unredeemed Captive*. For more recent examinations of Kanenstenhawi, see Demos, *The Redeemed Captive*, and Haefeli and Sweeney, *Captors and Captives*, 152–53, 222–23.

18. Castiglia, *Bound and Determined*, 6.

19. Ibid., 13.

20. Ibid.

21. Baym, *American Women Writers and the Work of History*. See Hawthorne, *The House of the Seven Gables, Tales of the Province House*, and *Grandfather's Chair*.

22. Bonnie G. Smith, *The Gender of History*, 26–27.

23. Parkman, *La Salle*, viii. Roosevelt's dedication in *The Winning of the West* reads: "This book is dedicated, with his permission, to Francis Parkman, to whom Americans who feel a pride in the pioneer history of their country are so greatly indebted" (1).

24. See Parkman, "The Woman Question" and "The Woman Question Again."

25. Parkman, *A Half-Century of Conflict*, 90.

26. Eventually, the New York Historical Society offered Baker membership. The MHS, however, never yielded. Baker's experience was not unique. For more on how gender biases inflected the professionalization of history, see Lindgren, *Preserving Historic New England*.

27. Sheldon to the Officers of the New York Historical Society, 4 November 1878. CAB.

28. Novick, *That Noble Dream*, 56.

29. Quoted ibid.

30. Ibid.

31. Quoted ibid.

32. Ibid., 44–46; on gender, the amateur, and history writing, see Bonnie G. Smith, *The Gender of History*, chapter 2.

33. This moment from *True Stories* echoes the unnamed narrator's visiting of Joanna Todd's grave in Sarah Orne Jewett's novel *Pointed Firs*. Like Baker's, Jewett's version of women's history and solitude is wrapped up with imperialism, captivity, conventual life, forms of affiliation, and empathy as part of a theory of white exceptionalism.

34. Dickinson, *The Complete Poems*, Poem 670, lines 1–4.

35. Baker's notion of an intellectual project driven by perpetual haunting looks a lot like Carla Freccero's notion of "queer spectrality," wherein "spectrality invokes a collectivity of unknown or known, 'uncanny' (both familiar and yet not) strangers who arrive to frequent us" ("Queer Spectrality," 196).

36. Sheldon, *Tribute to C. Alice Baker*, 9.

37. "Miss Baker's Papers," Pocumtuck Valley Historical Association Papers, Pocumtuck Valley Memorial Association Library.

38. Baker imagined her written work as being performed in the future, too. In the chapter from *True Stories* on Esther Wheelwright, she writes, "My fondest ambition in writing this story is that in some hour of recreation, it may be read to the novices by the Mother Assistant" (68).

39. Coleman, "Concerning Frary House," 59, ELC. Baker hosted many community events at Frary house, including the Bizarre Bazaar (a hospital benefit) in 1908 and the Wednesday Mornings series wherein women would gather and read from their fiction or historical research (Coleman, "Concerning Frary House," 64, 65, ELC). According to Miller and Lanning, Baker hoped to create "a sort of common parlor for the town [of Deerfield]" and used Frary house to do just that ("'Common Parlors,'" 441).

40. Hufnagel, "Emma Lewis Coleman," 152.

41. For a reading of race and reproduction in Barthes, see Shawn Michelle Smith, *At the Edge of Sight*, chapter 1.

42. Shawn Michelle Smith, *At the Edge of Sight*, 16.

43. Taylor, *The Archive and the Repertoire*, 20.

44. Ibid., 28.

45. Ibid.

46. Quoted in Bonnie G. Smith, *The Gender of History*, 116, 119.

47. Quoted ibid., 119, 120.

48. Goode, *Sentimental Masculinity and the Rise of History*, 106.

49. Elizabeth Freeman, *Time Binds*, 63.

50. Ibid., 65.

51. Quoted in Batinski, *Pastkeepers in a Small Place*, 179; Miller and Lanning, "'Common Parlors,'" 439.

52. Shawn Michelle Smith, *American Archives*, 137, 140.

53. *Oxford English Dictionary Online*, s.v. "scion," http://www.oed.com/view/Entry/172749, November 24, 2013.

54. Boeckmann, *A Question of Character*, 4.

55. Salazar, *Bodies of Reform*, 163.

56. Baker writes of "how it stirs the dissenting blood in one's veins to read" her own Deerfield ancestors John and Dorothy Stebbins named "Independants [*sic*]" in the Catholic church records (208). Baker, in representing her French great-grandfather Jacques de Noyon's history, reminds readers that his birthplace, Noyon, France, was most famous "as the birthplace of Jean Chauvin, or John Calvin, the great reformer" and draws de Noyon as a "bushranger, discontented with his government [of New France] and seeking a new home"; he is an "outlaw" (212, 217). Baker is careful to prove, too, that de Noyon was not a scout for Hertel de Rouville, the French officer in charge of the raid on Deerfield. In short, de Noyon becomes another sort of dissenting ancestor, a Protestant–New England type trapped in a Catholic Frenchman's historical position.

57. Murphy, *Citizenship and the Origins of Women's History*, 28–30.

58. Ibid., 16.

59. Ibid., 39–40, 96.

60. Love, *Feeling Backward*, 31.

61. Baker, Lane, and Coleman were familiar with the old garrison thanks to their vacations to York, Maine. In fact, the garrison served as the stage for one of Baker's recollective rescues: the china closet door in Frary house she salvaged from the Junkins garrison (Coleman, "Concerning Frary House," 40, ELC). In 1896, the house burned to the ground (Candee, "'Logg' Houses of the Piscataqua Region," 26).

62. For an analysis of the abandoned house in modernist New England landscapes, see Paton, *Abandoned New England*.

63. Coleman, *New England Captives*, 1:1.

64. Coleman formed part of a later generation of women writers who, I argue in chapter 4, continued to work with New England regionalism through the modernist turn.

65. Coleman, *New England Captives*, 1:300, 369–70; 2:294–95, 312, 324, 347.

66. Benjamin, "Theses on the Philosophy of History."

67. Coleman, *New England Captives*, 1:preface.

CHAPTER 2

1. Blanchard, *Sarah Orne Jewett*, 84; Jewett, *Deephaven*, 8.
2. Freeman to Garland, 8 December 1887, 84.
3. Donovan, *New England Local Color Literature*, 119.
4. Brodhead, *Cultures of Letters*, 146.
5. Foote, *Regional Fictions*, 38, 27.
6. Rohy, *Anachronism and Its Others*, 50.
7. A few critics have attended to the multiple temporalities of Jewett's *Pointed Firs*: Murphy reads "The Queen's Twin" "by way of an achronologic notion of time—as existing continually, and not set in the past," and June Howard recognizes multiple temporalities at play in *Pointed Firs*. Murphy, "Replacing Regionalism," 669; Howard, "Unsettling Periods," 379.
8. Foote, *Regional Fictions*, 20.
9. Freeman's colonial plays include *Giles Corey, Yeoman* and "Red Robin." *Silence and Other Stories* is a short story collection set in colonial times, as is a novella depicting a young girl's time travel entitled *The Green Door*.
10. Quoted in Blanchard, *Sarah Orne Jewett*, 348.
11. Garland to Brooks, 14 December 1938, 412.
12. Luciano, *Arranging Grief*, 9; Kristeva, "Women's Time."
13. Fleissner, *Women, Compulsion, Modernity*, 23.
14. Stowe, *Oldtown Folks*; Sedgwick, *A New-England Tale*.
15. Trowbridge, "Dorothy in the Garret," lines 1–8.
16. *Oxford English Dictionary Online*, s.v. "grope," http://www.oed.com/view/Entry/81745, December 15, 2012.
17. These spinsters' literary ancestors include Stowe's rough-edged Miss Roxy and Miss Ruey from *The Pearl of Orr's Island* and her young, unmarried friends Rose Ferguson and Grace Seymour of *Pink and White Tyranny*, who share "the most perfect undressed intimacy," even though both those novels ultimately place

women in the service of dominant narratives of martyrdom, marriage, and motherhood (Stowe, *Poganuc People and Pink and White Tyranny*, 23).

18. Freeman, *A New England Nun*, 173. These are words spoken by the character Christmas Jenny.

19. Jewett, *Pointed Firs*, 48, hereafter cited parenthetically in the text by page number.

20. Cather, preface, 9.

21. James to Henshel, 22 January 1895, 230.

22. Brooks, *New England*, 86.

23. Brodhead, *Cultures of Letters*, 134; Fleissner, *Women, Compulsion, Modernity*, 121–22.

24. Stewart, "The Pickpocket," 1135.

25. Freeman, *A New England Nun*, 465.

26. For a critique of regionalism as turning away from empire and toward the domestic, see Kaplan, "Nation, Region, Empire."

27. Cooke, *Huckleberries*, 35–57.

28. Spofford, *The Amber Gods*, 119–52.

29. Freeman, "Dear Annie," 267. Other works of regionalist fiction that represent women who put off marriage in the name of freedom include Freeman's "One Good Time," Jewett's *A Marsh Island*, and Cooke's "Grit." See Freeman, *A New England Nun*, 143–59; Cooke, *Huckleberries*, 1–34. In Freeman's *The Heart's Highway* and Jewett's *The Tory Lover*—both works of New England regionalist historical fiction set in colonial times of revolt—leading young women Mary Cavendish and Mary Hamilton demonstrate their independence and mobility in defiant acts against the English, assertions of radical disaffiliation that appear to prove temporary as each ends up engaged to the leading man as part of a supposed progress toward the consolidation of the U.S. as nation-state.

30. See Freeman, *A New England Nun*; Jewett, "Martha's Lady"; Jewett, *Deephaven*; Jewett, *A Country Doctor*; Brown, *Tiverton Tales*.

31. Older, unmarried characters of New England regionalism include Freeman's Candace Wheeler ("A Village Singer"), Betsey Dole ("A Poetess"), Elvira ("A Pot of Gold"), Lucinda Moss ("An Innocent Gamester"), Luella Norcross ("Life Everlastin'"), the Babcock sisters ("A Gala Dress"), Sophia and Amanda Gill ("The Southwest Chamber"), Sister Liddy ("Sister Liddy"), and Jenny Wrayne ("Christmas Jenny"), all from *A New England Nun and Other Stories*. Other notable older unmarried women of Freeman's include Lydia Anderson of "Luella Miller" (from *The Wind in the Rose-Bush*) and the older Evelina of "Evelina's Garden" (from *Silence and Other Stories*). A very limited sampling from other regionalist fiction writers might include Jewett's Miss Chauncey of *Deephaven* and Mrs. Todd of *Pointed Firs* as well as Brown's older Dilly Joyce and Amanda Green from *Meadow-Grass*. For readings that attend to issues of age in regionalism, see Turkes, "Must Age Equal Failure?"

32. Cooke, "How Celia Changed Her Mind," 151, hereafter cited parenthetically in the text by page number.

33. Fetterley and Pryse, *Writing Out of Place*, 321.

34. Sarah Josepha Hale, who was also keen on colonial revival commemoration, spearheaded the effort to establish Thanksgiving as a federal holiday. The daughter of an American Revolutionary War veteran, Hale led the completion of the Bunker Hill Monument and was longtime editor of the influential women's magazine *Godey's Lady's Book*. Her work demonstrates a yearning for national union, an interest in claiming New England history as the model for national history, and a concern for women's role in history making.

35. Celia's old maid Thanksgiving attests to the range of same-sex affiliative forms that might be made possible by the unmarried state. According to the narrator's listing of guests, it appears a same-sex couple (Nabby and Sarah), women who live alone (Ann, Celestia, and Delia), as well as cohabitating sisters (Sophronia Ann and Adelia Ann) are present (152).

36. Freeman, *A New England Nun*, 394, 173.

37. Freeman, "A Church Mouse," 344, hereafter cited parenthetically in the text by page number.

38. Games, *Witchcraft in Early North America*, 8.

39. Ibid., 42.

40. Ibid., 40. For more on colonial New England witches as predominantly menopausal women, see Demos, *Entertaining Satan*.

41. Freeman's narrator also refers to Hetty having "made her sacred castle impregnable except to violence," which further links this scene of violence to the sexual and historical, particularly along distinct gender lines (353).

42. Fassett, *Colonial Life in New Hampshire*, 13. According to Fassett's account, during the spring of 1706, Indians attacked a few sites by Oyster River. In one of these, "there was not a man in the fort at the time. The women, however, not at all daunted, loaded their guns and prepared for a stubborn fight. That the Indians might think they were men, they undid their hair and allowed it to hang loosely over their shoulders. . . . The fire which they poured upon the attacking force was so sharp and so accurate that after a short time the Indians withdrew, having lost many of their best warriors."

43. Daniel, "Redefining Place," 73.

44. Fetterley and Pryse read "A Church Mouse" as demonstrating a concern with "a feminist standpoint epistemology" (*Writing Out of Place*, 252). And though their focus is not on how history gets reenacted, they include their most detailed analysis of this story in a section entitled "Revolution."

45. The role played by the garrison house in "A Church Mouse" anticipates C. Alice Baker, Susan Minot Lane, and Emma Lewis Coleman choosing to place such emphasis on that architectural structure as central to colonial life and their own historical interest in it.

46. Jewett, *Pointed Firs*, 64, hereafter cited parenthetically in the text by page number.

47. Fetterley, "Reading *Deephaven* as a Lesbian Text," 170.

48. *Oxford English Dictionary Online*, s.v. "dismal," http://www.oed.com.mutex.gmu.edu/view/Entry/54731?rskey=tiZrzK&result=1&isAdvanced=false, August 2, 2013; Jewett, *Deephaven*, 27, 27–28, hereafter cited parenthetically in the text by page number.

49. Fetterley, "Reading *Deephaven* as a Lesbian Text," 168.

50. The photos reproduced here are the only four of the collection that depict Kate and Helen. Harvard University's Houghton Library currently has the photos listed as unattributed, but my work with archivists at the Museums of Old York (MOY), which houses a collection of Emma Lewis Coleman's photos, demonstrates that they are, in fact, Coleman's work. Ravage claims that this edition of *Deephaven* was published and attributes the photos to Coleman, but I have not been able to locate a copy of the book in published form, even after correspondence with the editors of the volume in which the claim was made and conversations with the archivists at MOY ("Sarah Orne Jewett," *Deephaven*, 180). I believe the volume was never published and, instead, exists only as a tipped book in the Sarah Orne Jewett Compositions and Other Papers, 1847–1909 at Harvard's Houghton Library.

Coleman was a friend of Jewett and herself a member of a triadic same-sex domestic configuration that included C. Alice Baker and Susan Minot Lane. As I note in the introduction of this volume, Baker and Lane were supposedly involved in the creation of these photographs along with Jewett and Coleman.

51. This image anticipates both the title of Jewett's later novel *Pointed Firs* and the description of "the thick growth of dark pines and firs" found therein (100).

52. Ammons, "Material Culture," 92, 97.

53. Fetterley and Pryse, *Writing Out of Place*, 125, 134.

54. Tompkins, *Sensational Designs*, 128–29. Stowe offers a similarly idealized Christ-like girl character in her novel *The Pearl of Orr's Island*, which had a keen influence on Jewett as a writer (Fields, preface).

55. Stowe, *Uncle Tom's Cabin*, 273, 265, hereafter cited parenthetically in the text by page number.

56. Brown, *Domestic Individualism*, 38.

57. For readings of sexuality in *Uncle Tom's Cabin*, see Foreman, "'This Promiscuous Housekeeping'"; Borgstrom, "Passing Over."

58. Sánchez-Eppler, *Touching Liberty*, 19.

59. For readings that attend to this aspect of "The Foreigner," see Foote, *Regional Fictions*, 29–34; Gleason, "Sarah Orne Jewett's 'The Foreigner.'"

60. I would argue that this queer cosmopolitanism is also the basis for Mrs. Todd's representation as an ideal democratic figure. I agree with Patrick Gleason that in the landscape of Dunnet Landing and, I would add, in Mrs. Todd's own economic and sociosexual independence, we have suggested "a counter-history ... [that] make[s] apparent the centrality of colonial markets and the slave trade in the material underpinnings of the town and its history" (41). Gleason and I differ, however, in that I read these not as repressed or forgotten or something that *despite the regionalists best efforts* can never fully be erased but as part of a legacy overtly claimed by Jewett in her stories.

61. The Ladies of Llangollen were the eighteenth-century Anglo-Irish aristocrat proto-lesbians Eleanor Butler and Sarah Ponsonby. For more on the ladies, see Faderman, *Surpassing the Love of Men*, chapter 2.

62. Alice Brown, "[Review of *The Country of the Pointed Firs*]," 37.

63. Coviello, *Tomorrow's Parties*, 81.

64. Kate Upson Clark, "Keeping City Boarders," 11.

65. Denison, "One State and the 'Summer People Industry,'" 2383.

66. Quoted in Cary, prologue, 16.

67. See Arnold, "A Swimming Lesson"; Ludlum, "The Other Boarder"; M. E. W. S., "Bell's Beehives"; "The Young Lady from Boston."

68. See Daisy Rhodes Campbell, "A Maid of the Sea"; Brett, "One Summer Day."

69. For other examples, see Grant, "A Wind of Fate"; Birney, "Ephraim's Idea"; Rowe, "Marjorie's Knight," "Farmer Bassett's Romance," and "Farmer Bassett's Romance II."

70. See Winchester, "Summer Boarders and Their Hosts"; Hooker, "On Boarders and Boarding"; Armstrong, "A Few Words with the Landlady"; Maybelle, "Summer Boarders"; Herrick, "Country Boarding"; Kate Upson Clark, "Keeping City Boarders"; Burrell, "Keeping Summer Boarders with Success."

71. Hooker, "On Boarders and Boarding," 139.

72. Coviello, *Tomorrow's Parties*, 83.

73. Jewett to Scudder, 13 July 1873, 29.

74. Critics such as Ammons have not recognized the mobility central to *Pointed Firs* but have theorized, instead, the novel's stasis in relation to an essential femaleness (*Conflicting Stories*, 46). Similarly, Joseph Boone suggests that the centric structure of Jewett's novel is "predicated upon static loci or settings that become emblematic of the rooted values and outwardly 'still' lives of their female protagonists" (*Tradition, Counter Tradition*, 286). Rather than as still, I read Mrs. Todd, the narrator, and Mrs. Fosdick as in constant motion.

75. McCullough, *Regions of Identity*, 30.

76. Bill Brown, *A Sense of Things*, 90. Brown ultimately contends that Jewett's use of plants makes *Pointed Firs* "cohere as a novel" (88).

77. See Donovan, *New England Local Color Literature*; Zagarell, "Narrative of Community"; Ammons, "Material Culture"; Zagarell, "*Country's* Portrayal of Community."

78. Bravmann, *Queer Fictions*, 50, 47. As Judith Butler has it, "Antigone's power . . . has to do not only with how kinship makes its claim within the language of the state but with *the social deformation of both idealized kinship and political sovereignty that emerges as a consequence of her act*"; "the disturbance of kinship appears to destabilize gender throughout the play" (Butler, *Antigone's Claim*, 6, 10).

79. Ammons, "Jewett's Witches."

80. Ammons, "Material Culture," 92.

81. These stories include "A Dunnet Shepherdess" (1899), "The Queen's Twin" (1899), "The Foreigner" (1900), and "William's Wedding" (1910).

CHAPTER 3

1. Sloboda, "Porcelain Bodies," 24; Auslander, "The Gendering of Consumer Practices," 86.

2. For a detailed account of how to hunt for china, see Moore, *The Old China Book*, 40.

3. For more on du Pont's collections, see Fuchs, "A Passion for China." On Rockefeller's collection, see Castille, "Remembering the Japan Society"; and Abe, "Rockefeller Home Decorating and Objects from China." On Walters' collecting, see Mann, "Exporting China." The archival legacies and endowments of high-profile collectors help ensure that scholars will continue to consider these collections as central: du Pont supported the creation of the Winterthur, for instance.

4. "The Fever of China Hunting." The *Times* borrows this idea from Earle herself, who also hypothesizes "most of the large collections of china have been owned by men" ("The Fever of China Hunting"). My own research seems to bear Earle's claims out, and I would add to it that men tended to publish compendiums on china understood in an international frame with the exception of Jennie J. Young's *The Ceramic Art*. But even though small-scale china hunting focused on acquiring china locally, ultimately, it was no less global or imperial in its conception.

5. Robie, *By-Paths in Collecting*, 60.

6. Slosson's characters live in "Littleville," a fictional version of Hartford, Connecticut, and go "in twos and threes to neighboring villages in search of plunder" while Earle, who took her own experiences as the basis for *China Collecting in America*, hunted in New England and New York (*The China Hunters Club*, 19; Susan Reynolds Williams, *Alice Morse Earle*, 92).

7. These other guides include Robie, *By-Paths in Collecting* and *The Quest of the Quaint*; Camehl, *The Blue-China Book*; Carrick, *Collector's Luck*; Robert and Elizabeth Shackleton, *The Charm of the Antique* and *The Quest of the Colonial*; Walter A. Dyer, *The Lure of the Antique*; and the works of N. Hudson Moore (Hannah "Nannie" Woodbridge Hudson, a woman whose books were published later in London under the name Mrs. Hannah Woodbridge Hudson Moore), among them *The Old China Book*. Antique collecting continued to be popular after 1915 and many more works were published through the 1930s and 1940s, some retrospective like Skiff, *Adventures in Americana*.

8. Slosson was featured in an *Atlantic Monthly* review essay, "New England in the Short Story," which also took up the fiction of Jewett and Freeman. For more on Slosson, see Edward Ifkovic, *Annie Trumbull Slosson*.

9. Susan Reynolds Williams, *Alice Morse Earle*, 108.

10. Castiglia, *Interior States*, 256.

11. See Susan Reynolds Williams, especially chapter 4, and Thomas S. Michie, "'Bought . . . of nobody for almost nothing.'"

12. Robie, *The Quest of the Quaint*, 82.

13. Mary Wilkins Freeman, *The Jamesons*, 110.

14. Kowaleski-Wallace, "Women, China, and Consumer Culture," 156, 153–54.

15. Auslander, "The Gendering of Consumer Practices," 86.

16. Quoted in Sloboda, "Porcelain Bodies," 20; Auslander, "The Gendering of Consumer Practices," 89.

17. Slosson does not mention it in "Women and Ceramics," but she knew of at least one, possibly two, early china-collecting women pioneers, both from New England. Anne Allen Ives (1810–84) of Providence, Rhode Island, amassed an

extensive collection of china in the 1840s and 1850s, and Slosson's sister, Mary Trumbull Prime, was a noted collector. With her husband, William Cowper Prime, Mary Trumbull Prime created a ceramic collection already so well known by the 1870s that it was consistently cited in informational books about china such as Jennie J. Young's *The Ceramic Art*.

18. As late as 1877, when the New England regionalist and historian of colonial America C. Alice Baker was nominated for membership in the MHS, she was denied. For more, see the discussion of Baker, Francis Parkman, and the MHS in chapter 1 of this volume.

19. Peck, "The Attic and Its Treasures," 280.

20. "The Fever of China Hunting."

21. Earle, *China Collecting in America*, 1, hereafter cited parenthetically in the text by page number.

22. Kim, "Being Modern," 383.

23. China-collecting women positioned themselves as cosmopolitan connoisseurs whose intimacy with history allowed them to shape the future by preserving the past. Theirs was certainly an antimodern enterprise as defined by T. J. Jackson Lears: "Far from being the nostalgic flutterings of a 'dying elite,' as historians have claimed," Lears insists, "antimodernism was a complex blend of accommodation and protest which tells us a great deal about the beginnings of present-day values and attitudes" (*No Place of Grace*, xv).

24. Slosson, *The China Hunters Club*, 213, 214, hereafter cited parenthetically in the text by page number.

25. "Aunt Charry's Boarder" is a rare case in Slosson in which a male collector ends up walking home with the coveted piece of china. Jane Forsythe, an urban china hunter, acts as a translator between the rural landlady and her ceramic-crazed male boarder. Jane pulls a prank on the urban man and ultimately loses a coveted platter as a result, but the sketch makes clear that the male collector would have had no chance at all if it had not been for Jane's ability to understand both women and men, country and city.

26. Part of the boldness requisite to the hunt, according to Earle, has to do with historical changes in collecting since Slosson wrote *The China Hunters Club*. Earle writes, "times have changed since 1876." "I have not found," Earle continues, "as did the members of the China Hunters' [*sic*] Club, that country housekeepers would, as a rule, rather have money than china" (*China Collecting in America*, 11).

27. By 1890, antique shops began popping up along tourist thoroughfares throughout New England as part of an effort made by local entrepreneurs to get in on this expanding market. One example of a pioneer in the field of antique sales is Fred Bishop Tuck. After peddling antiques in various parts of New England privately and through auctions, he opened the first antique shop in Maine in Kennebunkport in 1893 (Fales, introduction, v). See Tuck, *Antiqueman's Diary*. The antique-selling tradition is still a visible part of the twenty-first-century New England tourism economy along main roads such as route 1 in Maine.

28. Stowe, *Oldtown Folks*, 31.

29. Earle also sometimes refers to her female companion on the hunt. This was her unmarried sister, Frances Clary Morse, to whom Earle dedicated *China Collecting in America*.

30. Browne and Austin, *Who's Who on the Stage*, 120.

31. Earle also mentions a "specially comical portrait-plaque, painted in China, [that] shows an almond-eyed Washington with his hair *à la chinoise*, with feminine hair ornaments" (257).

32. Slosson and Earle were themselves New England daughters. Slosson was from Hartford and, widowed young, spent the remainder of her life unmarried. Earle was originally from Worcester, Massachusetts, but lived in Brooklyn, New York, with her husband and children.

33. Freeman, "The Willow-Ware," 147, hereafter cited parenthetically in the text by page number.

34. Porcelain, which is the type of ceramic imported from China, has a white body. The colored scenes transferred or glazes used on it might obscure that foundational white to some extent, but it is still has a white body. (If you were to break a piece of china, you would see the white porcelain exposed.) The same is true of English ceramics. Potters in the eighteenth century in England discovered how to create white or cream-colored wares from red clays, and so these wares, such as Staffordshire, Liverpool, and the like have white bodies, too.

35. Shackleton and Shackleton, *The Charm of the Antique*, 3–4.

36. Baudrillard, *The System of Objects*, 88.

37. Marx, *Capital*, 128.

38. Stewart, *On Longing*, 164.

39. Ibid., 164–65.

40. Ibid., 164.

41. Bourdieu, *Distinction*, 100.

42. Carrick, *Collector's Luck*, 15–16.

43. Slosson, like many of her Hartford friends, had black servants throughout her life. According to Ifkovic, "generations of the same Batson family served her, and were integral parts of her household" (*Annie Trumbull Slosson*, 130).

44. Leach, *Land of Desire*, 104.

45. Rujivacharakul, "China and china," 15, 16.

46. Lindgren, "'That Every Mariner May Possess the History of the World,'" 182, 198.

47. Ibid., 196, 197, 198.

48. Ibid., 197.

49. For more on Schliemann, see Maurer, "Archeology as Spectacle." For more on Cesnola, see McFadden, *The Glitter and the Gold*.

50. Lyle, "The China-Closet."

51. Ibid.

52. Leach, *Land of Desire*, 20–22.

53. Ironically, New England was at the forefront of the modernization that made regionalist collecting necessary. Stephen Nissenbaum writes, "By 1860, when the New England small town was first being sentimentalized as a seat of pastoral

Yankee stability, New England as a whole had become the single most urban part of the nation—the most industrial, the most Catholic, the most heavily immigrant in population, and the most rapidly changing area in the United States" ("New England as Region and Nation," 39–40).

54. Women china collectors redefined their relationship to the contemporary market, differentiating themselves from the urban women who were beginning to shop at department stores like Siegel-Cooper in New York City. William Leach writes, "Before 1880 businesses like department stores did not exist.... In the next twenty years, however, cities throughout the country would be filled with large retail establishments—multifloored, multiwindowed buildings of great concentrated selling power" (*Land of Desire*, 20). But there were antecedents such as the Marble Palace in New York City that, in the 1860s and 1870s, took up an entire city block (Leach, *Land of Desire*, 21).

55. Cook, *The House Beautiful*, 238.

56. Ibid.

57. Norton, "The Lack of Old Homes in America," 639.

58. Halttunen, "From Parlor to Living Room."

CHAPTER 4

1. Gilman's work has been linked to western regionalism: see Tuttle, "Gilman's *The Crux* and Owen Wister's *The Virginian*."

2. Rich, "From Near-Dystopia to Utopia," 168. See also Linett, "Modernist Women's Literature,"

3. Thadious M. Davis, "Black Women's Modernist Literature," 96.

4. Gilman, *The Living*, 325. Gilman short stories that explicitly represent New England womanhood include "The Giant Wistaria," "The Yellow Wall-Paper," "The Unexpected," "Turned," and "His Mother," all reprinted in Gilman, *Herland*, *"The Yellow Wall-Paper," and Selected Writings*.

5. Parrish, *Currents of the Nineties*, chapter 2.

6. Quoted in Parrish, *Currents of the Nineties*, 302–3.

7. Lois Brown, *Pauline Elizabeth Hopkins*, 34, 41–42. For readings of Hopkins's regionalist investments, see Carby, *Reconstructing Womanhood*, and Lois Brown, *Pauline Elizabeth Hopkins*.

8. Sundquist, *To Wake the Nations*, 570.

9. Barnard, "Modern American Fiction," 53–54. Although, as McGarry has pointed out, "Spiritualism held enormous appeal for women and men who inhabited gender and sexuality in transgressive ways," Gilman, Brown, and Hopkins appear not to have affiliated themselves with the Spiritualist movement proper (*Ghosts of Futures Past*, 154).

10. Baker, *True Stories*, 222; Slosson, *The China Hunters Club*, 125.

11. Butler, *The Psychic Life of Power*, 34. Frecerro offers a reading of melancholic incorporation as a form of haunting in "Queer Spectrality," 205–6.

12. Butler, *The Psychic Life of Power*, 34.

13. Gordon, *Ghostly Matters*, 8.

14. Freeman, *Time Binds*, 63.

15. In these reorientations, Gilman, Brown, and Hopkins might fairly be said to anticipate some of the questions that motivate Ahmed's exploration of queer phenomenology.

16. Luciano, "Geological Fantasies," 298. Luciano, in this article, discusses "The Amber Gods," a short story by Harriet Prescott Spofford who was an important intellectual leader in the community of women writers in and around Boston. Alice Brown, for instance, knew and admired Spofford so much she went out of her way to pay out of pocket for a special gift for Spofford from the Poetry Club, of which Brown was a member ("A Poem in Free Verse to A. F. B.," Papers of Alice Brown, 1899–1948, University of Virginia Library).

17. Bennett, "Confronting Continuity," 88.

18. Brown's Lucy Ann Cummings offers a useful counterpoint to the melancholic incorporation of the mother as part of subjection to heterosexuality wherein, as Butler explains it, "The girl becomes a girl through being subject to a prohibition which bars the mother as an object of desire and installs that barred object as a part of the ego, indeed, as a melancholic identification" (*The Psychic Life of Power*, 136).

19. James to Henshel, 22 January 1895, 230.

20. Quoted in Campbell, *Resisting Regionalism*, 4; quoted in Gebhard, "The Spinster in the House of American Criticism," 80.

21. Campbell, *Resisting Regionalism*, 7.

22. Ibid., 12.

23. Ibid., 9–12.

24. Fleissner, *Women, Compulsion, Modernity*, 115.

25. Quoted ibid., 121.

26. Ibid., 122.

27. For one of many examples of work reflecting on periodization and literary history, see Stein, "American Literary History and Queer Temporalities."

28. David Harvey points to various possible origin points—1848, 1910, and 1914—for modernism's beginning. See Harvey, *The Condition of Postmodernity*, chapter 2.

29. Gilman, *Diaries*, 411.

30. Lewis, "An Old New England Village."

31. "Good Form and Entertainment."

32. Beverly Gordon, "Costumed Representations of Early America," 6.

33. Gilman, *Diaries*, 412. For the sake of clarity and consistency, I have chosen to refer to Charlotte Perkins Stetson Gilman as Gilman, even though in 1890 she had not yet married Gilman. Similarly, I refer to Grace Ellery Channing Stetson as Stetson, even though when she collaborated with Gilman on "In the Name of the King!" she was Grace Ellery Channing. In doing this, I am following the lead of the Schlesinger Library's electronic finding aid, which uses the names by which the authors are most widely known.

34. See Knight, "New Evidence."

35. Carroll, "Forefathers' Day Dinners," 347.

36. Weinbaum, *Wayward Reproductions*, 77.

37. Lanser, "Feminist Criticism," 423, 425.

38. Gilman, "The Yellow Wall-Paper," 166, 167, 169, hereafter cited parenthetically in the text by page number.

39. Fleissner proposes that the yellow of the yellow wallpaper may be read "in the most straightforward terms, as merely a sign of age" (*Women, Compulsion, Modernity*, 80).

40. Hawthorne, *The Scarlet Letter*, 30, 33.

41. Focusing on literary tradition rather than cultural context, Sandra M. Gilbert and Susan Gubar have argued that the attics or upper floors of houses figure throughout nineteenth-century women's literature as the nether-regions to which rebellious female characters are relegated, and they cite "The Yellow Wall-Paper" as one of their examples (*The Madwoman in the Attic*, 85, 89).

42. In the 1890s, for example, the noted antiquarian and bibliophile Frederick Skiff searched his family attic for evidence to justify his membership in the Sons of the American Revolution. His search led to his lifelong obsession with antique collecting. See Skiff, *Adventures in Americana*.

43. Barrows, "In an Old Attic," 100.

44. Ibid.

45. See Castiglia, *Interior States*.

46. Gilman, *Women and Economics*, 36 (emphasis added). As Helen Lefkowitz Horowitz, in her discussion of evolutionary science in Gilman's thinking, has pointed out, in "A Dramatic View," published in April 1890, Gilman uses similar language: the character "He" commands "She" "Get behind, I tell you! . . . I will fight till I die to keep you behind!" (*Wild Unrest*, 239–40).

47. *Oxford English Dictionary Online*, s.v. "smooch," http://www.oed.com/view/Entry/182742, November 24, 2013.

48. Gilman, "The Giant Wistaria," 155, hereafter cited parenthetically in the text by page number.

49. The carpenters called in to fix the porch report that the pillars are rotten, the "creeper" being "about all that holds the thing up" (158). Thus, Jenny's creeping when thinking about the creeper reinforces the idea that she and Dwining are intertwined. Gilman also uses the term "creep" throughout "The Yellow Wall-Paper" (177, 179, 181, 182).

50. Potassium bromide was used as a common sedative in the nineteenth century. As early as 1866, this medicine was reported to be one that "neutralizes the sexual appetite" (Bartholow, "Experimental Investigations," 188), and, by 1905, *The National Standard Dispensatory* noted that bromide "is also of value in cases of sexual excitement or nymphomania" (Hare et al., *The National Standard Dispensatory*, 1229).

51. Golden has confirmed that Hatfield was the staff illustrator who drew this image for the *New England Magazine* ("Speaking a Different Story," 61).

52. Knight, "'You are getting to be a famous woman my dear!,'" 430; Gilman to Stetson, 3 December 1890, 87.

53. As Seitler has pointed out, Gilman's narrator's repetitive creeping at the end of "The Yellow Wall-Paper" alludes to notions of "primitive" behaviors of the sort Gilman hoped to see bred out of the white race by way of eugenics ("Unnatural Selection," 70).

54. Howard, *Publishing the Family*, 268–69.

55. Westbrook, in *Acres of Flint*, considers the work of little-known women New England regionalists that I consider in this study, including that of Annie Trumbull Slosson and Alice Brown. For the other published scholarship on Brown, see Walker, *Alice Brown*; Fisken, "Within the Limits of Alice Brown's 'Dooryards'"; Toth, "A Forgotten View from Beacon Hill."

56. Watt, "Modern American Drama," 110. For more on Browne's Little Theatre, see Lock, "Maurice Browne and the Chicago Little Theatre."

57. Walker, *Alice Brown*, 78.

58. Alice Brown, *Meadow-Grass*, 200, hereafter cited parenthetically in the text by page number; Somerville, *Queering the Color Line*, 17.

59. Diggs, "Romantic Friends," 334, 335.

60. Other examples of stories featuring female characters who, though they seem racially other, end up being crucial members of regional history and community, include Freeman's "Christmas Jenny" (Jenny Wrayne) and "A Church Mouse" (Hetty Fifield), as well as Jewett's *Deephaven* (i.e., Mrs. Bonny).

61. Alice Brown, *Tiverton Tales*, 166, 154, hereafter cited parenthetically in the text by page number.

62. Fisken, "Within the Limits of Alice Brown's 'Dooryards,'" 22.

63. Carby, *Reconstructing Womanhood*, 161; Doreski, "Inherited Rhetoric," 73.

64. Lois Brown, *Pauline Elizabeth Hopkins*, 288.

65. Ibid., 109–13.

66. Ibid., 89; Bullock, *The Afro-American Periodical Press*, 118.

67. Carby, *Reconstructing Womanhood*, 125.

68. For more on Hopkins and William James, see Schrager, "Pauline Hopkins and William James."

69. For how Hopkins influenced Fauset and Holt, see Marek, "Women Editors and Little Magazines." As Carby points out, "the late nineteenth and early twentieth centuries . . . were the years of the first flowering of black women's autonomous organizations and a period of intense intellectual activity" (*Reconstructing Womanhood*, 6–7).

70. See Sundquist, *To Wake the Nations*; Carby, *Reconstructing Womanhood*; Lois Brown, *Pauline Elizabeth Hopkins*.

71. Tuhkanen, "'Out of Joint,'" 337.

72. Carby, *Reconstructing Womanhood*, 149.

73. Ibid., 146.

74. Hopkins, *The Magazine Novels of Pauline Hopkins*, 33, hereafter cited parenthetically in the text by page number.

75. Gillian Brown, *Domestic Individualism*, 16.

76. For Stowe, *Household Papers*, 149; Cook, *The House Beautiful*, 272.

77. duCille, *The Coupling Convention*, 32.

78. Kowaleski-Wallace, "Women, China, and Consumer Culture," 154–55.

79. As Susan Hays Bussey notes, in this scene Hopkins "intimates that her character [Hagar] may stray from the norm by allowing her some self-awareness.... Hopkins's description of Hagar's dreams suggests that her heroine has the potential to be a *subjective* character" ("Whose Will Be Done?," 307).

80. Shawn Michelle Smith has argued that Hopkins relies on pictorial representations in *Hagar's Daughter,* but she focuses on the mixed-race character Aurelia and concludes that the white male bodies of Cuthbert Sumner and the young orphan boy are the visual foci of the novel's end; "By leaving Hagar present, but just off-screen, as it were, Hopkins refuses to repeat the objectification of the biracial woman, the fetish of colonial desire" (*American Archives*, 192). Smith does not, however, examine pictorial aspects of our first view of Hagar.

81. *Oxford English Dictionary Online,* s.v. "wood-nymph," http://www.oed.com/view/Entry/230057, November 24, 2013.

82. DeLamotte, "'Collusions of the Mystery,'" 74.

83. Tuhkanen, "'Out of Joint,'" 349.

84. Garber, *Vested Interests,* 186.

85. Hopkins, "Address," 355.

86. Lois Brown, *Pauline Elizabeth Hopkins,* 56–57.

87. Nell, *Colored Patriots,* 23.

88. Mossell, *The Work of the Afro-American Woman,* 26.

89. Lois Brown, *Pauline Elizabeth Hopkins,* 402.

90. My source for Sampson's history is Young, *Masquerade.*

91. Ibid., 300. The debate about Gannett's race is ongoing. In fact, Young adamantly maintains that Gannett was not black and also rejects claims that Gannett was proto-lesbian or bisexual (*Masquerade,* chapter 11).

EPILOGUE

1. Judith Newton insists in "History as Usual?" that there is not much new about new historicism, that feminists had long been working with history. For other reflections on the relationship between feminism and new historicism, see Pollak, "Feminism and the New Historicism"; Dimock, "Feminism, New Historicism, and the Reader"; and Fleissner, "Is Feminism a Historicism?" Two of the most famous new historicist critiques of feminist scholarship in American literary studies include Michaels, *The Gold Standard and the Logic of Naturalism,* and Brodhead, *Cultures of Letters.*

2. Combahee River Collective, "The Combahee River Collective Statement," 273.

3. Humez, *Harriet Tubman,* 56–58. In an editorial note on the "Statement," Barbara Smith writes that this "guerilla action [was] conceptualized and led by Harriet Tubman . . . and is the only military campaign in American history planned and led by a woman" (*Home Girls,* 272).

4. Combahee River Collective, "The Combahee River Collective Statement," 280.

5. *But Some of Us Are Brave* follows in the tradition of the political feminist anthology spearheaded by Cherríe Moraga and Gloria Andalzúa's *This Bridge*

Called My Back, understood as part of a "broad-based political movement" among "Third World women in the U.S." (Moraga and Andalzúa, introduction, xxiv).

6. Tuttle, "Looking Back, Looking Forward," 199. Much has been made, both in the 1970s and 1980s and after, of the rift that existed between white and black feminists. One representative critique of white literary feminist's ignoring of black women writers is Barbara Smith's "Toward a Black Feminist Criticism." For a history of racial tension in the feminist movement, see Breines, *The Trouble between Us*.

7. Tuttle, "Looking Back, Looking Forward," 212.

8. Ibid., 229.

9. Donovan, "The Unpublished Love Poems," 28. It is instructive to compare the reception of Donovan's archival findings regarding Jewett to Hull's near-simultaneous presentation of Angelina Weld Grimké as a queer black woman writer of the Harlem Renaissance, published in 1979 in *Conditions: a feminist magazine of writing by women with an emphasis on writing by lesbians* and reprinted in Smith, *Home Girls*, 73–82. Jewett has received considerably more scholarly attention.

10. Fetterley, introduction, 21.

11. This complaint echoes across early feminist recovery scholarship, as in Warren's introduction to Fanny Fern's *Ruth Hall and Other Stories*, which formed part of the important Rutgers reprint series American Women Writers: "Fanny Fern's contemporaries would not have recognized her in this twentieth-century portrait [authored by male critics inattentive to the archive]. The majority of her writings were far from sentimental; they were regarded as unfeminine by her contemporaries" (Warren, introduction, x). Feminist intellectuals dedicated to black women and queer studies, like Smith, similarly complained of male scholars, black and white, being "virulently sexist in their treatment of Black women writers" such as Zora Neale Hurston (Smith, "Toward a Black Feminist Criticism," 162).

12. Torsney, "In Anticipation," 72–73.

13. Hull, "Researching Alice Dunbar-Nelson," 190.

14. Ibid.

15. Walker, *In Search of Our Mothers' Gardens*, 234.

16. Ibid., 238–40.

17. Weidlich, "Quilt Scholarship," 1.

18. See Hedges, "Quilts and Women's Culture," "The Nineteenth-Century Diarist and Her Quilts," and *Hearts and Hands*. Ulrich's "Presidential Address," meanwhile, offers an object-based microhistory approach of the sort found in her book *The Age of Homespun*. For a more recent scholar's engagement of women's history and research as linked to quilting, see Riché Richardson, "Journeying with Toni Morrison's Writings and My Toni Morrison Quilt." Quilting also came in this era to be linked with mourning and the present as it figured prominently in the LGBTQ community in the form of the AIDS Memorial Quilt, which began in 1987 and quickly became a community art project of tremendous scale.

19. We might think these implicit theorizations as on a spectrum with Freccero's notion of queer spectrality. See Freccero, "Queer Spectrality."

20. Morrison, *Beloved*, xv.

21. Ibid., xvi.

22. Ibid., xviii.
23. Ibid., xvi, xix.
24. Fetterley, introduction, 35.
25. Ibid., 35.
26. Ibid., 36–37.
27. Ibid., 37.
28. Ibid., 37.
29. Hull, "Researching Alice Dunbar-Nelson," 191.
30. Ibid., 195.
31. Hull, "'Under the Days,'" 81.
32. Smith, "Toward a Black Feminist Criticism," 173.
33. See Zagarell, "Narrative of Community," "Crosscurrents," "*Country*'s Portrayal of Community and the Exclusion of Difference," "Troubling Regionalism," and "Old Women and Old Houses."
34. Love, *Feeling Backward*, 43.
35. *OED Online*, s.v. "recovery," http://www.oed.com.mutex.gmu.edu/view/Entry/159940, March 9, 2015.
36. Love, *Feeling Backward*, 45. For other, rich meditations on the meanings of recovery, see Fetterley, "Commentary"; Harris, "'Across the Gulf'"; Harvey, "States of Recollection"; and Foreman and Sherrard-Johnson, "Racial Recovery, Racial Death."
37. *OED Online*, s.v. "recognition," http://www.oed.com.mutex.gmu.edu/view/Entry/159646, March 9, 2015.
38. Brodhead, *Cultures of Letters*, 144.
39. Ibid. (emphasis mine).
40. Ibid., 143, 144. Brodhead also happens to ignore efforts among white feminist critics such as Sandra Zagarell and Susan Gillman to think gender analyses in relation to race, region, nation, and global imperialism and does not seem to branch beyond white feminist analyses of Jewett. I call Brodhead's move characteristic because, as Fleissner has noted, he was one of a number of new historicists who critiqued feminist critics while questioning nineteenth-century women writers' place in new canons.
41. Fleissner, "Is Feminism a Historicism?," 55.
42. Ibid., 60. Similarly, scholars working within what has become known as the temporal turn in queer studies have, from various angles, been mounting a case against a certain kind of historicism as a deadening, normalizing force. See especially Goldberg and Menon, "Queering History," and Traub's response: "The New Unhistoricism in Queer Studies."

Bibliography

ARCHIVAL SOURCES

Cambridge, Mass.
    Houghton Library, Harvard University
        Sarah Orne Jewett Compositions and Other Papers, 1847–1909

Charlottesville, Va.
    The Clifton Waller Barrett Library, University of Virginia
        Papers of Alice Brown, 1899–1948
        Sarah Orne Jewett Collection

Deerfield, Mass.
    Pocumtuck Valley Memorial Library
        C. Alice Baker Papers
        Emma Lewis Coleman Papers
        Historic Deerfield Summer Fellowship Papers
        Pocumtuck Valley Historical Association Papers
        Susan Minot Lane Papers

York, Maine
    Museums of Old York
        Elizabeth Bishop Perkins Collection
        Piscataqua Garden Club Collection

PUBLISHED WORKS

Abe, Stanley K. "Rockefeller Home Decorating and Objects from China." In *Collecting China: The World, China, and a History of Collecting*, edited by Vimalin Rujivacharakul, 107–23. Newark: University of Delaware Press, 2011.

Adams, Henry. *The Education of Henry Adams*. 1907. Boston: Riverside Press, 1918.

Ahmed, Sara. *Queer Phenomenology: Orientations, Objects, Others*. Durham: Duke University Press, 2006.

Anderson, Benedict. *Imagined Communities: Reflections on the Origin and Spread of Nationalism*. 1983. London: Verso, 1992.

Ammons, Elizabeth. *Conflicting Stories: American Women Writers at the Turn into the Twentieth Century*. New York: Oxford University Press, 1991.

———. "Jewett's Witches." In *Critical Essays on Sarah Orne Jewett*, edited by Gwen L. Nagel, 165–84. Boston: G. K. Hall, 1984.

———. "Material Culture, Empire, and Jewett's *Country of the Pointed Firs*." In *New Essays on The Country of the Pointed Firs*, edited by June Howard, 81–99. Cambridge: Cambridge University Press, 1994.

Ammons, Elizabeth, and Valerie Rohy, eds. *American Local Color Writing 1880-1920*. New York: Penguin Books, 1998.

Armstrong, Ruth. "A Few Words with the Landlady." *Good Housekeeping*, July 1892, 26-27.

Arnold, George. "A Swimming Lesson." *Saturday Evening Post*, June 23, 1883, 10.

Auslander, Leora. "The Gendering of Consumer Practices in Nineteenth-Century France." In *The Sex of Things: Gender and Consumption in Historical Perspective*, edited by Victoria de Grazia, 79-112. Berkeley: University of California Press, 1996.

Baker, C. Alice. *True Stories of New England Captives Carried to Canada during the Old French and Indian Wars*. 1897. Bowie, Md.: Heritage Books, 1990.

Barnard, Rita. "Modern American Fiction." In *The Cambridge Companion to American Modernism*, edited by Walter Kalaidjian, 39-67. Cambridge: Cambridge University Press, 2005.

Barrows, John S. "In an Old Attic." *New England Magazine* 10 (March 1891): 100-107.

Barthes, Roland. *Camera Lucida: Reflections on Photography*. Translated by Richard Howard. New York: Hill and Wang, 1981.

Bartholow, Roberts. "Experimental Investigations into the Action of the Bromide of Potassium." *The Half-Yearly Abstract of the Medical Sciences* 44-45 (1866): 188-89.

Batinski, Michael C. *Pastkeepers in a Small Place: Five Centuries in Deerfield, Massachusetts*. Amherst: University of Massachusetts Press, 2004.

Baudrillard, Jean. *The System of Objects*. 1968. Translated by James Benedict. London: Verso, 1996.

Baym, Nina. *American Women Writers and the Work of History, 1790-1860*. New Brunswick: Rutgers University Press, 1985.

Benjamin, Walter. "Theses on the Philosophy of History." 1940. In *Illuminations*. Translated by Harry Zohn, 253-64. New York: Schocken Books, 1968.

Bennett, Judith M. "Confronting Continuity." *Journal of Women's History* 9 (Autumn 1997): 73-94.

Berlant, Lauren. Introduction to *Intimacy*, edited by Lauren Berlant, 1-8. Chicago: University of Chicago Press, 2000.

Bernstein, Robin. *Racial Innocence*. New York: New York University Press, 2011.

Bhabha, Homi K. "DissemiNation: Time, Narrative, and the Margins of the Modern Nation." In *Nation and Narration*, edited by Homi K. Bhabha, 291-322. London: Routledge, 1999.

Birney, Florence H. "Ephraim's Idea." *Godey's Lady's Book and Magazine* 103 (December 1881): 553-55.

Blanchard, Paula. *Sarah Orne Jewett: Her World and Her Work*. Cambridge: Perseus Publishing, 1994.

Blight, David W. *Race and Reunion: The Civil War in American Memory*. Cambridge: Harvard University Press, 2001.

Boeckmann, Cathy. *A Question of Character: Scientific Racism and the Genres of American Fiction, 1892-1912*. Tuscaloosa: University of Alabama Press, 2000.

Boone, Joseph. *Tradition, Counter Tradition: Love and the Form of Fiction.* Chicago: University of Chicago Press, 1987.

Borgstrom, Michael. "Passing Over: Setting the Record Straight in *Uncle Tom's Cabin.*" *PMLA* 118 (October 2003): 1290-1304.

Bourdieu, Pierre. *Distinction: A Social Critique of the Judgement of Taste.* 1979. Translated by Richard Nice. Cambridge: Harvard University Press, 2000.

Bravmann, Scott. *Queer Fictions of the Past: History, Culture, and Difference.* Cambridge: Cambridge University Press, 1997.

Breines, Winifred. *The Trouble between Us: An Uneasy History of White and Black Women in the Feminist Movement.* Oxford: Oxford University Press, 2006.

Brett, W. J. "One Summer Day." *Saturday Evening Post*, August 20 1881, 7.

Brodhead, Richard H. *Cultures of Letters: Scenes of Reading and Writing in Nineteenth-Century America.* Chicago: University of Chicago Press, 1993.

Brooks, Van Wyck. *New England: Indian Summer, 1865-1915.* New York: E. P. Dutton, 1940.

Brown, Alice. *Children of Earth: A Play of New England.* New York: Macmillan, 1915.

———. *Meadow-Grass: Tales of New England Life.* 1895. Boston: Copeland and Day, 1896.

———. "[Review of *The Country of the Pointed Firs*]." In *Critical Essays on Sarah Orne Jewett*, edited by Gwen L. Nagel, 37-38. Boston: G. K. Hall, 1984.

———. *Tiverton Tales.* Boston: Houghton Mifflin, 1899.

Brown, Bill. *A Sense of Things: The Object Matter of American Literature.* Chicago: University of Chicago Press, 2003.

Brown, Dona. *Inventing New England: Regional Tourism in the Nineteenth Century.* Washington: Smithsonian Institute Press, 1995.

Brown, Gillian. *Domestic Individualism: Imagining Self in Nineteenth-Century America.* Berkeley: University of California Press, 1992.

Brown, Lois. *Pauline Elizabeth Hopkins: Black Daughter of the Revolution.* Chapel Hill: University of North Carolina Press, 2008.

Browne, Walter, and F. A. Austin, eds. *Who's Who on the Stage: The Dramatic Reference Book and Biographical Dictionary of the Theatre.* New York: Walter Browne & F. A. Austin Publishers, 1906.

Bullock, Penelope L. *The Afro-American Periodical Press, 1838-1909.* Baton Rouge: Louisiana State University Press, 1981.

Burrell, Caroline Benedict. "Keeping Summer Boarders with Success." *Ladies' Home Journal*, May 1901, 20.

Bussey, Susan Hays. "Whose Will Be Done? Self-Determination in Pauline Hopkins's *Hagar's Daughter.*" *African American Review* 39 (Fall 2005): 299-313.

Butler, Judith. *Antigone's Claim: Kinship between Life and Death.* New York: Columbia University Press, 2000.

———. "Imitation and Gender Subordination." In *The Lesbian and Gay Studies Reader*, edited by Henry Abelove et al., 307-20. New York: Routledge, 1993.

———. *The Psychic Life of Power: Theories in Subjection.* Stanford: Stanford University Press, 1997.

Camehl, Ada Walker. *The Blue-China Book*. New York: E. P. Dutton, 1916.

Campbell, Daisy Rhodes. "A Maid of the Sea." *Ladies' Home Journal*, August 1890, 5–6.

Campbell, Donna. *Resisting Regionalism: Gender and Naturalism in American Fiction, 1885–1915*. Athens: Ohio University Press, 1997.

Candee, Richard M. "'Logg' Houses of the Piscataqua Region." In *"A Noble and Dignified Stream": The Piscataqua Region in the Colonial Revival, 1860–1930*, edited by Sarah L. Giffen and Kevin D. Murphy, 26–29. York, Maine: Old York Historical Society, 1992.

Carby, Hazel V. *Reconstructing Womanhood: The Emergence of the Afro-American Woman Novelist*. New York: Oxford University Press, 1987.

Carpenter, Cari. Introduction to *Selected Writings of Victoria Woodhull*, by Victoria Woodhull. Edited by Cari Carpenter. Lincoln: University of Nebraska Press, 2010.

Carrick, Alice Van Leer. *Collector's Luck; or, A Repository of Pleasant and Profitable Discourses Descriptive of the Household Furniture and Ornaments of Olden Time*. 1919. Garden City: Garden City Publishing, 1937.

Carroll, Abigail. "Forefathers' Day Dinners and Martha Washington Teas: Commemorative Consumption and the Colonial Revival." *Food, Culture & Society* 12 (2009): 335–56.

Carter, Sarah Anne. "Picturing Rooms: Interior Photography, 1870–1900." *History of Photography* 34 (July 2010): 251–67.

Cary, Richard. Introduction to *Sarah Orne Jewett Letters*, by Sarah Orne Jewett, edited by Richard Cary, 3–8. Waterville, Maine: Colby College Press, 1967.

———. Prologue to *Sarah Orne Jewett Letters*, by Sarah Orne Jewett, edited by Richard Cary, 13–16. Waterville, Maine: Colby College Press, 1967.

Castiglia, Christopher. *Bound and Determined: Captivity, Culture-Crossing, and White Womanhood from Mary Rowlandson to Patty Hearst*. Chicago: University of Chicago Press, 1996.

———. *Interior States: Institutional Consciousness and the Inner Life of Democracy in the Antebellum United States*. Durham: Duke University Press, 2008.

Cather, Willa. Preface to *The Country of the Pointed Firs and Other Stories*, by Sarah Orne Jewett, edited by Willa Cather, 6–11. New York: Doubleday, 1956.

Champney, Elizabeth W. *Great-Grandmother's Girls in New France: The History of Little Eunice Williams*. Boston: Estes and Lauriat, 1887.

Clark, Emily. *Masterless Mistresses: The New Orleans Ursulines and the Development of a New World Society, 1727–1834*. Chapel Hill: University of North Carolina Press, 2007.

Clark, Kate Upson. "Keeping City Boarders." *Ladies' Home Journal*, June 1891, 11.

Cleves, Rachel Hope. *Charity and Sylvia: A Same-Sex Marriage in Early America*. Oxford: Oxford University Press, 2014.

Cole, Donald B. *Immigrant City: Lawrence, Massachusetts, 1845–1921*. Chapel Hill: University of North Carolina Press, 1963.

Coleman, Emma Lewis. *New England Captives Carried to Canada between 1677 and 1760 during the French and Indian Wars*. 2 vols. Portland, Maine: Southworth Press, 1925.

Combahee River Collective, "The Combahee River Collective Statement." In *Home Girls: A Black Feminist Anthology*, edited by Barbara Smith, 272–82. New York: Kitchen Table—Women of Color Press, 1983.

Conforti, Joseph A. *Imagining New England: Explorations of Regional Identity from the Pilgrims to the Mid-Twentieth Century*. Chapel Hill: University of North Carolina Press, 2001.

Cook, Clarence. *The House Beautiful: Essays on Beds and Tables, Stools and Candlesticks*. New York: Charles Scribner's Sons, 1881.

Cooke, Rose Terry. "How Celia Changed Her Mind." In *American Women Regionalists, 1850–1910*, edited by Judith Fetterley and Marjorie Pryse, 137–53. New York: W. W. Norton, 1992.

———. *Huckleberries Gathered from New England Hills*. Boston: Houghton Mifflin, 1892.

Coviello, Peter. *Tomorrow's Parties: Sex and the Untimely in Nineteenth-Century America*. New York: New York University Press, 2013.

Daniel, Janice. "Redefining Place: *Femes Covert* in the Stories of Mary Wilkins Freeman." *Studies in Short Fiction* 33 (Winter 1996): 69–76.

Davis, Cynthia J. "The Two Mrs. Stetsons and the 'Romantic Summer.'" In *Charlotte Perkins Gilman and Her Contemporaries*, edited by Cynthia J. Davis and Denise D. Knight, 1–16. Tuscaloosa: University of Alabama Press, 2004.

Davis, Thadious M. "Black Women's Modernist Literature." In *The Cambridge Companion to Modernist Women Writers*, edited by Maren Tova Linett, 95–109. Cambridge: Cambridge University Press, 2010.

Degler, Carl N. *At Odds: Women and the Family in America from the Revolution to the Present*. New York: Oxford University Press, 1980.

DeLamotte, Eugenia. "'Collusions of the Mystery': Ideology and the Gothic in *Hagar's Daughter*." *Gothic Studies* 6 (May 2004): 69–79.

Demos, John P. *Entertaining Satan: Witchcraft and the Culture of Early New England*. New York: Oxford University Press, 2004.

———. *The Unredeemed Captive: A Family Story from Early America*. New York: Vintage Books, 1994.

Denenberg, Thomas Andrew. *Wallace Nutting and the Invention of Old America*. New Haven: Yale University Press, 2003.

Denison, D. "One State and the 'Summer People Industry.'" *The World's Work*, August 1902, 2383–84.

Des Jardins, Julie. *Women and the Historical Enterprise in America: Gender, Race, and the Politics of Memory, 1880–1945*. Chapel Hill: University of North Carolina Press, 2003.

Dickinson, Emily. *The Complete Poems of Emily Dickinson*. Edited by Thomas H. Johnson. Boston: Little, Brown, 1960.

Diggs, Marylynne. "'Romantic Friends or a 'Different Race of Creatures'? The Representation of Lesbian Pathology in Nineteenth-Century America." *Feminist Studies* 21 (Summer 1995): 317–40.

Dimock, Wai-Chee. "Feminism, New Historicism, and the Reader." *American Literature* 63 (December 1991): 601–22.

Dinshaw, Carolyn. *Getting Medieval: Sexualities and Communities, Pre- and Postmodern.* Durham: Duke University Press, 1999.

Doan, Laura L. Introduction to *Old Maids to Radical Spinsters: Unmarried Women in the Twentieth-Century Novel,* edited by Laura L. Doan, 1–16. Urbana: University of Illinois Press, 1991.

Donovan, Josephine. *New England Local Color Literature: A Women's Tradition.* New York: Frederick Ungar, 1983.

———. "The Unpublished Love Poems of Sarah Orne Jewett." *Frontiers* 4 (Autumn 1979): 26–31.

Doreski, C. K. "Inherited Rhetoric and Authentic History: Pauline Hopkins at the *Colored American Magazine.*" In *The Unruly Voice: Rediscovering Pauline Elizabeth Hopkins,* edited by John Cullen Gruesser, 71–97. Urbana: University of Illinois Press, 1996.

Drake, Samuel Adams. *Our Colonial Homes.* Boston: Lee and Shepard, 1894.

duCille, Ann. *The Coupling Convention: Sex, Text, and Tradition in Black Women's Fiction.* New York: Oxford University Press, 1993.

Dyer, Walter A. *The Lure of the Antique.* New York: Century, 1910.

Earle, Alice Morse. *China Collecting in America.* 1892. New York: Empire State Book, 1924.

———. *Old-Time Gardens: Newly Set Forth.* 1901. New York: MacMillan, 1922.

Faderman, Lillian. *Surpassing the Love of Men: Romantic Friendship and Love between Women from the Renaissance to the Present.* New York: William Morrow, 1981.

Fales, Dean A. Introduction to *Antiqueman's Diary: The Memoirs of Fred Bishop Tuck,* by Fred Bishop Tuck, v–x. Gardiner, Maine: Tilbury House Press, 2000.

"Farmer Bassett's Romance." *Scribner's Monthly* 13 (February 1877): 484–97.

"Farmer Bassett's Romance II." *Scribner's Monthly* 13 (March 1877): 609–18.

Fassett, James H. *Colonial Life in New Hampshire.* Boston: Ginn, 1899.

Fetterley, Judith. "Commentary: Nineteenth-Century American Women Writers and the Politics of Recovery." *American Literary History* 6 (Autumn 1994): 600–11.

———. Introduction to *Provisions: A Reader from Nineteenth-Century American Women,* edited by Judith Fetterley, 1–40. Bloomington: Indiana University Press, 1985.

———. "Reading *Deephaven* as a Lesbian Text." In *Sexual Practice / Textual Theory: Lesbian Cultural Criticism,* edited by Susan J. Wolfe and Julia Penelope, 164–83. Cambridge: Basil Blackwell, 1993.

Fetterley, Judith, and Marjorie Pryse, eds. *American Women Regionalists, 1850–1910.* New York: W. W. Norton, 1992.

———. *Writing Out of Place: Regionalism, Women, and American Literary Culture.* Urbana: University of Illinois Press, 2003.

"The Fever of China Hunting." *New York Times,* May 28, 1893.

Fields, Annie Adams. Preface to *Letters of Sarah Orne Jewett,* by Sarah Orne Jewett, 3–12. Boston: Houghton Mifflin, 1911.

Fisken, Beth Wynne. "Within the Limits of Alice Brown's 'Dooryards':
Introspective Powers in *Tiverton Tales*." *Legacy* 5 (Spring 1988): 15–25.
Fleenor, Juliann E. "The Gothic Prism: Charlotte Perkins Gilman's Gothic Stories
and Her Autobiography." In *The Female Gothic*, edited by Juliann E. Fleenor,
227–41. Montreal: Eden, 1983.
Fleissner, Jennifer L. "Is Feminism a Historicism?" *Tulsa Studies in Women's
Literature* 21 (Spring 2002): 45–66.
———. *Women, Compulsion, Modernity: The Moment of American Naturalism*.
Chicago: University of Chicago Press, 2004.
Foote, Stephanie. *Regional Fictions: Culture and Identity in Nineteenth-Century
American Literature*. Madison: University of Wisconsin Press, 2001.
Foreman, P. Gabrielle. "'This Promiscuous Housekeeping': Death, Transgression,
and Homoeroticism in *Uncle Tom's Cabin*." *Representations* 43 (Summer
1993): 51–72.
Foreman, P. Gabrielle and Cherene Sherrard-Johnson. "Racial Recovery, Racial
Death: An Introduction in Four Parts." *Legacy* 24 (2007): 157–70.
Freccero, Carla. *Queer/Early/Modern*. Durham: Duke University Press, 2006.
———. "Queer Spectrality: Haunting the Past." In *A Companion to Lesbian, Gay,
Bisexual, Transgender, and Queer Studies*, edited by George E. Haggerty and
Molly McGarry, 194–212. Malden, Mass.: Blackwell Publishing, 2007.
Freeman, Elizabeth. *Time Binds: Queer Temporalities, Queer Histories*. Durham:
Duke University Press, 2010.
Freeman, Mary Wilkins. "A Church Mouse." In *American Women Regionalists,
1850–1910*, edited by Judith Fetterley and Marjorie Pryse, 344–56. New York:
W. W. Norton, 1992.
———. "Dear Annie." In *A New England Nun and Other Stories*, edited by Sandra A.
Zagarell, 250–85. New York: Penguin Books, 2000.
———. *The Fair Lavinia and Others*. 1902. New York: Harper and Brothers, 1907.
———. *The Jamesons*. 1899. In *A New England Nun and Other Stories*, edited by
Sandra A. Zagarell, 79–142. New York: Penguin Books.
———. *A New England Nun and Other Stories*. New York: Harper and Brothers,
1891.
———. *Silence and Other Stories*. London: Harper and Brothers, 1898.
———. *The Wind in the Rose-Bush and Other Stories of the Supernatural*. New
York: Doubleday, Page, 1903.
Freeman, Ruth, and Patricia Klaus, "Blessed or Not? The New Spinster in England
and the United States in the Late Nineteenth and Early Twentieth Centuries."
Journal of Family History 9 (December 1984): 394–414.
Frisch, Michael H. *Town into City: Springfield, Massachusetts, and the Meaning of
Community, 1840–1880*. Cambridge: Harvard University Press, 1972.
Fuchs, Ronald W., Jr. "A Passion for China: Henry Francis du Pont's Collection
of Export Porcelain." In *Collecting China: The World, China, and a History of
Collecting*, edited by Vimalin Rujivacharakul, 124–29. Newark: University of
Delaware Press, 2011.

Games, Alison. *Witchcraft in Early North America*. Lanham, Md.: Rowman and Littlefield, 2012.

Garber, Marjorie. *Vested Interests: Cross-Dressing and Cultural Anxiety*. New York: Routledge, 1992.

Garland, Hamlin. *Selected Letters of Hamlin Garland*. Edited by Keith Newlin and Joseph B. McCullough. Lincoln: University of Nebraska Press, 1998.

Gatewood, Willard B. *Aristocrats of Color: The Black Elite, 1880-1920*. Bloomington: Indiana University Press, 1990.

Gebhard, Caroline. "The Spinster in the House of American Criticism." *Tulsa Studies in Women's Literature* 10 (Spring 1991): 79-91.

Giffen, Sarah L. "Old York Historical and Improvement Society." In *"A Noble and Dignified Stream": The Piscataqua Region in the Colonial Revival, 1860-1930*, edited by Sarah L. Giffen and Kevin D. Murphy, 91-93. York, Maine: Old York Historical Society, 1992.

Gilbert, Sandra M., and Susan Gubar. *The Madwoman in the Attic: The Woman Writer and the Nineteenth-Century Literary Imagination*. 1979. New Haven: Yale University Press, 2000.

Gilman, Charlotte Perkins. *1890-1935*, vol. 2 of *The Diaries of Charlotte Perkins Gilman*. Edited by Denise D. Knight. Charlottesville: University of Virginia Press, 1994.

———. "The Giant Wistaria." 1891. In *Herland, "The Yellow Wall-Paper," and Selected Writings*, by Charlotte Perkins Gilman, edited by Denise D. Knight, 154-62. New York: Penguin Books, 1999.

———. *Herland, "The Yellow Wall-Paper," and Selected Writings*. Edited by Denise D. Knight. New York: Penguin Books, 1999.

———. *The Living of Charlotte Perkins Gilman: An Autobiography*. 1935. Salem, N.H.: Ayer Company Press, 1987.

———. *The Selected Works of Charlotte Perkins Gilman*. Edited by Denise D. Knight and Jennifer S. Tuttle. Tuscaloosa: University of Alabama Press, 2009.

———. *Women and Economics: A Study of the Economic Relation between Men and Women as a Factor in Social Evolution*. 1898. London: Putnam, 1900.

———. "The Yellow Wall-Paper." 1892. In *Herland, "The Yellow Wall-Paper," and Selected Writings*, by Charlotte Perkins Gilman, edited by Denise D. Knight, 166-82. New York: Penguin Books, 1999.

Gleason, Patrick. "Sarah Orne Jewett's 'The Foreigner' and the Transamerican Routes of New England Regionalism." *Legacy* 28 (2011): 24-46.

Goldberg, Jonathan, and Madhavi Menon. "Queering History." *PMLA* 120 (October 2005): 1608-17.

Golden, Catherine J. "Speaking a Different Story: The Illustrated Text." In *"The Yellow Wall-Paper" by Charlotte Perkins Gilman: A Dual-Text Critical Edition*, edited by Shawn St. Jean, 61-72. Athens: Ohio University Press, 2006.

"Good Form and Entertainment." *Harper's Bazaar* 39, June 1905, 26.

Goode, Mike. *Sentimental Masculinity and the Rise of History, 1790-1890*. Cambridge: Cambridge University Press, 2009.

Gordon, Avery. *Ghostly Matters: Haunting and the Sociological Imagination.* Minneapolis: University of Minnesota Press, 1997.
Gordon, Beverly. "Costumed Representations of Early America: A Gendered Portrayal, 1850–1940." *Dress* 30 (2003): 3–20.
Grant, Georgia. "A Wind of Fate." *Peterson's Magazine,* October 1888, 321–25.
Guyette, Elise A. *Discovering Black Vermont: African American Farmers in Hinesburgh, 1790–1890.* Burlington: University of Vermont Press, 2010.
Haefeli, Evan, and Kevin Sweeney. *Captors and Captives: The 1704 French and Indian Raid on Deerfield.* Amherst: University of Massachusetts Press, 2003.
Halttunen, Karen. "From Parlor to Living Room: Domestic Space, Interior Decoration, and the Culture of Personality." In *Consuming Visions: Accumulation and Display of Goods in America, 1880–1920,* edited by Simon J. Bronner, 157–89. New York: W. W. Norton, 1989.
Hare, Hobart Amory, et al. *The National Standard Dispensatory.* Philadelphia: Lea, 1905.
Harris, Sharon. "'Across the Gulf': Working in the 'Post-Recovery' Era." *Legacy* 26 (2009): 284–98.
Harvey, David. *The Condition of Postmodernity: An Enquiry into the Origins of Cultural Change.* 1980. Cambridge: Basil Blackwell, 1990.
Harvey, Tamara. "States of Recollection: How Seventeenth-Century Women Thought about Recovery and the Atlantic World." *Legacy* 31 (2014): 25–32.
Hawthorne, Nathaniel. *Grandfather's Chair: A History for Youth.* New York: American Publication Corporation, 1840.
———. *The House of the Seven Gables.* 1851. New York: Penguin Books, 1986.
———. *The Scarlet Letter.* 1850. New York: Penguin Books, 2003.
———. *Twice-Told Tales.* 1837. Philadelphia: D. McKay, 1893.
Hedges, Elaine. Essay for *Hearts and Hands: The Influence of Women & Quilts on American Society.* San Francisco: The Quilt Digest Press, 1987.
———. "The Nineteenth-Century Diarist and Her Quilts." *Feminist Studies* 8 (Summer 1982): 293–99.
———. "Quilts and Women's Culture." *Radical Teacher* 4 (March 1977): 7–10.
Herrick, Christine Terhune. "Country Boarding." *Ladies' Home Journal and Practical Housekeeper,* August 1886, 10.
Hewitt, Sarah Cooper. "Fashions and Counterfeits of Bric-a-Brac." *Cosmopolitan,* June 1892, 175–84.
Holley, Marietta. "How the Boarders 'Took Us In.'" *Peterson's Magazine,* December 1881, 432–36.
———. "How We Took in Summer Boarders." *Peterson's Magazine,* November 1881, 367–70.
Hooker, Ellen Bliss. "On Boarders and Boarding." *Good Housekeeping,* July 23, 1887, 138.
Hopkins, Pauline E. "Address at the *Citizen's William Lloyd Garrison Centenary Celebration.*" In *Daughter of the Revolution: The Major Non-Fiction Works of Pauline E. Hopkins,* by Pauline E. Hopkins, edited by Ira Dworkin, 355–57. New Brunswick: Rutgers University Press, 2007.

———. *The Magazine Novels of Pauline Elizabeth Hopkins*. New York: Oxford University Press, 1988.
Horowitz, Helen Lefkowitz. *Wild Unrest: Charlotte Perkins Gilman and the Making of "The Yellow Wall-Paper."* New York: Oxford University Press, 2010.
Howard, June. *Publishing the Family*. Durham: Duke University Press, 2001.
———. "Unraveling Regions, Unsettling Periods: Sarah Orne Jewett and American Literary History." *American Literature* 68 (June 1996): 365–84.
———, ed. *New Essays on The Country of the Pointed Firs*. Cambridge: Cambridge University Press, 1994.
Howells, William Dean. "Editor's Study." *Harper's New Monthly Magazine* 75 (September 1887): 638–42.
———. "Literary Boston Thirty Years Ago." *Harper's New Monthly Magazine* 91 (November 1895): 865–79.
———. "The Southern States in Recent American Literature." In *Defining Southern Literature: Perspectives and Assessments, 1831–1952*, edited by John E. Bassett, 199–209. Madison, N.J.: Fairleigh Dickinson University Press, 1997.
Hufnagel, Amy Wilkinson. "Emma Lewis Coleman." In *"A Noble and Dignified Stream": The Piscataqua Region in the Colonial Revival, 1860–1930*, edited by Sarah L. Giffen and Kevin D. Murphy, 152–55. York, Maine: Old York Historical Society, 1992.
Hull, Gloria T. "Researching Alice Dunbar-Nelson: A Personal and Literary Perspective." In *All the Women Are White, All the Blacks Are Men, But Some of Us Are Brave*, edited by Gloria T. Hull et al., 189–95. New York: Feminist Press, 1982.
———. "'Under the Days': The Buried Life and Poetry of Angelina Weld Grimké." In *Home Girls: A Black Feminist Anthology*, edited by Barbara Smith, 73–82. New York: Kitchen Table—Women of Color Press, 1983.
Hull, Gloria T., et al. *All the Women Are White, All the Blacks Are Men, But Some of Us Are Brave*. New York: Feminist Press, 1982.
Humez, Jean McMahon. *Harriet Tubman: The Life and the Life Stories*. Madison: University of Wisconsin Press, 2003.
Ifkovic, Edward. *The Life and Work of Writer Annie Trumbull Slosson: A Connecticut Local Colorist*. Lewiston, N.Y.: Edwin Mellen Press, 2004.
Jagose, Annamarie. *Inconsequence: Lesbian Representation and the Logic of Sexual Sequence*. Ithaca: Cornell University Press, 2002.
———. *Queer Theory: An Introduction*. New York: New York University Press, 1996.
James, Henry. *The Bostonians*. 1886. New York: Penguin Books, 1984.
———. *The Letters of Henry James*. Vol. 1. Edited by Percy Lubbock. New York: Charles Scribner's Sons, 1920.
Jewett, Sarah Orne. *A Country Doctor*. 1884. New York: Penguin Books, 1986.
———. *The Country of the Pointed Firs and Other Stories*. 1896. New York: W. W. Norton, 1994.
———. *Deephaven*. 1878. Portsmouth: Peter E. Randall, 1993.
———. "Martha's Lady." In *The Queen's Twin and Other Stories*, by Sarah Orne Jewett, 135–69. Boston: Houghton Mifflin, 1899.

———. *Sarah Orne Jewett Letters*. Edited by Richard Cary. Waterville, Maine: Colby College Press, 1967.

———. *The Story of the Normans*. New York: G. P. Putnam's Sons, 1889.

Johns, Barbara A. "'Mateless and Appealing': Growing into Spinsterhood in Sarah Orne Jewett." In *Critical Essays on Sarah Orne Jewett*, edited by Gwen L. Nagel, 147–164. Boston: G. K. Hall, 1984.

Johnson, Thomas B. "Elizabeth Perkins House." In *"A Noble and Dignified Stream": The Piscataqua Region in the Colonial Revival, 1860–1930*, edited by Sarah L. Giffen and Kevin D. Murphy, 67–70. York, Maine: Old York Historical Society, 1992.

Joseph, Philip. *American Literary Regionalism in a Global Age*. Baton Rouge: Louisiana State University Press, 2007.

Kammen, Michael. *Mystic Chords of Memory: The Transformation of Tradition in American Culture*. New York: Vintage Books, 1993.

Kaplan, Amy. *The Anarchy of Empire in the Making of U.S. Culture*. Cambridge: Harvard University Press, 2002.

———. *The Social Construction of American Realism*. Chicago: University of Chicago Press, 1988.

Kent, Kathryn R. *Making Girls into Women: American Women's Writing and the Rise of Lesbian Identity*. Durham: Duke University Press, 2003.

Kim, Thomas W. "Being Modern: The Circulation of Oriental Objects," *American Quarterly* 58 (June 2006): 379–406.

Kingston, Maxine Hong. *The Woman Warrior: Memoirs of a Girlhood among Ghosts*. 1975. New York: Vintage Books, 1989.

Knight, Denise D. "'The dawn of my work' (January 1, 1890–December 31, 1890)." In *1890–1935*. Vol. 2 of *The Diaries of Charlotte Perkins Gilman*, edited by Denise D. Knight, 407–9. Charlottesville: University of Virginia Press, 1994.

———. "New Evidence about the Origins of Gilman's 'The Giant Wistaria.'" *American Literary Realism* 40 (Winter 2008): 173–79.

———. "'That pure New England stock': Charlotte Perkins Gilman and the Construction of Identity." In *Charlotte Perkins Gilman: New Texts, New Contexts*, edited by Jennifer S. Tuttle and Carol Farley Kessler, 27–43. Columbus: Ohio State University Press, 2011.

———. "'You are getting to be a famous woman my dear!' (January 1, 1891–June 4, 1891)." In *1890–1935*. Vol. 2 of *The Diaries of Charlotte Perkins Gilman*, by Charlotte Perkins Gilman, edited by Denise D. Knight, 429–30. Charlottesville: University of Virginia Press, 1994.

Koppelman, Susan. "About 'Two Friends' and Mary Eleanor Wilkins Freeman." *American Literary Realism* 21 (Fall 1988): 43–57.

Kowaleski-Wallace, Beth. "Women, China, and Consumer Culture in Eighteenth-Century England." *Eighteenth-Century Studies* 29 (Winter 1995/1996): 153–67.

Kristeva, Julia. "Women's Time." In *The Kristeva Reader*, edited by Toril Moi, translated by Alice Jardine and Harry Blake, 187–213. New York: Basil Blackwell, 1986.

Lanser, Susan S. "Feminist Criticism, 'The Yellow Wallpaper,' and the Politics of Color in America." *Feminist Studies* 15 (Autumn 1989): 415–41.

Larkin, Edward. "The Cosmopolitan Revolution: Loyalism and the Fiction of an American Nation." *Novel* 40 (Fall 2006/Spring 2007): 52-76.

Leach, William. *Land of Desire: Merchants, Power, and the Rise of a New American Culture*. New York: Pantheon Books, 1993.

Lears, T. J. Jackson. *No Place of Grace: Antimodernism and the Transformation of American Culture, 1880-1920*. Chicago: University of Chicago Press, 1994.

Lee, Maureen E. *Black Bangor: African Americans in a Maine Community, 1880-1950*. Durham, N.H.: University of New Hampshire Press, 2005.

Lewis, Mrs. A. G. "An Old New England Village." *Ladies' Home Journal* 12, January 1895, 19.

Lindgren, James M. *Preserving Historic New England: Preservation, Progressivism, and the Remaking of Memory*. New York: Oxford University Press, 1995.

———. "'That Every Mariner May Possess the History of the World': A Cabinet for the East India Marine Society of Salem," *New England Quarterly* 68 (June 1995): 179-205.

Linett, Maren Tova. "Modernist Women's Literature: An Introduction." In *The Cambridge Companion to Modernist Women Writers*, edited by Maren Tova Linett, 1-16. New York: Cambridge University Press, 2010.

Lock, Charles. "Maurice Browne and the Chicago Little Theatre." *Modern Drama* 31 (Spring 1988): 106-16.

Love, Heather. *Feeling Backward: Loss and the Politics of Queer History*. Cambridge: Harvard University Press, 2007.

———. "Gyn/Apology: Sarah Orne Jewett's Spinster Aesthetics." *ESQ* 55 (2009): 305-34.

Luciano, Dana. *Arranging Grief: Sacred Time and the Body in Nineteenth-Century America*. New York: New York University Press, 2007.

———. "Geological Fantasies, Haunting Anachronies: Eros, Time, and History in Harriet Prescott Spofford's 'The Amber Gods.'" *ESQ* 55 (2009): 269-303.

———. "Passing Shadows: Melancholic Nationality and Black Critical Publicity in Pauline E. Hopkins's *Of One Blood*." In *Loss: The Politics of Mourning*, edited by David L. Eng and David Kazanjian, 148-87. Berkeley: University of California Press, 2003.

Ludlum, J. K. "The Other Boarder." *New England Magazine* 6 (September 1888): 493-97.

Lutz, Tom. *Cosmopolitan Vistas: American Regionalism and Literary Value*. Ithaca: Cornell University Press, 2004.

Lyle, Ella. "The China-Closet." *Good Housekeeping* 10, January 18, 1890, 133.

Mann, C. Griffith. "Exporting China: The Collecting Taste of William and Henry Walters." In *Collecting China: The World, China, and a History of Collecting*, edited by Vimalin Rujivacharakul, 99-106. Newark: University of Delaware Press, 2011.

Marek, Jayne. "Women Editors and Little Magazines in the Harlem Renaissance." In *Little Magazines and Modernism: New Approaches*, edited by Suzanne W. Churchill and Adam McKible, 106-18. Hampshire, England: Ashgate, 2007.

Marx, Karl. *Capital: A Critique of Political Economy*. Vol. 1. Translated by Ben Fowkes. New York: Penguin Books, 1992.

Maurer, Kathrin. "Archeology as Spectacle: Heinrich Schliemann's Media of Excavation." *German Studies Review* 32 (May 2009): 303–17.

Maybelle. "Summer Boarders." *Ladies' Home Journal and Practical Housekeeper*, July 1884, 3.

McCullough, Kate. *Regions of Identity: The Construction of American Women's Fiction, 1885–1914*. Stanford: Stanford University Press, 1999.

McFadden, Elizabeth. *The Glitter and the Gold: A Spirited Account of the Metropolitan Museum of Art's First Director, the Audacious and High-Handed Luigi Palma di Cesnola*. New York: Dial Press, 1971.

McGarry, Molly. *Ghosts of Futures Past: Spiritualism and the Cultural Politics of Nineteenth-Century America*. Berkeley: University of California Press, 2008.

Michaels, Walter Benn. *The Gold Standard and the Logic of Naturalism: American Literature at the Turn of the Century*. Berkeley: University of California Press, 1987.

Michie, Thomas S. "'Bought . . . of nobody for almost nothing': Anne Allen Ives and China Collecting in Nineteenth-Century New England." In *New England Collectors and Collections*, edited by Peter Benes, 87–101. Boston: Boston University Press, 2006.

Miller, Marla R., and Anne Diggan Lanning. "'Common Parlors': Women and the Recreation of Community Identity in Deerfield, Massachusetts, 1870–1920." *Gender and History* 6 (November 1994): 435–55.

"Miss Brown and Miss Guiney." *The Critic*, December 5, 1896, 367–68.

Moore, Lisa. *Dangerous Intimacies*. Durham: Duke University Press, 1997.

Moore, N. Hudson. *The Old China Book, Including Staffordshire, Wedgewood, Lustre, and Other English Pottery and Porcelain*. 1903. New York: Tudor Publishing Company, 1944.

Moraga, Cherríe, and Gloria Andalzúa. Introduction to *This Bridge Called My Back: Writings by Radical Women of Color*, edited by Cherríe Moraga and Gloria Andalzúa, xxiii–xxvi. Watertown, Mass.: Persephone Press, 1981.

Morgan, Phillip. "The Problems of Rural New England: A Remote Village." *Atlantic Monthly* 79 (May 1897): 577–88.

Morrison, Toni. *Beloved*. 1987. New York: Vintage Books, 2004.

Mossell, Gertrude E. H. Bustill. *The Work of the Afro-American Woman*. 1894. New York: Oxford University Press, 1988.

Murphy, Jacqueline Shea. "Replacing Regionalism: Abenaki Tales and 'Jewett's' Coastal Maine." *American Literary History* 10 (Winter 1998): 664–90.

Murphy, Kevin D. "The Politics of Preservation: Historic House Museums in the Piscataqua Region." In *"A Noble and Dignified Stream": The Piscataqua Region in the Colonial Revival, 1860–1930*, edited by Sarah L. Giffen and Kevin D. Murphy, 193–204. York, Maine: Old York Historical Society, 1992.

———. "'Secure from All Intrusion': Heterotopia, Queer Space, and the Turn-of-the-Twentieth-Century American Resort." *Winterthur Portfolio* 43 (Summer/Autumn 2009): 185–228.

Murphy, Teresa Anne. *Citizenship and the Origins of Women's History in the United States.* Philadelphia: University of Pennsylvania Press, 2013.

Nash, Alice N. "Elizabeth Bishop Perkins (1879-1952)." In *"A Noble and Dignified Stream": The Piscataqua Region in the Colonial Revival, 1860-1930,* edited by Sarah L. Giffen and Kevin D. Murphy, 189-90. York, Maine: Old York Historical Society, 1992.

Nealon, Christopher. *Foundlings: Lesbian and Gay Historical Emotion before Stonewall.* Durham: Duke University Press, 2001.

Nell, William C. *Colored Patriots of the American Revolution.* Boston: Robert F. Wallcut, 1855.

"New England in the Short Story." *Atlantic Monthly* 67 (June 1891): 845-50.

Newman, Andrew. "Fulfilling the Name: Catherine Tekakwitha and Marguerite Kanenstenhawi (Eunice Williams)." *Legacy* 28 (2011): 232-56.

Newton, Judith. "History as Usual? Feminism and the 'New Historicism.'" *Cultural Critique* 9 (Spring 1988): 87-121.

Niering, William A., and Nancy C. Olmstead. *The Audubon Society Field Guide to North American Wildflowers, Eastern Region.* New York: Knopf, 1979.

Nissenbaum, Stephen. "New England as Region and Nation." In *All over the Map: Rethinking American Regions,* edited by Edward Ayers and Peter Onuf, 38-61. Baltimore: Johns Hopkins University Press, 1996.

Norton, Charles Eliot. "The Lack of Old Homes in America." *Scribner's Magazine* 5 (May 1889): 636-40.

Novick, Peter. *That Noble Dream: The "Objectivity Question" and the American Historical Profession.* Cambridge: Cambridge University Press, 1988.

Nylander, Richard C. "Hamilton House." In *"A Noble and Dignified Stream": The Piscataqua Region in the Colonial Revival, 1860-1930,* edited by Sarah L. Giffen and Kevin D. Murphy, 70-74. York, Maine: Old York Historical Society, 1992.

"Old Furniture in New England." *Atlantic Monthly* 69 (March 1892): 413-14.

Oliver, James, and Lois E. Horton. *Black Bostonians: Family Life and Community Struggle in the Antebellum North.* New York: Holmes and Meier Press, 1979.

Onuf, Peter. "Federalism, Republicanism, and the Origins of American Sectionalism." In *All over the Map: Rethinking American Regions,* edited by Edward Ayers and Peter Onuf, 11-37. Baltimore: John Hopkins University Press, 1996.

Parkman, Francis. *A Half-Century of Conflict, Part 6: France and England in North America.* 1892. Boston: Little, Brown, 1905.

———. *La Salle and the Discovery of the Great West, Part 3: France and England in North America.* 1869. Boston: Little, Brown, 1927.

Parrish, Stephen Maxfield. *Currents of the Nineties in Boston and London: Fred Holland Day, Louise Imogen Guiney, and Their Circle.* New York: Garland Publishing, 1987.

Paton, Priscilla. *Abandoned New England: Landscape in the Works of Homer, Frost, Hopper, Wyeth, and Bishop.* Hanover, N.H.: University Press of New England, 2003.

Pattee, Fred Lewis. *History of American Literature since 1870*. New York: Century, 1915.

Peck, Ada Marie. "The Attic and Its Treasures." *Good Housekeeping*, December 1891, 280.

Pollak, Ellen. "Feminism and the New Historicism: A Tale of Difference or the Same Old Story?" *The Eighteenth Century* 29 (Fall 1988): 281–86.

Prentiss, Benjamin F. *The Blind African Slave; or, Memoirs of Boyrereau Brinch, Nicknamed Jeffery Brace*. Edited by Kari J. Winters. Madison: University of Wisconsin Press, 2004.

Pryse, Marjorie. "Sex, Class, and 'Category Crisis': Reading Jewett's Transitivity." In *Jewett and Her Contemporaries: Reshaping the Canon*, edited by Karen Kilcup and Thomas S. Edwards, 31–62. Gainesville: University Press of Florida, 1999.

Puar, Jasbir K. *Terrorist Assemblages: Homonationalism in Queer Times*. Durham: Duke University Press, 2007.

Ravage, Jessie. "Sarah Orne Jewett, *Deephaven*." In *"A Noble and Dignified Stream": The Piscataqua Region in the Colonial Revival, 1860–1930*, edited by Sarah L. Giffen and Kevin D. Murphy, 180–82. York, Maine: Old York Historical Society, 1992.

Reichardt, Mary R. *A Web of Relationship: Women in the Short Stories of Mary Wilkins Freeman*. Jackson: University Press of Mississippi, 1992.

Renan, Ernest. "What Is a Nation?" 1882. Translated by Martin Thom. In *Nation and Narration*, edited by Homi K. Bhabha, 8–22. London: Routledge, 1999.

Renza, Louis A. *"A White Heron" and the Question of Minor Literature*. Madison: University of Wisconsin Press, 1984.

Rich, Charlotte. "From Near-Dystopia to Utopia: A Source for *Herland* in Inez Haynes Gillmore's *Angel Island*." In *Charlotte Perkins Gilman and Her Contemporaries*, edited by Cynthia J. Davis and Denise D. Knight, 155–70. Tuscaloosa: University of Alabama Press, 2004.

Richardson, Riché. "Journeying with Toni Morrison's Writings and My Toni Morrison Quilt," *Riché Richardson's Art Quilts* (blog), November 10, 2011, http://richerichardsonartquilts.blogspot.com/search?q=Morrison.

Robie, Virginia Huntington. *By-Paths in Collecting, Being Aids in the Quest of Rare and Unique Things Which Have Passed the Century Mark, Such as Old China, Furniture, Pewter, Copper, Brass, Samples and Sun-Dials, with Comments on Their Age, Decoration, and Value*. New York: Century, 1912.

———. *The Quest of the Quaint*. Boston: Little, Brown, 1916.

Rohy, Valerie. *Anachronism and Its Others: Sexuality, Race, Temporality*. Albany: State University of New York Press, 2009.

———. *Impossible Women: Lesbian Figures and American Literature*. Ithaca: Cornell University Press, 2000.

Roman, Judith. "A Closer Look at the Jewett-Fields Relationship." In *Critical Essays on Sarah Orne Jewett*, edited by Gwen L. Nagel, 119–34. Boston: G. K. Hall, 1984.

Roof, Judith. *Come as You Are: Sexuality and Narrative*. New York: Columbia University Press, 1996.

Roosevelt, Theodore. "The Parasite Woman; the Only Indispensable Citizen." In *Selected Speeches and Writings of Theodore Roosevelt*, edited by Gordon Hutner, 54–59. New York: Vintage Books, 2013.

——. *Winning the West*. 1889. New York: Review of Reviews, 1904.

Rowe, Mrs. H. G. "Marjorie's Knight." *Godey's Lady's Book*, February 1885, 169–79.

Rujivacharakul, Vimalin. "China and china: An Introduction to Materiality and a History of Collecting." In *Collecting China: The World, China, and a History of Collecting*, edited by Vimalin Rujivacharakul, 15–28. Newark: University of Delaware Press, 2011.

S., M. E. W. "Bell's Beehives." *Appletons' Journal: A Monthly Miscellany of Popular Literature*, July 1876, 68–74.

Salazar, James B. *Bodies of Reform: The Rhetoric of Character in Gilded Age America*. New York: New York University Press, 2010.

Sánchez-Eppler, Karen. *Touching Liberty: Abolition, Feminism, and the Politics of the Body*. Berkeley: University of California Press, 1993.

Scharnhorst, Gary. "Charlotte Perkins Gilman's 'The Giant Wistaria': A Hieroglyph of the Female Frontier Gothic." In *Frontier Gothic: Terror and Wonder at the Frontier in American Literature*, edited by David Mogen et al., 156–64. Rutherford, N.J.: Fairleigh Dickinson University Press, 1993.

Schrager, Cynthia D. "Pauline Hopkins and William James: The New Psychology and the Politics of Race." In *The Unruly Voice: Rediscovering Pauline Elizabeth Hopkins*, edited by John Cullen Gruesser, 182–210. Urbana: University of Illinois Press, 1996.

Schweninger, Lee. "Reading the Garden in Gilman's 'The Yellow Wallpaper.'" *ISLE* 2 (Winter 1996): 25–44.

Seaton, Beverly. "A Pedigree for a New Century: The Colonial Experience in Popular Historical Novels, 1890–1910." In *The Colonial Revival in America*, edited by Alan Axelrod, 273–93. New York: W. W. Norton, 1985.

Sedgwick, Catherine Maria. *A New-England Tale*. 1822. New York: Penguin Books, 2003.

Sedgwick, Eve Kosofsky. "Paranoid Reading and Reparative Reading; or, You're So Paranoid, You Probably Think This Introduction Is About You." In *Novel Gazing: Queer Readings in Fiction*, edited by Eve Kosofsky Sedgwick, 1–37. Durham: Duke University Press, 1997.

Seitler, Dana. Introduction to *The Crux: A Novel*, by Charlotte Perkins Gilman. 1911. Edited by Dana Seitler. Durham: Duke University Press, 2003.

——. "Unnatural Selection: Mothers, Eugenic Feminism, and Charlotte Perkins Gilman's Regeneration Narratives." *American Quarterly* 55 (March 2003): 61–88.

Shackleton, Robert, and Elizabeth Shackleton. *The Charm of the Antique*. New York: Hearst's International Library, 1914.

——. *The Quest of the Colonial*. New York: Century, 1907.

Shannon, Laurie. "The Country of Our Friendship: Jewett's Intimist Art." *American Literature* 71 (June 1999): 227–62.

Sheldon, Jennie M. Arms. *Tribute to C. Alice Baker*. Greenfield, Mass.: Recorder Press, 1910.

Skiff, Frederick Woodward. *Adventures in Americana: Recollections of Forty Years Collecting Books, Furniture, China, Guns, and Glass*. Portland, Ore.: Metropolitan Press, 1935.

Sloboda, Stacey. "Porcelain Bodies: Gender, Acquisitiveness, and Taste in Eighteenth-Century England." In *Material Cultures, 1740-1920: The Meanings and Pleasures of Collecting*, edited by John Potvin and Alla Myzelev, 19-36. Surrey, England: Ashgate, 2009.

Slosson, Annie Trumbull. *The China Hunters Club*. New York: Harper and Brothers, 1878.

Smith, Barbara. "Toward a Black Feminist Criticism." In *All the Women Are White, All the Blacks Are Men, But Some of Us Are Brave*, edited by Gloria T. Hull et al., 157-75. New York: The Feminist Press, 1982.

———, ed. *Home Girls: A Black Feminist Anthology*. New York: Kitchen Table—Women of Color Press, 1983.

Smith, Bonnie G. *The Gender of History: Men, Women, and Historical Practice*. Cambridge: Harvard University Press, 1998.

Smith, Shawn Michelle. *American Archives: Gender, Race, and Class in Visual Culture*. Princeton: Princeton University Press, 1999.

———. *At the Edge of Sight: Photography and the Unseen*. Durham: Duke University Press, 2013.

Smith-Rosenberg, Carroll. *Disorderly Conduct: Visions of Gender in Victorian America*. Oxford: Oxford University Press, 1986.

———. "The Female World of Love and Ritual: Relations between Women in Nineteenth-Century America." *Signs* 1 (Autumn 1975): 1-29.

Somerville, Siobhan B. *Queering the Color Line: Race and the Invention of Homosexuality in American Culture*. Durham: Duke University Press, 2000.

Spofford, Harriet Prescott. *The Amber Gods and Other Stories*. Boston: Ticknor and Fields, 1863.

Stein, Jordan Alexander. "American Literary History and Queer Temporalities." *American Literary History* 25 (Winter 2013): 855-69.

Stewart, Susan. *On Longing: Narratives of the Miniature, the Gigantic, the Souvenir, the Collection*. 1993. Durham: Duke University Press, 2001.

———. "The Pickpocket: A Study in Tradition and Allusion." *MLN* 95 (December 1980): 1127-54.

Stillinger, Elizabeth. *The Antiquers: The Lives and Careers, the Deals, the Finds, the Collections of the Men and Women Who Were Responsible for the Changing Taste in American Antiques, 1850-1940*. New York: Alfred A. Knopf, 1980.

Stowe, Harriet Beecher. *House and Home Papers*. 1864. Boston: Houghton Mifflin, 1896.

———. *Oldtown Folks*. 1869. New Brunswick: Rutgers University Press, 1987.

———. *The Pearl of Orr's Island*. Boston: Ticknor and Fields, 1862.

———. *Poganuc People and Pink and White Tyranny*. 1871. Vol 11 of *The Writings of Harriet Beecher Stowe*. New York: AMS Press, 1967.

———. *Uncle Tom's Cabin*. 1852. New York: Penguin Books, 1986.

"Summer Reading." *Legacy* 1 (Spring 1984): 8.

Sundquist, Eric J. *To Wake the Nations: Race in the Making of American Literature*. Cambridge: Belknap Press of Harvard University Press, 1993.

Tate, Claudia. *Domestic Allegories of Political Desire: The Black Heroine's Text at the Turn of the Century*. New York: Oxford University Press, 1992.

Taylor, Diana. *The Archive and the Repertoire: Performing Cultural Memory in the Americas*. Durham: Duke University Press, 2003.

Tompkins, Jane. *Sensational Designs: The Cultural Work of American Fiction, 1790-1860*. New York: Oxford University Press, 1985.

Torsney, Cheryl B. "In Anticipation of the Fiftieth Anniversary of Woolson House." *Legacy* 2 (Fall 1985): 72-73.

Toth, Susan. "A Forgotten View from Beacon Hill: Alice Brown's New England Short Stories." *Colby Library Quarterly* 10 (March 1973): 1-17.

Traub, Valerie. "The New Unhistoricism in Queer Studies." *PMLA* 128 (January 2013): 21-39.

———. *The Renaissance of Lesbianism in Early Modern England*. Cambridge: Cambridge University Press, 2002.

Trowbridge, J. T. "Dorothy in the Garret." *Atlantic Monthly* 26 (August 1870): 188-90.

Truettner, William, and Roger Stein, eds. *Picturing Old New England: Image and Memory*. New Haven: Yale University Press, 1999.

Tucker, Louis Leonard. *Clio's Consort: Jeremy Belknap and the Founding of the Massachusetts Historical Society*. Boston: Massachusetts Historical Society, 1990.

Tuhkanen, Mikko. "'Out of Joint': Passing, Haunting, and the Time of Slavery in *Hagar's Daughter*." *American Literature* 79 (June 2007): 335-61.

Turkes, Doris J. "Must Age Equal Failure? Sociology Looks at Mary Wilkins Freeman's Old Women." *ATQ* 13 (September 1999): 197-214.

Tuttle, Jennifer. "Gilman's *The Crux* and Owen Wister's *The Virginian*: Intertextuality and 'Woman's Manifest Destiny.'" In *Charlotte Perkins Gilman and Her Contemporaries*, edited by Cynthia J. Davis and Denise D. Knight, 127-38. Tuscaloosa: University of Alabama Press.

———. Introduction to *The Crux: A Novel*, by Charlotte Perkins Gilman. Edited by Jennifer Tuttle. Newark: University of Delaware Press, 2002.

———, ed. "Looking Back, Looking Forward: Two *Legacy* Roundtable Discussions." *Legacy* 26 (2009): 197-241.

Ulrich, Laurel Thatcher. *The Age of Homespun: Objects and Stories in the Creation of an American Myth*. New York: Vintage Books, 2001.

———. "Presidential Address: An American Album, 1857." *American Historical Review* 115 (February 2010): 1-25.

Vicinus, Martha. *Intimate Friends: Women Who Loved Women, 1778-1928*. Chicago: University of Chicago Press, 2004.

Vincenttelli, Moira. *Women and Ceramics*. Manchester: Manchester University Press, 2000.

Walker, Alice. "African-American Literature and Black Women Writers." In *All the Women Are White, All the Blacks Are Men, But Some of Us Are Brave*, edited by Gloria T. Hull et al., 376–78. New York: Feminist Press, 1982.

———. *In Search of Our Mothers' Gardens*. New York: Harcourt Brace Jovanovich, 1983.

Walker, Dorothea. *Alice Brown*. New York: Twayne Publishers, 1974.

Warren, Joyce W. Introduction to *Ruth Hall and Other Stories*, by Fanny Fern, ix–xxxix. New Brunswick: Rutgers University Press, 1986.

Watt, Stephen. "Modern American Drama." In *The Cambridge Companion to American Modernism*, edited by Walter Kalaidjian, 102–26. Cambridge: Cambridge University Press, 2005.

Weidlich, Lorre M. "Quilt Scholarship: The Quilt World and the Academic World." *Quilt Journal* 3 (1994): 1–4.

Weinbaum, Alys Eve. *Wayward Reproductions: Genealogies of Race and Nation in Transatlantic Modern Thought*. Durham: Duke University Press, 2004.

Weinstock, Jeffrey A. *Scare Tactics: Supernatural Fiction by American Women*. New York: Fordham University Press, 2008.

Westbrook, Perry D. *Acres of Flint: Sarah Orne Jewett and Her Contemporaries*. 1951. Revised edition. Metuchen, N.J.: Scarecrow Press, 1981.

Whitehill, Walter Muir. *Independent Historical Societies: An Enquiry into Their Research and Publication Functions and Their Financial Future*. Boston: Boston Athenaeum, 1962.

Williams, Susan Reynolds. *Alice Morse Earle and the Domestic History of Early America*. Amherst: University of Massachusetts Press, 2013.

Winchester, Mary. "Summer Boarders and Their Hosts." *Good Housekeeping*, August 8, 1885, 9.

Wood, Ann Douglas. "The Literature of Impoverishment: The Women Local Colorists in America, 1865–1914." *Women's Studies* 1 (December 1972): 3–45.

Wood, Joseph S. *The New England Village*. Baltimore: Johns Hopkins University Press, 1997.

Woods, Kate Tannatt. "The Old Maid Mothers of New England." *The Chautauquan; A Weekly Newsmagazine* 12 (December 1890): 375.

Young, Alfred F. *Masquerade: The Life and Times of Deborah Sampson, Continental Soldier*. New York: Alfred A. Knopf, 2004.

"The Young Lady from Boston." *Frank Leslie's Popular Monthly*, September 1879, 369–74.

Zagarell, Sandra A. "*Country*'s Portrayal of Community and the Exclusion of Difference." In *New Essays on The Country of the Pointed Firs*, edited by June Howard, 39–60. Cambridge: Cambridge University Press, 1994.

———. "Crosscurrents: Registers of Nordicism, Community, and Culture in Jewett's *Country of the Pointed Firs*." *Yale Journal of Criticism* 10 (Fall 1997): 355–70.

———. "Narrative of Community: The Identification of a Genre." *Signs* 13 (Spring 1988): 498–527.

———. "Old Women and Old Houses: New England Regionalism and the Specter of Modernity in Jewett's *Strangers and Wayfarers.*" *American Literary Realism* 34 (Spring 2002): 251–64.

———. "Troubling Regionalism: Rural Life and the Cosmopolitan Eye in Jewett's *Deephaven.*" *American Literary History* 10 (Winter 1998): 639–63.

Index

Page numbers in *italics* refer to illustrations.

Ackmann, Martha, 156
Activism, feminist, 140, 141, 148–49, 155–56
Adams, Abigail, 49
Adams, Henry, 19, 34
All the Women Are White, All the Blacks Are Men, But Some of Us Are Brave (Hull et al.), 156, 159
"'Almaqui' The House in the Woods" (Perkins), 4–5, 151–53
American Quilt study group, 159
Ammons, Elizabeth, 17, 77, 87, 165–66n5, 167n24, 180n74
Ancestry. *See* Genealogy (biological)
Architectural restoration: Baker's influence in, 25; of Frary house, 26; house of history and, 34, 36; Jewett's connection to, 10; Perkins and, 2–3, 4–5, 166n12
Archive and the Repertoire, The (Taylor), 39
Archives: Baker's research in, 39; as erotic spaces, 42–43; feminist scholarship and, 157–58; history making and, 14–15, 21–22; vs. repertoire, 11, 12
Art: *Hagar's Daughter* and, 147; influence on Coleman's photography, 37; Junkins garrison house, 51–53, 55; portrait exhibition in Baker's work, 41; quilts as, 159. *See also* China collecting; Photography
"At Sudleigh Fair" (Alice Brown), 133–34, 87
Attics (upper levels of houses), 60–61, 126–27, 148, 186n41

Autoeroticism, 129, 131, 132; china collecting and, 102, 103, 108; spectral fusions and, 135

Baker, C. Alice, 25–50; archival research of, 21; bedroom of, 27, *28*; collaborations of, 50–56; correspondence of, 26–27; on Deerfield attack, 173n8; Frary house renovation by, 26; hauntings and, 21, 31, 35–36; historical practice of, 34–35; intimacies of, 7, 9–10, 22, 117, 172n2; Massachusetts Historical Society and, 33, 174n26, 182n18; Parkman and, 32–33; performativity of, 36–39, 175n38; photographs of, 37–39, *38*, 55, *56*. *See also True Stories of New England Captives Carried to Canada during the Old French and Indian Wars* (Baker)
Barthes, Roland, 28, 38
Baudrillard, Jean, 104
Baym, Nina, 32
Belonging: of captives, 31, 35; cross-generational, 21, 27–28, 39, 135–36, 137–38; intimate historicism and, 10–11; women's history and, 22, 46, 49–50. *See also* Genealogy (adoptive)
Beloved (Morrison), 121, 159, 160
Benjamin, Walter, 20, 169n52; angel of history, 55
Bennett, Judith, 121
Berlant, Lauren, 10
Black women's studies, 156, 159
Blood. *See* Genealogy (biological)

Blue Cup, The (painting, DeCamp), 143, *144*

Body, the: in Baker's work, 35, 36–40, 43–45, 55; in *Beloved*, 160; in Alice Brown's work, 135–36, 138; china as symbol for, 101–2, 104–5, 122, 145, 183n34; in *Deephaven* photographs, 72–73, 76–77; in domestic spaces, 28; in Gilman's work, 128–29, 130; in Jewett's work, 23, 84–85; of old maids, 61, 67; Perkins and, 5; the senses and, 45, 85, 111; spectral fusions and, 120, 128, 130–33, 135–36, 137–38, 148–49, 153; temporal drag and, 45, 120. *See also* Fingers; Genitalia, female; Intimate historicism

Boeckmann, Cathy, 48

Bostonians, The (Henry James), 2

Boston marriages, 6, 7, 14, 84

Bourdieu, Pierre, 105–6

Bravmann, Scott, 87

Brodhead, Richard, 13, 17, 58, 62, 163, 190n40

Brooks, Van Wyck, 59, 61–62

Brown, Alice, 23, 132–39; "At Sudleigh Fair," 87, 133–34; *Children of Earth*, 133; colonial revival nonfiction of, 59; intimacies of, 7, 9, 117, 185n16; *Joint Owners in Spain*, 133; "A Last Assembling," 18, 133, 134–37, 170n63; *Meadow-Grass*, 132, 133; New England connections of, 118; on *Pointed Firs*, 80–81; spectral fusions and, 121; *Tiverton Tales*, 132, 133; "The Way of Peace," 137–38, 139, 153

Brown, Bill, 85, 167n24

Brown, Gillian, 78

Brown, Lois, 140, 150

Butler, Judith, 119, 180n78, 185n18

By-Paths in Collecting (Robie), 90

Camera Lucida (Barthes), 38

Campbell, Donna, 122

Capital (Marx), 105

Captives, female: agency of, 30–31, 48–49; Baker's account of, 25, 29–31, 173–74n16; Coleman's account of, 54–55; house of history and, 34; marriage of, 173–74n16; scenarios and, 40–42, 43–44

Carby, Hazel V., 139, 140, 141, 155, 187n69

Carrick, Alice Van Leer, 106

Castiglia, Christopher, 31, 90–91

Cather, Willa, 8–9, 61, 168n36

Catholicism, 30, 42, 47, 175n56

Catlin, Mary Baldwin, 42

Cesnola, Luigi Palma di, 112

Character, as racial inheritance, 18, 40, 46–49

Charm of the Antique, The (Shackleton and Shackleton), 104

Cheyney, Edward, 33–34

Children of Earth (Alice Brown), 133

China: as figure for female body, 92, 101–2, 103–4, 108, 109, 122, 145, 183n34; in *Hagar's Daughter*, 142, 143, 145; Washington pitchers, 99–101

"China-Closet, The" (poem, Lyle), 114

China collecting, 23, 89–116; in "A China Craze," 106–10; class and, 112–14; consumerism and, 89, 91, 95, 105–6, 114–15; in English culture, 89, 92, 93; eroticism of, 23, 91–92, 101–10; fantasies and, 23, 90–91, 97–98, 101, 103–5, 106, 108–9, 112–13; gender roles and, 23, 92–101; history of, 89–90; as imperialist adventuring, 23, 110–11, 112–13; in *The Jamesons*, 91; labor of, 105–6, 116

China Collecting in America (Earle), 90, 92–93, 93–95, 97, 99–101, 111–12, 112–13, 114

China collectors: men as, 92, 93–94, 96, 97–99; women as, 90, 91–92, 93, 95–96, 114–15

212 *Index*

China hunters. *See* China collecting; China collectors
China Hunters Club, The (Slosson), 90, 92–93, 95–96, 97–99, 106–10, 112
Chronobiopolitics, 14, 59
Chrononormativity, 102
"Church Mouse, A" (Mary Wilkins Freeman), 66–69, 87
Citizenship, women's, 16, 17, 30–31, 49–50, 62, 92–93, 148–49. *See also* Dissent; Patriotism
Civil War, 148–49
Clarke, Cheryl, 156
Climaxes, erotic: china collecting and, 101, 104, 108; in "The Giant Wistaria," 130; in "A Last Assembling," 135; in *Pointed Firs*, 85
"Codfish Ghost, The" (Perkins), 4
Coleman, Emma Lewis: *Gathering Faggots*, 37–38; "Homestead of Josiah Riseing and Abigail Nims," 36; intimacies of, 7, 9–10, 22, 25–26; *New England Captives Carried to Canada between 1677 and 1760 during the French and Indian Wars*, 26, 29, 30, 51, 54–55, 56; photograph of Baker's chamber by, 27, *28*; photographs for *Deephaven* by, 72–77, *73, 74, 75*, 79, 179n50; *True Stories* and, 36, 43
Colonial fancy dressing, 37, 123–24, *152*, 153. *See also* Costumes, colonial; Cross-generational dressing; Spectral fusions
Colonial revivalism: Baker and, 26, 37–38, 39–40, 45; china collectors and, 90, 103, 107, 112–13; in Gilman's work, 125–27, 129–30; in *Hagar's Daughter*, 140–41, 143; modernism and, 118–19; New England regionalists and, 1–2, 6, 58–59, 62, 63–69, 87–88, 167n24; Perkins and, 152–53; in *Pointed Firs*, 87–88
Colonial teas, 12, 123–24

Colored American Magazine, 140
Colored Patriots of the American Revolution (Nell), 149–50
Combahee River Collective (CRC), 155–56
Conforti, Joseph, 2, 16
Consumerism, china collecting and, 89, 91, 95, 105–6, 114–15
Cook, Clarence, 115, 142
Cooke, Rose Terry: colonial fiction of, 59; historical allusions in work of, 22–23, 62; "How Celia Changed Her Mind," 64–66; *Huckleberries Gathered from New England Hills*, 9; intimacies of, 7, 9, 117; "Mary Ann's Mind," 64
Cosmopolitanism: Baker's work and, 39–40; china collecting and, 89, 90, 96, 112–13, 115, 182n23; of *Colored American Magazine*, 140; empathetic identification and, 77, 80; Jewett's work and, 17, 69–70, 77, 80, 179n60; regional, 15–18, 20
Costumes, colonial, 37–38, 118, 123–24, 152–53. *See also* Colonial fancy dressing
Country of the Pointed Firs, The (Jewett), 82–88; Bowden reunion in, 85–87; Cather's preface to, 8, 61; eroticism in, 61, 85–87; imperialism in, 77; natural world in, 72, 80–81, 84–86; queerness in, 17, 69–70, 82–85; summer tourism and, 81–82, 84
Country Wife, The (Wycherley), 92
Coviello, Peter, 7, 81, 83
Cross-dressing. *See* Drag
Cross-generational dressing: Baker's, 45; in "A China Craze," 109; colonial fancy dressing as, 37, 123–24, *152*, 153; Perkins's, 5–6, *152*; spectral fusions and, 120; Washington pitcher and, 100; in "The Way of Peace," 137–38
"Custom-House, The" (Hawthorne), 126

Dandurand, Karen, 156
Daniel, Janice, 68
Daughters of the American Revolution (DAR), 46, 124, 150
Davidson, Elizabeth Burleigh, 2, 124
Davis, Thadious M., 118
"Dear Annie" (Mary Wilkins Freeman), 64
DeCamp, Joseph, 143, *144*
Deephaven (Jewett), 70–77, 79–80; photographs for unpublished edition of, 10, 14, 72–77, 79, 169n45, 179n50; preface to, 57
Deerfield, Massachusetts, 7, 25, 29, 173n8. *See also* Captives, female
DeLamotte, Eugenia, 147
Democracy: linked to recollection, 12–13; queerness and, 11; race and, 77–78. *See also* Citizenship, women's; Dissent; Patriotism
Department stores, 110, 184n54
Dickinson, Emily, 16, 35
Dissent: ancestry and, 46–49; as Anglo-American birthright, 16, 18–19; in "A Church Mouse," 66–69; in *Hagar's Daughter*, 140–41; refusal to marry as, 11, 62, 64, 136–37, 141; unmarried women and, 11, 18, 19–20, 64
Dobson, Joanne, 156
Domesticity/domestic space: African American women and, 143–45; Baker's bedroom, *27–28*; captives and, 44; china collecting and, 96; in *Deephaven*, 70, 71; in *Hagar's Daughter*, 142–45; history as, 34, 35–36, 49; in "A Last Assembling," 134–35, 136; as performance space, 28; repetition and, 148; as sensual site, 9; women's citizenship and, 49
Domestic labor, 114, 142–45
Domestic tourism. *See* Tourism
Donovan, Josephine, 58, 157
Doreski, C. K., 139

"Dorothy in the Garret" (Trowbridge), 60–61
Drag: in *Hagar's Daughter*, 141–42, 148–51; Washington pitchers and, 99–101. *See also* Cross-generational dressing; Spectral fusions
Dreiser, Theodore, 121
duCille, Ann, 144–45
Dunbar-Nelson, Alice, 158, 161

Earle, Alice Morse: career of, 90; on china collecting, 23, 103, 181n4, 182n26; intimacies of, 7, 9, 10, 117, 168n29. *See also China Collecting in America* (Earle)
East Indian Marine Society (EIMS), 110–11
Empathy, 76, 77, 79–80
Eroticism: of archives, 42–43; china collecting and, 91–92, 101–10, 113–14, 115; in "A China Craze," 106–10; in *Pointed Firs*, 85; in *True Stories*, 44–45. *See also* Autoeroticism; Climaxes, erotic; Sensuality
Erotohistoriography, 12, 14
Eugenics, 17, 171n75
Exceptionalism, 15–16, 17, 20, 23, 46, 47–48, 174n33

Families. *See* Genealogy (biological); Queer intimacies
Fantasies: china collecting and, 23, 90–91, 97–98, 101, 103–5, 106, 108–9, 112–13; of colonial times, 145–46; of heterosexual reproduction, 143; of imperialist adventures, 110–11, 112–13; of living in colonial houses, 4–5, 151
Feeling Backward (Love), 50
Female friendship: in "A Church Mouse," 69; in *Deephaven*, 70; in "How Celia Changed Her Mind," 65; in *Pointed Firs*, 83. *See also* Queer intimacies

214 *Index*

Feminist literary scholarship, 13–14, 24, 155–57, 159–62, 163–64
Fetterley, Judith, 17–18, 65, 70, 77, 79, 155, 157, 160–61, 165–66n5
Fields, Annie, 7
Fingers: archives and, 43; in *Deephaven* photographs, 72–73; in "Dorothy in the Garret," 61; in "The Giant Wistaria," 130; in *Hagar's Daughter*, 145, 146; in photograph of Baker, 55; *Pointed Firs* and, 80–81. *See also* Body, the; Genitalia, female; Senses, the
Fisken, Beth, 138
Flaubert, Gustave, 57
Fleissner, Jennifer, 14, 60, 62, 122–23, 163–64, 190n40
Foote, Stephanie, 9, 14, 15, 58
"Foreigner, The" (Jewett), 80
Fourth of July, 63–64
Fradenburg, Louise, 12, 162
France and England (Parkman), 32–33
Frary house, 26–27, 37, 46, 153, 175n39
Freccero, Carla, 12, 162, 174n35
Freeman, Elizabeth, 12, 14, 45, 102, 120
Freeman, Mary Wilkins: "A Church Mouse," 66–69, 87; colonial fiction of, 58–59, 176n9; correspondence of, 9, 10, 57, 169n42; "Dear Annie," 64; Fleissner on, 122–23; *The Heart's Highway*, 59, 177n29; historical allusions in work of, 62, 63, 64, 66–69; intimacies of, 7, 117; *The Jamesons*, 2, 12, 91; "The Revolt of 'Mother,'" 63; "Silence," 10; temporality and, 57–58; "The Willow-Ware," 101–3
French, Thomas, 47
Frontiers (journal), 157
Fuller, Margaret, 49

Gannett, Deborah Sampson. *See* Sampson, Deborah
Garland, Hamlin, 57, 59
Garrison house: in "A Church Mouse," 66, 67–68, 69, 178n45; history as, 36, 50–55; Junkins house, 26, 36, 51, 51–53, *52*, 176n61
Gathering Faggots (photograph, Coleman), 37–*38*
Gay. *See* Queer intimacies; Queerness
Genealogy (adoptive), 46–49, 92–93, 94, 97, 138, 147
Genealogy (biological), 18–19, 46–48, 97, 134–35, 138, 143, 147
Generations: of New England regionalists, 24, 54, 117, 119–20, 153. *See also* Belonging; Cross-generational dressing
Genitalia, female: china bowl as figure for, 92, 108, 109; in *Deephaven* photographs, 72, 76–77; well as figure for, 130; womb images, 61, 129, 135, 136
Ghosts, 5, 7, 28, 39; in Baker's life, 35, 36; in "A China Craze," 109; in "The Giant Wistaria," 130; scholarly subjects as, 161; spectral fusions, 119–21; spinsters as, 60–61, 71. *See also* Hauntings; Spectral fusions
"Giant Wistaria, The" (Gilman), 125, 129–31
Gillman, Susan, 14, 190n40
Gilman, Charlotte Perkins, 123–32; colonial revivalism and, 123–26; colonial teas and, 12, 123, 124–25; "The Giant Wistaria," 125, 129–31; "In the Name of the King!," 125; intimacies of, 117; New England connections of, 118; *Women and Economics*, 128; "The Yellow Wall-Paper," 21, 118, 125–29, 131–32, 146–47
Good Housekeeping, 2, 82, 93
Gordon, Avery, 120
Gothic, the, 32, 34; cathedral and history writing, 33; in *Hagar's Daughter*, 147–48; in *The Junkins Garrison*, 53. *See also* Ghosts; Hauntings
Greek culture, 86–87
Grimké, Angelina Weld, 161
Guiney, Louise Imogen, 7, 9, 118

Hagar's Daughter (Hopkins), 140–49; colonial revivalism and, 118–19, 143; domesticity in, 142–45; drag in, 148–49, 151, 153; the Gothic in, 147–48
Hamilton house, 10
Hands. *See* Fingers
Hauntings: Baker and, 21, 31, 35–36; *The Junkins Garrison* and, 53. *See also* Ghosts; Gothic, the; Spectral fusions
Hawthorne, Nathaniel, 2, 60, 126
Heart's Highway, The (Mary Wilkins Freeman), 59, 177n29
Hedges, Elaine, 159
Heritage tourism, 2–3, 7, 25
Hertel brothers, 41–42
Heterosexuality: archives and, 42–43; spinster narratives and, 8, 9, 59, 64. *See also* Queer intimacies; Reproduction (heterosexual)
"Hidden Self, The" (William James), 140
Historical allusions, 22–23, 62–69, 84, 86–87, 139
Historical preservation societies, 1, 93
History: as a building, 33–34, 35–36, 49, 50–51; china collecting and, 111–12; making of, 12, 21–22; professionalization of, 32, 33–34, 54; as progressive, 17–18, 33–34, 55, 63, 70, 127; women's, 49–50, 121, 127–28, 155–56. *See also* Intimate historicism
Homer, Winslow, 37, 51–52, 53
"Homestead of Josiah Riseing and Abigail Nims" (photograph, Coleman), 36
Homonationalism, 20
Hopkins, Pauline Elizabeth: career of, 140; New England connections of, 118; *Of One Blood*, 140; *The Slaves' Escape (Peculiar Sam)*, 140; spectral fusions and, 121, 139. See also *Hagar's Daughter* (Hopkins)
House and Home Papers (Stowe), 142
House Beautiful, The (Cook), 142
House books, 27
House of the Seven Gables, The (Hawthorne), 60
Houses, colonial: in "'Almaqui' The House in the Woods," 4–5, 151–53; in *Deephaven*, 70, 71; Frary house, 26–27, 37, 46, 153, 175n39; in "The Giant Wistaria," 129, 130; in *Hagar's Daughter*, 146–47, 148; Hamilton house, 10; history as, 35–36, 49, 50–55; Junkins garrison house, 26, 36, *51*, 51–53, *52*, 176n61; in "A Last Assembling," 134–35; Perkins house, 2, 3–4, 153, 166n12; renovation of, 26; as sensual sites, 4–5, 7, 8–9; as stages for intimate historicism, 4, 5–6, 9, 26–28, 134–35; in "The Yellow Wall-Paper," 126, 127, 128. *See also* Architectural restoration; Domesticity/domestic space; Garrison house
Howard, June, 15, 176n7
"How Celia Changed Her Mind" (Cooke), 64–66
Howells, William Dean, 8, 18, 83, 132, 171–72n79
Huckleberries Gathered from New England Hills (Cooke), 9
Hull, Akasha Gloria (Gloria T.), 156, 158, 161

Immigrants, 114, 170–71n65
Imperialism, 15–20; in Baker's *True Stories*, 30; china collecting and, 103, 110–11, 112–13; in Coleman's *New England Captives*, 54; in Jewett's work, 77; in Mary Wilkins Freeman's work, 63, 66, 68, 170n63; of New England, 15–16; New England men and, 170n63; in *Robert Junkins' Garrison House, York, Maine*, 52; women's citizenship and, 66, 68. *See also* Sectionalism
Imprisonment, of women, 127–28, 146–47, 148. *See also* Mobility

"In Anticipation of the Fiftieth Anniversary of Woolson House" (Torsney), 158
Industrialization, 105, 115, 183–84n53
Inheritance. *See* Genealogy (adoptive); Genealogy (biological)
"In the Name of the King! A Colonial Romance" (play, Gilman and Stetson), 125
Intimacies. *See* Queer intimacies
Intimate historicism, 8; Baker's, 26–28, 34–36, 36–41, 43–44, 45; in china-collecting guides, 91; definition of, 10–12; of late twentieth-century feminist scholars, 158–59, 160–62, 163–64; in Mary Wilkins Freeman's work, 63, 66, 68–69; as methodology, 14–15, 123; Perkins house and, 3–4; in Perkins photograph, 5–6; in *Pointed Firs*, 84–85, 87–88; recovery vs. recognition and, 162–64; the repertoire and, 12; in *True Stories*, 29; in "The Yellow Wall-Paper," 128, 131

Jagose, Annamarie, 14, 166n8
James, Henry, 2, 61, 121
James, William, 140
Jameson, J. Franklin, 34
Jamesons, The (Mary Wilkins Freeman), 2, 12, 91
Jewett, Sarah Orne, 2; "The Foreigner," 80; intimacies of, 7, 9–10, 117, 169n42; *A Marsh Island*, 82; on narrative, 83–84; New England regionalism of, 18–19, 57–58; queerness in writings of, 69–77, 157; *The Tory Lover*, 10, 59, 177n29; on tourism, 81; women's cosmopolitanism and, 17; writing process of, 8–9. *See also Country of the Pointed Firs, The* (Jewett); *Deephaven* (Jewett)
"Jewett's Witches" (Ammons), 87
Joint Owners in Spain (Alice Brown), 133

Junkins Garrison, The (painting, Lane), 51–53, 55
Junkins garrison house, 26, 36, *51*, 51–53, *52*, 176n61

Kammen, Michael, 19
Kanenstenhawi, Marguerite (originally Eunice Williams), 30, 48, 174n17
Kelley, Mary, 157
Kim, Thomas W., 95
Kingston, Maxine Hong, 159
Knapp, Adeline E., 132
"Knitting Sale-Socks" (Spofford), 64
Kristeva, Julia, 59

Labor: archival work as, 43; in *Beloved*, 160; china collecting as, 105–6, 115, 116; New England regionalism and, 6, 10–11, 12. *See also* Reproduction (heterosexual)
Ladies' Home Journal, 2, 81, 124
Lamb, Charles, 94–95
Lane, Susan Minot: contribution to *True Stories*, 36; intimacies of, 7, 9–10, 22, 25–26, 27, 172n2; *The Junkins Garrison*, 50–51, 52–53, 55
Lanser, Susan S., 125
"Last Assembling, A" (Alice Brown), 18, 133, 134–37, 170n63
Leach, William, 110, 184n54
Legacy (journal), 156–57, 157–58
Lesbians. *See* Queer intimacies; Queerness
Lewis, Sinclair, 121
Lindgren, James, 110–11
Literary history: modernism in, 24, 122–23; naturalism in, 117, 121–22; regionalism in, 13, 24, 61–62, 117, 121–23, 153, 165–66n5. *See also* Feminist literary scholarship; Regionalism, literary
Little Theatre, 133
Love, Heather, 50, 162
Luciano, Dana, 13, 14, 59, 121
Lutz, Tom, 17

Index 217

Margry, M. Pierre, 32
Marie-Joseph of the Infant Jesus (originally Esther Wheelwright), 30, 48
Marriage: independence and, 63–64; in *Pointed Firs*, 82. *See also* Boston marriages; Unmarried women
Marsh Island, A (Jewett), 82
Marx, Karl, 105
"Mary Ann's Mind" (Cooke), 64
Massachusetts Historical Society, 33, 93
Masturbation. *See* Autoeroticism
McCullough, Kate, 14, 15, 84
Meadow-Grass (Alice Brown), 132, 133
Melancholic incorporation, 119, 185n18
Mobility: as Anglo-American birthright, 16; china collecting and, 90–91, 96, 101; in colonial-revival fiction, 177n29; in *Deephaven*, 70, 71–72, 76, 77, 79–80; in *Hagar's Daughter*, 145; in *Pointed Firs*, 82, 84, 180n74. *See also* Imprisonment, of women
Modernism, 13, 24; Alice Brown and, 117, 132, 133; colonial revivalism and, 117, 119; Gilman and, 117; Hopkins and, 117–18, 140; literary history and, 122–23; Perkins and, 151–53
Morrison, Toni, 121, 159, 160
Mossell, Gertrude E. H. Bustill, 150
Murphy, Kevin D., 3, 4, 169n46
Murphy, Teresa Anne, 49
Museums of Old York, 179n50

Native Americans, 15, 29, 30, 48, 134, 173–74n16
Nativism, 1, 46, 86, 125, 142
Naturalism, 117, 118, 121–22
Natural world: in *Deephaven*, 71–73, 76; in *Pointed Firs*, 80–81, 84–86, 87–88
Nealon, Christopher, 14
Nell, William C., 149–50
New England Captives Carried to Canada between 1677 and 1760 during the French and Indian Wars (Coleman), 26, 29, 30, 51, 54–55, *56*
New England Magazine, 127, 131, *132*
New England Nineteenth-Century American Women Writers study group, 156–57
New Essays on the Country of the Pointed Firs (Howard), 15
New historicism, 13, 15, 163, 188n1, 190n40
New York Times, 90, 93
Nissenbaum, Stephen, 1, 167n24, 183–84n53
Norris, Frank, 121
Norton, Charles Eliot, 115
Novick, Peter, 34
Noyon, Abigail de, 36, 40, 46
Noyon, Jacques de, 175n56
Nuclear family, the, 19, 136–37, 138–39
Nutting, Wallace, 1

Of One Blood (Hopkins), 140
Old maids. *See* Unmarried women
Oldtown Folks (Stowe), 98
Old York Historical and Improvement Society, 3
O'Neill, Eugene, 133
Onuf, Peter, 16
Otis, Christine (originally Margaret Otis), 29–30
Oyster River raid, 68, 178n42

Parkman, Francis, 25, 32–33, 174n23
Passing (racial), 140–41
Past, the. *See* History
Patriotism: china collecting and, 93; female captives and, 30–31; in *Hagar's Daughter*, 149; housekeeping and, 142–43; in *Pointed Firs*, 86; queerness and, 11, 36, 137. *See also* Citizenship, women's; Democracy; Dissent
Pattee, Fred Lewis, 122–23
Peculiar Sam (Hopkins), 140

Penetration: in Baker's work, 42–43; china collecting and, 101, 107, 109–10; in "A Church Mouse," 67; in "The Codfish Ghost," 4; in *Hagar's Daughter*, 147; in *Pointed Firs*, 80–81; in "The Yellow Wall-Paper," 131

Performance: Baker and, 36–40, 175n38; domestic spaces and, 4, 5–6, 9, 26–28, 134–35; Gilman and, 12; in Mary Wilkins Freeman's work, 68–69; Perkins and, 5–6, 167n20; Washington pitchers and, 99–101

Perkins, Elizabeth Bishop, 2–6, *5*, *152*; "'Almaqui' The House in the Woods," 4–5, 151–53; architectural restoration and, 2–3, 4–5, 166n12; "The Codfish Ghost," 4; colonial revivalism of, 5–6, 151–53; intimacies of, 10; intimate historicism of, 3–4; performance and, 167n20

Perkins, Mary Sowles, 2, 10, 124

Perkins house, 2, 3–4, 153, 166n12

Photography: archival records compared to, 43; of Baker, 37–*38*, 55, *56*; of colonial dressing, 5–6, *124*, *152*, 153; death and, 27, 28; for *Deephaven* edition, 10, 72–77, *79*, 179n50; *Gathering Faggots*, 37–*38*; of interior rooms, 27, 28, 39; race and, 38–39

Pink and White Tyranny (Stowe), 142, 170n63, 176n17

Piscataqua Garden Club, 3, 166–67n13

Plessis, Joseph-Octave, 47–48

Pocumtuck Valley Memorial Association (PVMA), 37

Pope, Alexander, 92

Present, the. *See* Temporality

Protolesbians. *See* Queer intimacies; Queerness

Provisions: A Reader from Nineteenth-Century American Women (Fetterley), 157, 160–61

Pryse, Marjorie, 17–18, 65, 77, 79, 155, 165–66n5

Puar, Jasbir, 19, 20

Queer cosmopolitanism, 69–70, 77, 80, 179n60

Queer intimacies: Baker-Lane-Coleman family, 22, 25–26, 50–56; Boston marriages, 6, 7, 14, 84; china collecting and, 91–92, 106, 116; in *Deephaven*, 70–72, 76–77; Gilman's, 132; in "How Celia Changed Her Mind," 65; of New England regionalists, 6–7; in *Pointed Firs*, 82–83, 84; range of, 7–8; scale of, 10–11. *See also* Female friendship

Queerly colonial, the, 8, 60

Queerness: in "At Sudleigh Fair," 133–34; of captive women's lives, 30–31; cultural narratives of, 20; defined, 30, 166n8; democratic life and, 11; in Jewett's work, 17, 69–70, 157; in "A Last Assembling," 136; linked with witches, 87; New England regionalism and, 20; in *Uncle Tom's Cabin*, 78

Queer studies, 9, 14, 21, 50, 157, 160–61, 168n39, 190n42

Quilts, 159, 189n18

Race: in "At Sudleigh Fair," 133–34; attics and, 127; in Baker's work, 46–50; character as synonymous with, 18, 40, 46–49; china and, 112–13, 122, 145; democracy and, 77–80; domestic ideal and, 143–45; in *Gathering Faggots*, 38–39; in Gilman's work, 125–26; in *Hagar's Daughter*, 141, 142, 147; in *Pointed Firs*, 86–87

Racial inheritance. *See* Genealogy (biological)

Raizenne, Jean Baptiste, 43, 44

Ranke, Leopold von, 42

Rape of the Lock, The (Pope), 92

Index   219

Realism, 117, 118, 121, 132
Regional cosmopolitanism, 15–20
Regional Fictions (Foote), 15
Regionalism, literary: generations of women writers and, 117; as historiographical, 22–23, 23–24, 57–60; in literary history, 121–23; as women's tradition, 2, 165–66n5. *See also* individual authors
Regions of Identity (McCullough), 15
Relationships. *See* Queer intimacies
Renovation/restoration. *See* Architectural restoration; Houses, colonial
Repertoire, the, 11–12, 15, 39
Reproduction (heterosexual): celebration of, 44; china collecting and alternatives to, 115; housekeeping and, 143; in "How Celia Changed Her Mind," 65; old maid stereotypes and, 59–60; white women's, 17–18, 19–20, 30–31, 137
"Researching Alice Dunbar-Nelson: A Personal and Literary Perspective" (Hull), 161
"Revolt of 'Mother,' The" (Mary Wilkins Freeman), 63
Rich, Charlotte, 117
Robert Junkins' Garrison House, York, Maine (painting, Homer), 51–52, 53
Robie, Virginia Huntington, 90, 91
Rohy, Valerie, 58, 166n8
Romantic historicism, 32, 34
Roosevelt, Theodore, 17, 19, 32
Rujivacharakul, Vimalin, 110

Salazar, James, 48
Sampson, Deborah, 149–51, 188n91
Sánchez-Eppler, Karen, 78
Santayana, George, 121–22
Sayward, Esther, 53
Sayward, Mary, 53
Scarlet Letter, The (Hawthorne), 2, 126
Scenario: definition of, 39; of heritage, 40, 43–44; of heroism, 40–41; of the historian, 40, 41–43

Schliemann, Heinrich, 112
Scott, Patricia Bell, 156
Sectionalism, 1, 8, 18–19, 20, 165–66n5
Sedgwick, Eve Kosofsky, 24
Seitler, Dana, 125, 186–87n53
Senses, the, 45, 85, 111. *See also* Body, the; Fingers
Sensuality: architectural spaces and, 4–5; in "The Giant Wistaria," 130–31; in *Hagar's Daughter*, 145; in Jewett's work, 69, 70, 80–81, 85; in "The Yellow Wall-Paper," 129, 131. *See also* Eroticism; Fingers
Sentimentalism, 82, 96, 103, 112
Sexuality: autoeroticism, 102, 103, 108, 129, 131, 132, 135; climaxes, erotic, 85, 101, 104, 108, 130, 135. *See also* Eroticism; Fingers; Penetration; Queerness; Sensuality
Shackleton, Elizabeth, 104
Shackleton, Robert, 104
Sheldon, George, 29, 33
Sheldon, Jennie Arms, 29, 37, 172n2
Sheldon, John, 40–41
Shonatakakwani, Ignace, 43, 45, 173n16
Shopping. *See* Consumerism, china collecting and
"Silence" (Mary Wilkins Freeman), 10
Silver, 145
Slavery, 78, 80, 120–21, 141, 149
Slaves' Escape, The; or, The Underground Railroad (*Peculiar Sam*) (Hopkins), 140
Slosson, Annie Trumbull: career of, 90; china-collecting women and, 23, 181–82n17; *The China Hunters Club*, 90, 92–93, 95–96, 97–99, 106–10, 112; intimacies of, 7, 9, 117, 168n29
Smith, Barbara, 156, 161–62, 188n3
Smith, Bonnie G., 34, 171n73
Smith, Shawn Michelle, 39
South, the, 1, 15, 141, 148, 165n5
Spectral fusions: feminist action through, 119–21; in "The Giant

Wistaria," 129–30; in *Hagar's Daughter*, 148–49, 151; in "A Last Assembling," 134, 135–37; Perkins's, 5–6, 153; in "The Way of Peace," 137–38; in "The Yellow Wall-Paper," 126, 128–29, 131–32

Spinsters. *See* Unmarried women

Spofford, Harriet Prescott, 64, 169n41, 185n16

Staël, Germaine de, 32, 171n73

Stetson, Grace Ellery Channing, 125, 132

Stewart, Susan, 62–63, 105

Stowe, Harriet Beecher, 77–78, 98, 142, 170n63, 176n17, 179n54

Summer boarding. *See* Tourism

Sundquist, Eric, 140

Taylor, Diana, 11–12, 15, 39

Teacups. *See* China

Temporal drag, 45, 120

Temporality: "behind" as physical vs. temporal position, 128, 131, 147, 186n46; in *Beloved*, 160; china collecting and, 94–95; in "A China Craze," 108–9; in *Deephaven*, 57; in *Deephaven* photographs, 73, 76; generations of women and, 54, 117; in *Hagar's Daughter*, 148; intimate historicism and, 14; models of, 59–60, 102; past in relation with present, 20–21, 57–58; in *Pointed Firs*, 69–70, 83, 85–86; reparative practices and, 24; in "The Way of Peace," 138; in "The Yellow Wall-Paper," 127–28. *See also* Spectral fusions

Thanksgiving, 65, 178n34

Time. *See* Temporality

Tiverton Tales (Alice Brown), 132, 133

Tompkins, Jane, 77

Torsney, Cheryl B., 158

Tory Lover, The (Jewett), 10, 59, 177n29

Tourism: antique shops and, 182n27; china collecting and, 91, 96, 97, 107, 112; in "The Giant Wistaria," 129; heritage tourism, 2–3, 7, 25; *Pointed Firs* and, 81–82, 84; summer boarding, 2, 81–82

"Toward a Black Feminist Criticism" (Smith), 161–62

Travel. *See* Mobility; Tourism

Trowbridge, J. T., 60–61

True Stories of New England Captives Carried to Canada during the Old French and Indian Wars (Baker), 25, 39–49; belonging in, 46–49; "A Day at Oka" (chapter), 43–45; intimate historicism and, 34–36, 37; "My Hunt for the Captives" (chapter), 40–43; "A Scion of the Church in Deerfield: Joseph-Octave Plessis, First Archbishop of Quebec" (chapter), 47–48; stories of captives in, 29–31; women's cosmopolitanism and, 17, 47

Tuhkanen, Mikko, 140, 147

Tuttle, Jennifer S., 125

Twatogwach, Elizabeth (originally Abigail Nims), 30, 43, 48, 173n16

Tyson, Elise, 10

Tyson, Emily, 10

Ulrich, Laurel Thatcher, 159

Uncle Tom's Cabin (Stowe), 77–78

Uncoverings (journal), 159

Unmarried women: age and, 60; belonging and, 19; in Alice Brown's work, 133–35, 137; in china-collecting guides, 106–7; in *Deephaven*, 71; dissent of, 8, 11, 18, 19–20, 64; intimacies of, 59; labors of, 11, 12–13, 36; in literary scholarship, 61–62; literary stereotypes of, 60–61, 172n86; in New England regionalist fiction, 58, 59–64, 177n31; race and, 11, 18–19; temporality and, 59–60; in *Uncle Tom's Cabin*, 78; in "The Willow-Ware," 102–3; as witches, 66, 67, 87, 133–34

Index 221

"Unpublished Love Poems of Sarah Orne Jewett, The" (Donovan), 157

Urban-rural relations: china collecting and, 89, 96, 97, 106, 107, 112; in summer boarding fiction, 81–82

Violence: captives and, 50, 54, 55; in *The China Hunters Club*, 96; in "A Church Mouse," 68, 178n41; in "The Giant Wistaria," 129–30

Walker, Alice, 159
Washington, George, 99
Washington pitchers, 99–101, *100*
"Way of Peace, The" (Alice Brown), 137–38, 139, 153
Weidlich, Lorre M., 159
Weinbaum, Alys Eve, 125
Whiteness: in Baker's work, 40; china and, 113, 122, 145; New England associated with, 16; photography and, 38–39. *See also* Race
Whole Family, The (Howells), 132

"Willow-Ware, The" (Mary Wilkins Freeman), 101–3
Winning of the West, The (Roosevelt), 32
Witches, unmarried women as, 66, 67, 87, 133–34
Woman Warrior, The: Memoirs of a Girlhood among Ghosts (Kingston), 159
Womb, images of, 61, 129, 135, 136
Women and Economics (Gilman), 128
Wood, Ann Douglas, 62
Wood, Joseph, 3
Woolson, Constance Fenimore, 158
Work of the Afro-American Woman, The (Mossell), 150
Wycherley, William, 92

Yankees, 16, 97–98
"Yellow Wall-Paper, The" (Gilman), 21, 118, 125–29, 131–32, 146–47
York, Maine (Old York Village), 2–3
Young, Pauline A., 158

Zagarell, Sandra, 14, 162, 167n24, 190n40

www.ingramcontent.com/pod-product-compliance
Lightning Source LLC
Chambersburg PA
CBHW030648230426
43665CB00011B/1000